PUERTO RICAN WRITERS AT HOME IN THE USA

PUERTO RICAN WRITERS
at home in the USA

AN ANTHOLOGY

Edited by
Faythe Turner

OPEN HAND PUBLISHING INC.
Seattle, Washington

OPEN HAND PUBLISHING INC.
P.O. Box 22048
Seattle, WA 98122-0048

Distributed by:
The Talman Company, Inc.
131 Spring Street, Suite 201 E-N
New York, NY 10012
(212)431-7175
(212)431-7215 FAX

First published in 1991 in simultaneous hardcover and paperback editions.

Copyright ©Faythe Turner, 1991
Cover photos by Jerome Liebling
Book design by Deb Figen

Pages 343-347 constitute an extension of this copyright page.

Library of Congress Cataloging-in-Publication Data

Puerto Rican writers at home in the USA : an anthology/edited by
  Faythe Turner.
      p.   cm.
    Includes bibliographical references.
    ISBN 0-940880-32-6 : $39.95. — ISBN 0-940880-31-8 (pbk.) : $19.95
    1. American literature—Puerto Rican authors.   2. Puerto Ricans-
  -United States—Literary collections.   I. Turner, Faythe E. (Faythe
  Elaine)
  PS508.P84P8   1991
  810.8'08687295—dc20   91-2141
                                                                      CIP

ISBN 0-940880-32-6 cloth cover
ISBN 0-940880-31-8 paperback

95 94 93   6 5 4 3 2

*For the writers
whose words you are about to read.*

Table of Contents

Anthology

xiii

Acknowledgments

My thanks to all those in the Puerto Rican community who have so generously taken me into their homes and hearts.

My gratitude to my family and friends who shared my enthusiasm for the work and the writers in this anthology, most particularly to poet Anne Halley for her assistance in the poetry selections at the outset and to Professor Richard Haven for his tireless help and encouragement.

My appreciation to Nichols College for a sabbatical leave to work on this anthology.

Introduction

My journey into Puerto Rican culture began after reading Piri Thomas' autobiographical narrative, **Down These Mean Streets.** Later when I wrote asking if I might meet and talk with him about his work, he graciously invited me to his home in New York City. The time I spent with Piri during that first of many visits was invaluable. We talked of poetry and song, and he showed me some of the bountiful literature that was coming from the Puerto Rican community in New York. Through him I became acquainted with many of the Puerto Rican writers in New York, including Jose Angel Figueroa, Pedro Pietri, Sandra Maria Esteves and others. This community of writers was full of activity. There was always a reading or event being presented somewhere—at a writer's home, as street theater or legitimate theater, in museums or cafés—for those interested as I was. Esteves, who has played a part in all these, suggests to us in her poem "Transference" how best to approach this life-filled literature.

. . .

So when you come to me, don't assume
That you know me so well as that
Don't come with preconceptions
Or expect me to fit the mold you have created
Because we fit no molds
We have no limitations
And when you do come, bring me your hopes
Describe for me your visions, your dreams
Bring me your support and your inspiration
Your guidance and your faith
Your belief in our possibilities
Bring me the best that you can

Give me the chance to be
Myself and create symphonies like
The pastel dawn or the empty canvass
Before the first stroke of color is released

Come in a dialogue of we
You and me reacting, responding
Being, something new
Discovering.

The nineteen seventies saw the emergence in New York of a number of young Puerto Rican writers who had been born or had grown up in that city and who often wrote in English. Many of them were associated with the Nuyorican Poets' Cafe. Opened on the Lower East Side by poet Miguel Algarín, the cafe was originally intended as an alternative meeting place for poets and other writers who had taken to gathering at Algarín's home. It was housed in what looked like an abandoned storefront church. A big storefront window and an open door beckoned passers-by to stop and come in for an hour or an evening of poetry and the rhythm of *salsa*. Inside at the back were a few tables to sit at and in front of them some rows of chairs and an open space where some people could perform while others sat on the floor to watch and listen. To one side was a refrigerator from which beer, wine, and soda were sold. Audience, performers, and the ever present master of ceremonies were nearly all Latino, mostly Puerto Rican. They were there to have a good time.

A cafe or bar on the Lower East Side may seem an unlikely place for writers to present their work or to find an enthusiastic audience, but in Puerto Rico, as in many other societies, poetry, song, and story are pleasures central to the pattern of daily life. Puerto Ricans recall the tradition of *El Lector,* the Reader, an important person to each community, who was hired by the workers, most often *tabaqueros,* to read aloud from both the newspapers of the day and the classical literature of the past while the *tabaqueros* carried on their work of rolling cigars. What they listened to during the day became matter for discussion in village squares after the working day was done. So it was that people who came to the Nuyorican Poets' Cafe and to other such gathering places, came expecting that what they heard was not only to be listened to but commented on, that it should circulate through people's ears and mouths. It was a working, participating audience, one both responsive and critical. As the writers and singers examined in words and melody the contours and depths of their experience, the listeners debated the truth or falsity of what they heard.

In January of 1978, I gave a paper on "Puerto Rican Writers in New York" at a meeting of the Modern Language Association at the New York Hilton. The paper was sponsored by MELUS (Multi-Ethnic Literature in the United States), a newly established group in the Association, dedicated to expanding the definition of American Literature. This was the first time a slot had been set aside for a discussion of the work of Puerto Ricans writing in the United States. To most of the people attending the meeting, the idea of a body of literature focused in New York and written by Puerto Ricans was quite new. Aside from Piri Thomas and Miguel Piñero, both of whom had attracted attention by that time, Puerto Rican writers had little audience outside the Puerto Rican community. After the discussion which followed my paper, I went downtown to the Nuyorican Poets' Cafe to talk with Algarín and other friends. On hearing of the day's events, Miguel Piñero gave an

2

exuberant shout, calling across the Cafe, "Hey! They're talkin' about us at the Hilton!" It seemed as though the moment was perhaps at hand when the work of these Puerto Rican writers would be recognized for what it already was: a new and vital part of contemporary American literature.

The seventies had seemed filled with promise for New York's Puerto Rican writers. Thomas' much-extolled **Down These Mean Streets** had appeared in 1967, and in 1969 Victor Hernández Cruz had published his first volume of poetry, **Snaps**, with Random House, heralding a new turn of events,

> . . .
>
> a day of great joy
> when they stop poems
> in the mail & clap
> their hands & dance to
> them . . . when poems start to
> knock down walls . . .
> begin to break the air . . .
> it is a great day.

He followed this with **Mainland** in 1973 and **Tropicalization** in 1976. Nineteen seventy-three brought forth Pedro Pietri's poems in **Puerto Rican Obituary** and Jose Angel Figueroa's in **East 110 Street** as well as Nicholasa Mohr's novel for young people, **Nilda**. It was followed by a collection of her stories, **El Bronx Remembered,** in 1975. Piñero's brilliant prison play, **Short Eyes**, was published in 1974, later to be performed at Lincoln Center and made into a film. The vitality of this group, the flurry of publishing in the early seventies, and the often stunning quality of their work led to the expectation that these writers, these Nuyoricans, as some of them described themselves, would soon be highly visible and recognized.

This has not proved to be the case. Although all of these writers are active today, with the exception of Piñero who died in 1988, and although a new generation has increased their numbers, they are still published mostly by journals with limited distribution, and by small presses, chiefly Nicolas Kanellos' Arte Publico Press at the University of Houston. As vital as it is, and as much as it deserves our attention, their work remains, as Earl Shorris suggested recently in "In Search of the Latino Writer," "secret, available mostly in ghetto bookstores and arcane corners of college campuses." (*New York Times Book Review*, July 15, 1990).

But the year just past (1989) seems again to provide grounds for hope. Judith Ortiz Cofer's novel, **The Line of the Sun**, published by the University of Georgia Press, was nominated for a Pulitzer prize; the

National Endowment for the Arts gave fellowships in poetry and fiction respectively to Cofer and Ed Vega, and Martin Espada received a PEN fellowship for his poetry. Distinguished publications like *The New York Review of Books* and *The Massachusetts Review* have published Victor Hernández Cruz and Magdalena Gomez respectively; Cofer, Hernández Cruz, Mohr, and Pietri are included in the new *Heath Anthology of American Literature*, a good measure of what is recently beginning to be included in the canon of American Literature. *Puertoricaanse Literatuur in Nueva York* which includes work by Pietri, Piñero, Thomas, and Vega has just been published in Holland. These are again signs of recognition beyond the Puerto Rican community which will lead to a lasting awareness that the contributions of these writers have a permanent place in American Literature.

In 1978, Puerto Rican writing in this country was concentrated heavily in New York, produced by members of the Puerto Rican community there who knew each other and frequently saw and talked with each other. In 1990, that geographical concentration has weakened. While some, like Ed Vega, a long-time resident of New York, have only recently become visible, others have moved away: Jose Angel Figueroa to Hartford, Piri Thomas first to Puerto Rico and then to San Francisco, Victor Hernández Cruz first to San Francisco and then recently to Puerto Rico, Luz Maria Umpierre to Bowling Green, Kentucky, Magdalena Gomez to Hadley, Massachusetts. And new voices have appeared in places other than New York: Martín Espada and Rosario Morales in Boston, Judith Ortiz Cofer in Savannah, and Aurora Levin Morales in Berkeley. Although dispersed geographically, these writers remain in some important ways a group, however distinct their individual voices may be. Reflected in their work are a common cultural heritage and for the most part a common social background. So much might, of course, be said of many earlier groups of immigrants. But unlike other immigrants, Puerto Ricans are citizens of the United States by birth; Puerto Rico is, at this writing, part of the United States without being a state. Travel to the Island does not require a passport, and, unlike earlier generations of European immigrants, Puerto Ricans have not left "the old country" with little or no expectation of returning and often with little wish to do so.

Puerto Rico has its own distinct and complex culture, which has evolved over several centuries (its capital of San Juan is older than any city in the continental United States). In it are interwoven strands from the Taino Indians, a branch of the Arawak who migrated from South America to what was known as Borinquen; from the Spanish, who ruled the island from the time of Columbus until 1898; and from the Africans who were brought to work on the sugar and coffee plantations. Poet Victor Hernández Cruz captures the essence of this composite that makes up the Puerto Rican people:

> african juice warming
> the centuries and centuries
> of sea exploration and mixing.

4

Perhaps the proper point of departure for modern Puerto Rican history is the year 1897, the eve of the Spanish American War. Throughout the 1800's there had been pressure put on Spain by Puerto Ricans for more freedom. As her empire crumbled around her, Spain gratuitously offered self-determination. Many Puerto Ricans today feel that their country's liberty was imminent just as the United States intervened in 1898 with what Theodore Roosevelt called "that splendid little war," the Spanish American War, after which the island of Puerto Rico was ceded to the United States.

During the first half of the twentieth century the plantation system collapsed. With this many of the country people, the *campesinos* or *jíbaros*, were forced to leave the countryside to look for work in the urban areas where industry was developing. In the years following World War II hundreds of thousands of Puerto Ricans moved on to the continental United States in search of better economic conditions. They moved most often to the ghettos of New York and other eastern cities where they found themselves confronted with linguistic, ethnic, and racial barriers. The writers who share this background are not so much people in the process of leaving one world and entering another as they are people living in two worlds at once. An issue which recurs in one guise or another in the work of nearly all of these writers is the question of identity. One of the many strengths of their writing is the frequency with which that question appears as a matter of affirmation and celebration, as in the poem with which this collection begins, "Ending Poem," by Rosario Morales and Aurora Levins Morales:

> I am what I am.
> *A child of the Americas*
> A light-skinned mestiza of the Caribbean.
> *A child of many diaspora, born into this continent at a crossroads.*
> I am Puerto Rican. I am U.S. American.
> *I am New York Manhattan and the Bronx.*
> A mountain-born, country-bred, homegrown jíbara child.
> . . . .
> *History made us.*
> We will not eat ourselves up inside anymore.
>
> *And we are whole.*

In reading the work of the writers included in this anthology we become aware of the unique background which they hold in common. We recognize and delight in their individuality and in the strength arising from the diversity of their voices. The opening section of the anthology is a sampler whose purpose is to give a sense both of what these writers share and of their individuality, their diversity. It is intended to provide some context for the work which follows. The remainder of the anthology offers more substantial selections from individual authors arranged chronologically by publication. With the single exception of Jesus Colon, they were born or arrived in the continental United States after World War II. Colon, from whom we can derive some impression of what confronted the earlier generation, was one of the first Puerto Ricans to come here not as a traveler but in search of expanded opportunities. He came as a stowaway in 1918 when he was seventeen, confident that as a trained artisan he could find work in a small factory. Instead, he found himself one of many immigrants looking for work and forced to take the meanest positions. His *A Puerto Rican in New York,* published in 1961 and familiar to most of the post-war Puerto Rican writers, covers the years from the twenties to the mid-fifties and attempts "to throw a little light on how Puerto Ricans in this city *really* feel, think, work, and live because Puerto Ricans remain unsung, unheralded, and practically unknown to their fellow New Yorkers." His pieces included here are very direct, if gentle, accounts of what will confront the new immigrant: language and race discrimination, deceitful advertising, exploitation, and the erosion of cultural and spiritual values.

While Colon belongs to and in some ways reflects an earlier generation, he also sounds a note developed by the next generation of writers and sharply distinct from the rosy optimism expressed twenty years earlier by Pedro Labarthe in his autobiography, *The Son of Two Nations* (1931). Labarthe had arrived already convinced that the "country was one of opportunities, she opened her doors for everybody. . . . If these people lead a clean-cut life and are ambitious, the United States will accept them as her real children." He is a victim of what has been considered one route to a truly American identity: the losing of one's own. Colon's tone, on the other hand, is that of one who feels a part of a strong community that he hopes to alert to the possibilities, but also to the problems, of life in this country.

Since the years of which Colon was writing, the ethnic composition of the United States has changed markedly. Nearly two million Puerto Ricans live here today, and instead of one lone voice like Colon's speaking for his people, there is an increasing number of keenly conscious writers for whom ethnicity is not a liability but a source of pride and strength.

Faythe Turner
Amherst, Massachusetts

POETS' SAMPLER

Ending Poem

Rosario Morales
Aurora Levins Morales

I am what I am.
A child of the Americas.
A light-skinned mestiza of the Caribbean.
A child of many diaspora, born into this continent at a crossroads.
I am Puerto Rican. I am U.S. American.
I am New York Manhattan and the Bronx.
A mountain-born, country-bred, homegrown jíbara child,
up from the shtetl, a California Puerto Rican Jew
A product of the New York ghettos I have never known.
I am an immigrant
and the daughter and granddaughter of immigrants.
We didn't know our forbears' names with a certainty.
They aren't written anywhere.
First names only or mija, negra, ne, honey, sugar, dear.

I come from the dirt where the cane was grown.
My people didn't go to dinner parties. They weren't invited.
I am caribeña, island grown.
Spanish is in my flesh, ripples from my tongue, lodges in my hips,
the language of garlic and mangoes.
Boricua. As Boricuas come from the isle of Manhattan.
I am of latinoamerica, rooted in the history of my continent.
I speak from that body. Just brown and pink and full of drums inside.

I am not African.
Africa waters the roots of my tree, but I cannot return.

I am not Taína.
I am a late leaf of that ancient tree,
and my roots reach into the soil of two Americas.
Taíno is in me, but there is no way back.

I am not European, though I have dreamt of those cities.
Each plate is different.
wood, clay, papier mâché, metals, basketry, a leaf, a coconut shell
Europe lives in me but I have no home there.

The table has a cloth woven by one, dyed by another,
embroidered by another still.
I am a child of many mothers.
They have kept it all going

9

All the civilizations erected on their backs.
All the dinner parties given with their labor.

We are new.
They gave us life, kept us going,
brought us to where we are.
Born at a crossroads.
Come, lay that dishcloth down. Eat, dear, eat.
History made us.
We will not eat ourselves up inside anymore.

And we are whole.

Felipa, La Filosofa de Rincon que Nació a los 98 Años

Jose Angel Figueroa

She had life in the blood of her eyes, history in her body. With a cigar half-strangled by her aged fingerprints, she jawed my eyes and put my words to pulsate with the night. She was very tranquil. This bulk of life never took her eyes off my mind. She never left me alone: I was filled with her voice every sun-baked afternoon beneath a tree of quenepas. Her strength raised me like a breeze whose skin was made from the old prophets of our history.

Felipa, The Philosopher, was slowly sewing my consciousness. Era el quinque de la noche. Her voice was a lantern that held my small hand and walked with my mind toward the blue face of the sky. The sun-light always waited for her. The conversations were warm, gentle, but absorbing. I became her private seed and listened to what was going around me with my eyes.

Little did I know Felipa was sculpturing my roots. I can still seep the memories of that last afternoon together, when the small valleys paid attention to our footsteps, when the hills surrounding us gave their ears, when the spirit of the wind stopped playing with the humid wigs of palm trees as the sound of patience colored our meeting place with solitude. My soul was spread all over this island as she blew history into my ears. LISTEN:

I remember, my child, when jíbaros woke up the tired mornings and poured their sweat into the hungry soil of our homeland. Those were happier days when our people danced to the emotional songs of Spanish guitars as if inviting Yukiyu to bear and breed our future. The tempor and the tastebuds of the sun fed the fruits of distant years while

10

our smiles endured or fertilized any dent or torn out days. Tripping on love was our only thirst and luxury.

I listened to Felipa but could not imagine the tears drowning in her throat. I was a child insulated from pain and could not weigh her long-winded words, then. Come, let me take you back before my memory runs away from me and feel her voice dive into your ears:

Ours was a life-filled island where dreams and an engine of smiles could be found, my son, until a thick black cloud invaded the ever silent faces of long hours. Our dreams have been tortured ever since our soil has been docked with strangers who sleep with our future. MIJO: we have become hostages inside a hurricane of torturous rain and the unbearable sun of an uprooted earth. Look up and see a bullet-hole in the sky. Freedom is no longer on the guest list of the infinite wind.

After mi abuelita said this I had seen that the scars were suffocating her prunish body and I looked at her as if I'd seen her soul leaving her massive skeleton, knowing my own soul would not be home for many days, many nights. Then we walked back the narrow dirt road when an orange cloud began blindfolding the sun. The island was mute.

She filled my eyes with philosophy. And the history she blew inside my ears taught me never to let hope get stuck in my ribs: For hope is harmony. And Felipa, La Filosofa, once said:
You could always kill a hurricane with harmony.

Murdered Luggage

Jose Angel Figueroa

I STILL REMEMBER that first day. We got off with our splintered shopping bags & half-panicky, the entire family walked out like some rainbow: i was the skinny dark blue suit, purple shirt with thin black tie, red socks with rings around the heels, and always hungry for bubble gum drops; tall lanky carlos stood out the most because his rooster-like hairstyle made him look cocky; and ruben: he was the chubby hick who loved reading gene autry comic books and who never got used to wearing long-sleeve shirts cause they always fatigued him; and i remember snow skinned shy celia, always hiding & fencing those smiles cause one of her teeth ran out on her; and little sister miriam was the best Puerto Rican thumbsucker in the airport; (talking about sucking, i didn't get to eat bubble gum drops that day,) my brother hector was the meanest vacuum cleaner from Rincon, and he took them from me.

UUMMHHH, AND MI MOTHER, MILAGROS: have you ever seen a proud rose with indented cheekbones before? i will always see her as a piece of wind, scratching on my windows & feeding my thoughts

11

with the wonders of when & how & why tree leaves fall in a child's past dream.

AND I DREAMT OF THAT FIRST DAY: when we got to the baggage terminal, my mother saw our luggage murdered and sprawled all over the cold city floor; i remember that day like some blade, knifing my memory: it was the first time i had ever seen a rose sighing while melting inside
SNOW.

Puertoricanness

Aurora Levins Morales

It was Puerto Rico waking up inside her. Puerto Rico waking her up at 6:00 a.m., remembering the rooster that used to crow over on 59th Street and the neighbors all cursed "that damn rooster," but she loved him, waited to hear his harsh voice carving up the Oakland sky and eating it like chopped corn, so obliviously sure of himself, crowing all alone with miles of houses around him. She was like that rooster.

Often she could hear them in her dreams. Not the lone rooster of 59th Street (or some street nearby . . . she had never found the exact yard though she had tried), but the wild careening hysterical roosters of 3:00 a.m. in Bartolo, screaming at the night and screaming again at the day.

It was Puerto Rico waking up inside her, uncurling and shoving open the door she had kept neatly shut for years and years. Maybe since the first time she was an immigrant, when she refused to speak Spanish in nursery school. Certainly since the last time, when at thirteen she found herself between languages, between countries, with no land feeling at all solid under her feet. The mulberry trees of Chicago, that first summer, had looked so utterly pitiful beside her memory of flamboyan and banana and. . . . No, not even the individual trees and bushes but the mass of them, the overwhelming profusion of green life that was the home of her comfort and nest of her dreams.

The door was opening. She could no longer keep her accent under lock and key. It seeped out, masquerading as dyslexia, stuttering, halting unable to speak the word which will surely come out in the wrong language, wearing the wrong clothes. Doesn't that girl know how to dress? Doesn't she know how to date, what to say to a professor, how to behave at a dinner table laid with silver and crystal and too many forks?

Yesterday she answered her husband's request that she listen to the whole of his thoughts before commenting by screaming "This is how we talk. I will not wait sedately for you to finish. Interrupt me back!" She drank pineapple juice three or four times a day. Not Lotus, just Co-op brand, but it was piña, and it was sweet and yellow. And she was letting the clock slip away from her into a world of morning and afternoon and night, instead of "five-forty-one-and-twenty seconds—beep."

There were things she noticed about herself, the Puertoricanness of which she had kept hidden all these years, but which had persisted as habits, as idiosyncracies of her nature. The way she left a pot of food on the stove all day, eating out of it whenever hunger struck her, liking to have something ready. The way she had lacked food to offer Elena in the old days and had stamped on the desire to do so because it was Puerto Rican: Come, mija . . . ¿quieres cafe? The way she was embarrassed and irritated by Ana's unannounced visits, just dropping by, keeping the country habits after a generation of city life. So unlike the cluttered datebooks of all her friends, making appointments to speak to each other on the phone days in advance. Now she yearned for that clocklessness, for the perpetual food pots of her childhood. Even in the poorest houses a plate of white rice and brown beans with calabaza or green bananas and oil.

She had told Sally that Puerto Ricans lived as if they were all in a small town still, a small town of six million spread out over tens of thousands of square miles, and that the small town that was her country needed to include Manila Avenue in Oakland now, because she was moving back into it. She would not fight the waking early anymore, or the eating all day, or the desire to let time slip between her fingers and allow her work to shape it. Work, eating, sleep, lovemaking, play—to let them shape the day instead of letting the day shape them. Since she could not right now, in the endless bartering of a woman with two countries, bring herself to trade in one-half of her heart for the other, exchange this loneliness for another perhaps harsher one, she would live as a Puerto Rican lives en la isla, right here in north Oakland, plant the bananales and cafetales of her heart around her bedroom door, sleep under the shadow of their bloom and the carving hoarseness of the roosters, wake to blue-rimmed white enamel cups of jugo de piña and plates of guineo verde, and heat pots of rice with bits of meat in them on the stove all day.

There was a woman in her who had never had the chance to move through this house the way she wanted to, a woman raised to be like those women of her childhood, hardworking and humorous and clear. That woman was yawning up out of sleep and into this cluttered daily routine of a Northern California writer living at the edges of Berkeley. She was taking over, putting doilies on the word processor, not bothering to make appointments, talking to the neighbors, riding miles on the bus to buy bacalao, making her presence felt . . . and she was all Puerto Rican, every bit of her.

Immigrants

Aurora Levins Morales

For years after we left Puerto Rico for the last time, I would wake from a dream of something unbearably precious melting away from my memory as I struggled desperately to hold on, or at least to remember that I had forgotten. I am an immigrant, and I forget to feel what it means to have left. What it means to have arrived.

There was hail the day we got to Chicago and we joked that the city was hailing our arrival. The brown brick buildings simmered in the smelly summer, clenched tight all winter against the cold and the sooty sky. It was a place without silence or darkness, huddled against a lake full of dying fish whose corpses floated against the slime-covered rocks of the south shore.

Chicago is the place where the slack ended. Suddenly there was no give. In Indiera there was the farm: the flamboyan tree, the pine woods, the rainforest hillsides covered with alegría, the wild joyweed that in English is called impatiens. On the farm there were hideouts, groves of bamboo with the tiny brown hairs that stuck in your skin if you weren't careful. Beds of sweet-smelling fern, drowsymaking under the sun's heat, where the new leaves uncurled from fiddleheads and tendrils climbed and tangled in a spongy mass six feet deep. There were still hillsides, out of range of the house, where I could watch lizards hunt and reinitas court, and stalk the wild cuckoos, trying to get up close. There were mysteries and consolations. There was space.

Chicago was a wasteland. Nowhere to walk that was safe. Killers and rapists everywhere. Police sirens. Ugly, angry looks. Bristling hostility. Worst of all, nowhere to walk. Nowhere to go if it was early morning and I had to get out. Nowhere to go in the late afternoon or in the gathering dusk that meant fireflies and moths at home. Nowhere to watch animal life waking into a new day. The animal life was rats and dogs, and they were always awake because it never got dark here: always that sickly purple and orange glow they call sky in this place. No forest to run wild in. Only the lot across 55th Street with huge piles of barren earth, outlines of old cellars, and a few besieged trees in a scraggly row. I named one of them Ceres, after the goddess of earth and plenty who appeared in my high school production of *The Tempest*: bounteous Ceres, queen of the wasteland. There were no hills to race down, tumbling into heaps of fern, to slide down, on a slippery banana leaf: no place to get muddy. Chicago had grime, but no mud. Slush, but no slippery places of the heart, no genuine moistness. Only damp alleyways, dank brick, and two little humps in the middle of 55th Street over which grass had been made to grow. But no real sliding. No slack.

There are generations of this desolation behind me, desolation, excitement, grief, and longing all mixed in with the dirty air, the noise, seasickness, and the strangeness of wearing a winter coat.

My grandmother Lola was nineteen the day she married my grandfather and sailed away to Nueva York in 1929. She had loved someone else, but his family disapproved and he obeyed their orders to leave for the States. So her family married her to a son of a neighboring family because the family store was doing poorly and they could no longer support so many children. Two months after her first love left, she found herself married and on the boat. She says: "I was a good Catholic girl. I thought it was my duty to marry him, that it was for the good of my family." I have pictures of her, her vibrant beauty wrapped up but not smothered in the winter coats and scarves. In my grandfather's violent possessiveness and jealousy. She is standing in Central Park with her daughters, or with her arms around a friend or cousin. Loving the excitement. Loving the neighbors and the hubbub. In spite of racist landlords. In spite of the girdle factory. In spite of Manolin's temper and the poverty and hunger. Now, retired to Manolin's dream of a little house in Puerto Rico with a yard and many plants to tend, she longs for New York or some other U.S. city where a woman can go out and about on her own, live among many voices speaking different languages, out of the stifling air of that house, that community, that family.

My mother, the child in that Central Park photo, grew up an immigrant child among immigrants. She went to school speaking not a word of English, a small Puerto Rican girl scared out of her wits, and learned fast: learned accentless English in record time, the sweet cadence of her mother's open-voweled words ironed out of her vocabulary, the edges flattened down, made crisp, the curls and flourishes removed. First generation.

The strangeness. The way time worked differently. The way being on time mattered. Four second bells. Four minutes of passing time between classes. A note from home if you were ten minutes late, which you took to the office and traded for a late pass. In Indiera the classroom emptied during coffee season, and they didn't bother to send the inspector up unless we were out for longer than four or five weeks. No one had a clock with a second hand. We had half days of school because there were only four rooms for six grades. Our room was next to the bakery, and the smell of the warm pan de agua filled our lungs and stomachs and mouths. Things happened when they were ready, or "cuando Dios quiere." The público to town, don Paco's bread, the coffee ripening, the rain coming, growing up.

The stiffness. The way clothing mattered with an entirely different kind of intensity. In Indiera, I wore the same wine-colored jumper to school each day with the same white blouse, and only details of the buttons or the quality of the cloth or the presence or absence of earrings, only the shoes gave information about the homes we left at dawn each day, and I was grateful to be able to hide my relative wealth. In Chicago, there were rituals I had never heard of. Knee socks and paid skirts and sweaters matching each other according to a secret code I didn't understand. Going steady and wearing name tags. First date, second date, third date, score. The right songs to be listening to. The right dances. The coolness.

In the middle of coolness, of stiffness, of strangeness, my joyful rushing up to say, "I come from Puerto Rico, a nest of beauty on the top of a mountain range." Singing "beauty, beauty, beauty." Trying to get them to see in their minds' eyes the perfected edge of a banana leaf against a tropical blue sky, just wanting to speak of what I longed for. Seeing embarrassed faces turning away, getting the jeering voices, singing "Puerto Rico, my heart's devotion . . . let it sink into the ocean!" Learning fast not to talk about it, learning excruciatingly slowly how to dress, how to act, what to say, where to hide. The exuberance, the country-born freshness going quietly stale. Made flat. Made palatable. Made unthreatening. Not different, really. Merely "exotic."

I can remember the feelings, but I forget to give them names. In high school we read novels about immigrant families. In college we discussed the problems of other first generations, talked about displacement, talked about families confused and divided, pride and shame. I never once remembered that I was an immigrant, or that both my parents are the first U.S.-born generations of their families.

Today Is a Day of Great Joy
Victor Hernández Cruz

when they stop poems
in the mail & clap
their hands & dance to
them
when women become pregnant
by the side of poems
the strongest sounds   making
the river go along

it is a great day

as poems fall down to
movie crowds   in restaurants
in bars

when poems start to
knock down walls   to
choke politicians
when poems scream &
begin to break the air

that is the time of
true poets   that is
the time of greatness

a true poet   aiming
poems   & watching things
fall to the ground

it is a great day.

Traffic Misdirector

Pedro Pietri

the greatest living poet
in new york city
was born in Puerto Rico
his name is Jorge Brandon
he is over 70 years old
he carries his metaphor
in brown shopping bags
inside steel shopping cart
he travels around with
on the streets of manhattan
he recites his poetry
to whoever listens
& when nobody is around
he recites to himself
he speaks the wisdom
of unforgotten palm trees
the vocabulary of coconuts

that wear overcoats
the traffic lights
of his poems function
without boring advice
from ac or dc current
book stores & libraries
are deprived of his vibes
to become familiar
with this immortal poet
you have to hang-out
on street corners
building stoops rooftops
fire escapes bars parks
subway train stations
bodegas botanicas
iglesias pawn shops
card games cock fights
funerals valencia bakery
hunts point palace
pool halls orchard beach
& cuchifrito stands
on the lower eastside
the admission is free
his presence is poetry

Christmas Eve: Nuyorican Café
Miguel Algarín   December 24, 1975

Slow by slow people come
to celebrate the birth of
    jesus rodriguez,
John comes in releasing joyous vibes,
has a beer, gives me a rap about his
party in the Bronx and how he's coming
down with everybody later on to celebrate
Noche Buena at the café,
one more night of people searching to make
contact with each other and jesus is
the living pretext,
    jesus,
    jesus rodriguez
hoy es tu cumpleaño,
tonight on the eve of your birth
I sit weaving electrical impulses
with Willy One, Ruben and the talking
coconut, el Señor Jorge Brandon, who
bears the flag of poetry on his tongue
and purest love in his heart giving it
away on the impulse of the moment,
generously to anybody ready to control
the ego and become a listener to a master
painter with words, today jesus rodriguez
was born and el gran poeta Brandon
brings words that change
the listener as he tells in word paintings
the pain of falling in love with woman
and the disaster that jealousy
initiates when man and woman
do not trust each other,
    but here it is and it is
    Christmas day and today
    jesus rodriguez is born
and men and women will cease
to be jealous and green will only
mean spring, rejuvenation,

not evil
disintegrating
jealousy,
jesus is born speaking Nuyorican
eating tortillas con salchichas
to the rhythms of winter hot
conga drums that
lament an ice cold Christmas
that slips away under a slight
blanket of Christmas snow.

This Is Not the Place
Where I was Born
Miguel Piñero

puerto rico 1974
this is not the place where i was born
remember—as a child the fantasizing images my mother planted
within my head—
the shadows of her childhood recounted to me many times
over welfare loan on crédito food from el bodeguero
i tasted mango many years before the skin of the fruit
ever reached my teeth
i was born on an island about 35 miles wide 100 miles long
a small island with a rainforest somewhere in the central
regions of itself
where spanish was a dominant word
& signs read by themselves
i was born in a village of that island where the police
who frequented your place of business-hangout or home came as
servant or friend & not as a terror in slogan clothing
i was born in a barrio of the village on the island
where people left their doors open at night
where respect for elders was exhibited with pride
where courting for loved ones was not treated over confidentially
where children's laughter did not sound empty & savagely alive
with self destruction . . .

i was born on an island where to be puerto rican meant to be
part of the land & soul & puertorriqueños were not the
minority
puerto ricans were first, none were second
no, i was not born here . . .
no, i was not born in the attitude & time of this place
this sun drenched soil
this green faced piece of earth
this slave blessed land
where the caribbean seas pound angrily on the shores
of pre-fabricated house/hotel redcap hustling people gypsy taxi cab
fighters for fares to fajardo
& the hot wind is broken by fiberglass palmtrees
& highrise plátanos mariano on leave & color t.v.
looneytune cartoon comicbook characters with badges
in their jockstraps
& foreigners scream that puertorriqueños are foreigners
& have no right to claim any benefit on the birthport
this sun drenched soil
this green faced piece of earth
this slave blessed land
where nuyoricans come in search of spiritual identity
are greeted with profanity
this is insanity that americanos are showered
with shoe shine kisses
police in stocking caps cover carry out john wayne
television cowboy law road models of new york city detective
french connection/death wish instigation ku-klux-klan mind
panorama screen seems
in modern medicine is in confusion needs a transfusion quantity
treatment if you're not on the plan the new stand
of blue cross blue shield blue uniform master charge
what religion you are
blood fills the waiting room of death
stale air & qué pasa stares are nowhere
in sight & night neon light shines bright
in el condado area puerto rican under cover cop
stop & arrest on the spot puerto ricans who shop for the flag
that waves on the left-in souvenir stores—
puertorriqueños cannot assemble displaying the emblem

nuyoricans are fighting & dying for in newark, lower east side
south bronx where the fervor of being
puertorriqueños is not just rafael hernández
viet vet protest with rifle shots that dig into four pigs
& sociable friday professional persons rush to the
golf course & martini glasses work for the masses
& the island is left unattended because the middle class
bureaucratic cuban has arrived spitting blue eyed justice
at brown skinned boys in military khaki
compromise to survive is hairline length
moustache trimmed face looking grim like a soldier
on furlough further cannot exhibit contempt for what is
not cacique born this poem will receive a burning
stomach turning scorn nullified classified racist
from this pan am eastern first national chase manhattan
puerto rico . . .

The Idea of Islands

Judith Ortiz Cofer

The place where I was born,
that mote in a cartographer's eye,
interests you?
Today Atlanta is like a port city
enveloped in mist. The temperature
is plunging with the abandon
of a woman rushing to a rendezvous.
Since you ask, things were simpler
on the island. Food and shelter
were never the problem. Most days,
a hat and a watchful eye were all
one needed for protection, the climate being
rarely inclement. Fruit could be plucked
from trees languishing under the weight
of their own fecundity. The thick sea
spewed out fish that crawled into the pots
of women whose main occupation was to dress

each other's manes with scarlet hibiscus,
which as you may know, blooms
without restraint in the tropics.
I was always the ambitious one, overdressed
by my neighbors' standards, and unwilling
to eat mangoes three times a day.
In truth, I confess to spending my youth
guarding the fire by the beach, waiting
to be rescued from the futile round
of paradisial life.
How do I like the big city?
City lights are just as bright
as the stars that enticed me then;
the traffic ebbs and rises like the tides
and in a crowd,
everyone is an island.

Poem
Victor Hernández Cruz

The greater cities are
surrounded by woods
Jungles secretly
of America

Behind lights
the green
Green eyes of Tree gods
Rhythm we would call it Puerto Rico
But it doesn't begin to be as real

Silver of the moon
On the upper Hudson
Green Quiet night
Night island wish
Outside the stars
get fatter and louder
Secret Jungle where

the moon is closer
Highway to the skies
Secret
Outside getting cold
We talk to the wind
That moves the world
before it becomes foul
Over the heads of
the buildings

We take it in our mouths
Drunk outside great
Electrical Apple / Nueva York
No Puerto Rico
Nueva York
No Puerto Rico/

The Man Who Came to the Last Floor

Victor Hernández Cruz

There was a Puerto Rican man who
came to New York
He came with a whole shopping bag
full of seeds strange to the big
city
He came and it was morning
and though many people thought the
sun was out this man wondered:
"Where is it"
"Y el sol donde esta" he asked
himself
He went to one of the neighborhoods
and searched for an apartment
He found one in the large somewhere
of New York
with a window overlooking a busy avenue
It was the kind of somewhere that is
usually elevatorless
Somewhere near wall/less

stairless
But this man enjoyed the wide space
of the room with the window that
overlooked the avenue
There was plenty of space
looking out of the window
There is a direct path to heaven
he thought
A wideness in front of the living
room
It was the sixth floor so he lived
on top of everybody in the building
The last floor of the mountain
He took to staring out of his sixth
floor window
He was a familiar sight every day
From his window he saw legs that
walked all day
Short and skinny fat legs
Legs that belonged to many people
Legs that walk embraced with nylon socks
Legs that ride bareback
Legs that were swifter than others
Legs that were always hiding
Legs that always had to turn around
and look at the horizon
Legs that were just legs against
the grey of the cement
People with no legs
He saw everything hanging out
from his room
Big city anywhere and his smile
was as wide as the space in front of him

One day his dreams were invaded by spirits
People just saw him change
Change the way rice changes when it is
sitting on top of fire
All kinds of things started to happen
at the top of the mountain

Apartamento number 32
All kinds of smells started to come out
of apartamento number 32
All kinds of visitors started to come
to apartamento number 32
Wild looking ladies showed up
with large earrings and bracelets
that jingled throughout the hallways
The neighborhood became rich in legend
One could write an encyclopedia if one
collected the rumors
But nothing bothered this man who was
on top of everybody's heads
He woke one day and put the shopping bag
full of seeds that he brought from the island
near the window
He said "para que aproveche el fresco"
So that it can enjoy the fresh air
He left it there for a day
Taking air
Fresh air
Grey air
Wet air
The avenue air
The blue legs air
The teenagers who walked below
Their air
With their black hats with the red
bandana around them full of cocaine
That air
The heroin in the young girls that
moved slowly toward their local
high school
All the air from the outside
The shopping bag stood by the window
inhaling
Police air
Bus air
Car wind
Gringo air

Big mountain city air anywhere
That day this man from Puerto Rico
had his three radios on at the same time
Music coming from anywhere
Each station was different
Music from anywhere everywhere

The following day the famous
outline of the man's head once again showed
up on the sixth floor window
This day he fell into song
and his head was in motion
No one recalls exactly at what point
in the song he started flinging the
seeds of tropical fruits down to
the earth
Down to the avenue of somewhere big
city
But no one knew what he was doing
So all the folks just smiled
"El hombre esta bien loco, algo le
cogio la cabeza"
The man is really crazy
something has taken his head
He began to throw out the last of the
Mango seeds
A policeman was walking down the avenue
and all of a sudden took off his hat
A mango seed landed nicely into his
curly hair
It somehow sailed into the man's
scalp
Deep into the grease of his curls
No one saw it
And the policeman didn't feel it
He put his hat on and walked away
The man from Puerto Rico
was singing another pretty song
His eyes were closed and his head waved.

Two weeks later the policeman felt

a bump coming out of his head
"Holy shit" he woke up telling his wife
one day
"this bump is getting so big I can't
put my hat on my head"
He took a day off and went to see his
doctor about his growing bump
The doctor looked at it and said
it'll go away
The bump didn't go away
It went toward the sky
getting bigger each day
It began to take hold of his whole head
Every time he tried to comb his hair
all his hair would fall to the comb
One morning when the sun was really hot
his wife noticed a green leaf sticking
out from the tip of his bump
Another month passed and more and more
leaves started to show on this man's head
The highest leaf was now two feet above
his forehead
Surely he was going crazy he thought
He could not go to work with a mango
tree growing out of his head
It soon got to be five feet tall
and beautifully green
He had to sleep in the living room
His bedroom could no longer contain him
Weeks later a young mango showed up
hanging from a newly formed branch
"Now look at this" he told his wife
He had to drink a lot of water or he'd
get severe headaches
The more water he drank the bigger
the mango tree flourished over his head
The people of the somewhere city heard
about it in the evening news and there was
a line of thousands ringed around his
home

They all wanted to see the man who
had an exotic mango tree growing from
his skull
And there was nothing that could be done.
Everyone was surprised when they
saw the man who lived at the top of
the mountain come down with his shopping
bag and all his luggage
He told a few of his friends that
he was going back to Puerto Rico
When they asked him why he was going back
He told them that he didn't remember
ever leaving
He said that his wife and children
were there waiting for him
The other day he noticed that he was
not on his island he said
almost singing
He danced toward the famous corner
and waved down a taxi
"El Aire port" he said
He was going to the clouds
To the island
At the airport he picked up a newspaper
and was reading an article about a mango
tree
At least that's what he could make out of
the English
Que cosa he said   Wao
Why write about a Mango tree
There're so many of them
and they are everywhere
They taste goooooood
Como eh.

African Things

Victor Hernández Cruz

o the wonder man   rides his space ship/
                              brings his power through
many moons
                    carries in soft blood   african spirits
dance & sing in my mother's house. in my cousin's house.
black as night can be/   what was Puerto Rican all about.
                                        all about the
indios & you better believe it the african things
                                        black & shiny
grandmother speak to me & tell me of african things
                                    how do latin
boo-ga-loo sound   like you
                        conga drums in the islands   you know
the traveling through many moons
                        dance & tell me black african things
i know you know.

For South Bronx

Sandra Maria Esteves

I live amidst hills of desolate buildings
rows of despair
crowded together
in a chain of lifeless shells

Every five minutes the echoing roar
of the racing elevated train
sears thru the atmosphere
floating low over the horizon

But at every moment
like magic the shells breathe
and take on the appearance of second cousins
or sometimes even look like old retired ladies
who have nothing more to do
but ride empty subways from stop to stop

At night
hidden away from the city
the youngbloods invade the trainyards
laiden with colors of dreams
crying for existence
on the empty walls of desolation's subway cars
for old ladies to read on and on . . .

Getting Out Alive
Rosario Morales

1.

The South Bronx appears on the TV screen:
I'm looking down Beck Street toward my block.
I stare in shock.

Oh, I'd known things were rough there
After I left,
And that after my parents left it was called Korea
That it was a war zone of sorts.
I'd known
and I hadn't known.

God!
On both sides of the street houses are leveled
Rubble lies on the ground.
Where the grocery store stood—only rubble on an empty lot.
Buildings empty
Their bare plumbing showing through the wounds in the walls
Tile floors covered with plaster and porcelain.
Houses lying there helpless
while children enter and poke and hurt
Use her as a latrine.

I look quickly toward Tiffany
Searching for my old home.
The picture flicks
away.

2.

I moved away from El Barrio
I moved away from the Bronx
I left when the signs showed increasing danger.
Stores with large boards across their gashed windows
Streets full of debris, paper blowing into doorways
I knew the signs,
The smell of death permeating the brick like urine
The occasional casualty spilling brick and glass onto the pavement.
Did I get out in time?

"Puerto Rico" Made in Japan

Jose Angel Figueroa

SOMEWHERE in the mountains
of Caguas, streams looking
flat, flow in every tide
painful reflexions down
the river and to my home.
Touristas push each other
with starving cameras to
show Boston they have seen
Winterless Wonders: like
San Juan natives dressed
in creamy vanilla sunshine
suits and Carmen Mirandas
eating uncle ben's minute
rice. And sometimes,
smiling Puerto Rican door-

men.

And they go home in Eastern
Cielos with gorged cameras
& leave with juggled images
of my homeland.

SOMEDAY our wind will mis-
behave & the rough edges of
the sea will thicken & the
Puerto Rican doormen will
continue smiling when La
Isla Del Encanto pushes
them off the e c h o e s of
h o t e l c i v i l i z a t i o n s.

Borinkins in Hawaii

Victor Hernandez Cruz

for Norma Carr, Blaise Sosa
and Ayala and his famous corner

In 1900
A ship left San Juan Harbor
Full of migrant workers
Of the fields
Enroute to what they believed
To be California
Instead something like C&H
Which managed the vessel
With strings like a puppet
From afar
Took them to Hawaii

When Toño who was one of them
And Jaime who was another
And Felipe who was a third
Of the many 8,000 who took
This spin
Saw Hawaii they thought they
Were still in Puerto Rico
It took movement of time
Show up of the wind
It took the Japanese currents
To convince them
That in somewhere they were

Sugar was the daddy on the
Commercial horizon
Donuts for everybody
Ah history was getting sweet
If you wasn't a cane worker
With sores on your feet
And corns on your hands
Under the sun for how much
A day
Sugar was gonna blow flesh up
Sugar mania

Sugar come from cane
Get some cane
Get some workers
Get some land

The United States talked to the
Old Hawaiian queen
It was a polite conversation
The gringo merely pointed
To where the Marines
Were casually placed
Just that
The Hawaiian Kingdom
Pieces of cake
Littered on the Pacific

"What in the mountain got
Into you Toño to wanna come
From where you were
To jump on this boat
To come to this other planet.
Looka a volcano to lite your
Cigar, a desert for your
Camel, what is this the
End of the world, HA"

"Well Jaime look a guava
And coconut is coconut
See that tree where a Pana
Hangs. Smell the flowers
Fragrance like Aguas Buenas."
Thru each Pana-pen a metropolis
Of juices and texture
Ulus are Pana-pens in Puerto Rico
Ulus: Hawaii
Pana-pen: Puerto Rico
Breadfruit for you
Ulus hang like earrings
From the ears of women

On the tree
A blue dress on top
The curve is the horizon
A reminder that we all live
On a Pana-pen

Hawaii feudal 19th century
Catholic liturgy
Thru the flower tops
The best years of
Tomas-Toñon
Jaime
Felipe and the full migration
Living in camps
Box homes for workers
And their families
Early risers
Church on Sunday
Machete on Monday
Orange curtains thru
The greenery
Cuatro strings
With the bird speech
The pick pickers of
Pineapple stress the
Decima
As back in Borinkin
Ya se men
In ten lines you hem
A skirt
In Kohala they call it
Cachy-cachy

People jumpy-jumpy
Like roosters
The cuatro guitar chirps
Squeeky its note in the
Upper C high nose pitch

Sound of the Arawak
Garganta of the Areyto
Song gallery of
the Ancient inhabitants
Of the boat Borinkin

Broken guitars navigating
Vessels
Arrive like seed onto the
Ground
Whatever is in the dirt
Will come out
We're gonna finger pop
The pineapple
The cane is gonna fly
The majordomos will whip
Ankles
Secret hidden wood
Will get them
There are dark passages of night
Roads under the kona trees
In the dark the sound kaploosh
On the skull
The majordomos are paid
By the plantation owners
The wood is made by nature

At Ayalas Place
3rd & 4th generation Puerto Rican
Hawaiian
Eat rice and beans prepared
By Japanese woman
Soya sauce on the tables
Hawaii only Puerto Rican
Oriental community in the
World

A ship which left San Juan
Turn of the century
Transported workers music
And song
They thought they were
California bound
But were hijacked by
Corporate agriculture
Once they got to land
They folded over
They grew and mixed
Like Hawaii can mix
Portuguese sausage slit
Inside banana leaf
Filipino Japanese eyes
Stare from mulatto faces

The Portuguese brought
The ukulele to anxious fingers
Who looked at the motion of
Palm leaves to help them search
For a sound
They studied the designs of
The hula dancers
And made
A guitar which sounds like
It's being played by the
Fingers of the breeze

They all dance cachy cachy
And jumpy-jumpy
In places like Hilo
And Kohala
You hear the shouts
You hear the groans
You feel the wind of the
Cane workers' machete
And in the eyes you see
The waves of the oceans
You see beads
Which form a necklace

Of islands
Which have emerged out of
The tears.

Thursday

Victor Hernández Cruz

Water is Manhattan
The trains and the buses they sail
Stores and the lights
In the water wet
Thursday far and near strange
A dream Thursday and island
There are two in the memory

What forces elevated me today
To look for what I need
This corner of this earth
Searching for a way to know you
Venus
Thursday Jupiter
Land of somebody's fathers

Wet lines between us all
as the city is bombarded by rain
Young as you are
Young as I am   young as the world
Young History

Now we open doors
Now we remember continents and how they
Danced under the water
Under the ground

Was it Thursday
Was it Thursday

Let me look at you Thursday
Let me look all inside your secret

Open your arms
Elevate
Like rising music
Like that music
that I love so much

Like that Spanish that you like to talk
Like the way you walk

I hold Thursday all in my arms
In the deep tunnel I hear your hair
As it brushes against your neck
As you move
As a dance
Coming to see what it is all about

I build bridges in the sky
Send waves of thoughts
Do you hear them?

Today I eat guineo
With my hands
Under a palm tree by the beach
Where I am not
Do you see the dance that could begin
Evolve.

David Leaves the Saints for Paterson
Martín Espada

David's arm hung near-paralyzed
after the stabbing,
and there was no work in the coffee
of barrio Hills Brothers,
so he learned to smoke with the other hand
and plotted to leave Puerto Rico.

His mother sponge-washed the plaster santos
every week, draped statues crowded

with flowers. Then Tata, la abuela,
would nod with ceremony, foretelling
money and sickness, mouth quavering ajar
with the dialects of the many dead.
In spite of prophecy at Jardines del Paraíso
housing project, no one could stop drinking.

David left the saints for Paterson:
the boot factory, then a hospital job
wheeling carts of delicate bottles
through light-bleached corridors on late shift.

Together with his father at the Paterson hospital,
the gallo-man who learned to box in prison,
who also pushes the medicine carts to impatient doctors
and cannot stop drinking.

Discovery

Victor Hernández Cruz

Watching a thousand smiles
that were full of sadness
standing in a wall
all sideways
My ears are the walls
No one can see me there
I am quiet
Still
Like the owls who sit atop
telephone polls

The traffic between
the walls
Those smiles that come
and go
Those darkened whiskers
suspended in the air

Those souls
Spirits
Coming from one thing
and going to another
but belonging nowhere

The walls breathe
My ears are hung like
blankets
My legs disappear into the
roof
My hands touch the building
next door

I swing from the walls
to the ceilings
No one hears me

I watch a yellow dress
that floats across
the rooms and stares
out of the windows
The Saints walk through
the walls
San Martin has a whole bowl
of grapes sitting on
the altar
he eats one every time
he walks by

Words come out of the rooms
like millions of fire crackers
They slam
Dance against the walls

On a clear Jupiter
The sun enters
Works its way in
Through the parted curtains
It moves inside the yellow
dress that hangs on
Yolanda

So
If you see a yellow dress
flying
Looking down on those
who walk the earth
with borrowed shoes
It's only Yolanda
cooking food
In through the door
and out through
the roof

My ears are the walls
And they hear it all
The yellow dress
It sometimes slips
and falls
Way in there
Where a smile
is six hundred miles
Way in there
where the Indians went to/

Weaver

Sandra Maria Esteves
for Phil George

Weave us a song of many threads

Weave us a red of fire and blood
that tastes of sweet plum
fishing around the memories of the dead
following a scent wounded
our spines bleeding with pain

Weave us a red of passion
that beats wings against a smoky cloud
and forces motion into our lungs

Weave us a song
of yellow and gold and life itself

a wildgrowth
into the great magnetic center
topaz canyons
floral sweatseeds
in continuous universal suspension

Weave us a song of red and yellow and brown
that holds the sea and sky in its skin
the bird and mountain in its voice
that builds upon our graves a home
with fortifications
strength, unity and direction

And weave us a white song to hold us
when the wind blows so cold to make our children wail
submerged in furious ice
a song pure and raw
that burns paper
and attacks the colorless venom stalking hidden
in the petal softness of the black night

Weave us a rich round black that lives
in the eyes of our warrior child
and feeds our mouths with moon breezes
with rivers interflowing
through ALL spaces of existence

Weave us a song for our bodies to sing
a song of many threads
that will dance with the colors of our people
and cover us with the warmth of peace.

ANTHOLOGY

Jesus Colon

Born: 1901
Died: 1974

Jesus Colon has left a valuable record, the first written in English, of what life was like for the first Puerto Ricans to migrate to the United States as permanent residents. His valuable recollections of the years between the mid-twenties and mid-fifties in **A Puerto Rican in New York** (Masses and Mainstream, 1961) are in the form of autobiographical sketches, fictional vignettes, and articles. Colon came from his home in Cayey, Puerto Rico, to the United States in 1918 at the age of seventeen. He was part of a migration made up of artisans, many of them *tabaqueros*, trained cigar makers, who came to work in the small shops in New York. Having had his political consciousness raised by the Bolshevik Revolution in Russia and participation in the labor movement in Puerto Rico, he was keenly aware of the common lot of workers and wrote in part to give them recognition that otherwise would not have been forthcoming. He was a contributor to two socialist newspapers in Puerto Rico, **Union Obrera** and **Justicia**, and to the following newspapers in New York: **El Machete Criollo**, **El Nuevo Mundo**, **The Worker**, **Mainstream**, **The Daily Worker**, **Grafico**, and **Liberation**.

Hiawatha into Spanish

The old *New York World* was a great paper. I bought it mainly for the Heywood Broun column "It Seems To Me," and for the pages and pages of Help Wanted Ads. I got many a "good" porter job through these Help Wanted pages of the *New York World*. Once, I also got myself a job as a translator from these same pages.

Those were the days of the silent films. A film agency somewhere in the Times Square area was asking for a person who could translate the explanatory material like "One Year Later," into Spanish, so that the films could be used in Latin America. Half a penny a word was to be paid. The translator was to work in his own home and all transactions were to be done through the mail. The agency gave a post office box number to which you were supposed to write.

I wrote. The agency mailed me the material to be translated for one short film. I returned the completed translation. Then they sent me a small check, and more work. It seems that they were satisfied.

Time passed. My old Oliver typewriting machine continued to grind translations of inspirational thoughts such as: "The morning after," "One week after," "Five years after." Sometimes a description or historical paragraph such as an introduction to a striking panorama or a scene helped to break the monotony of the hackneyed phrase and the routine short dialogue.

During the early twenties, the episode or chapter of a serial was a standard feature accompanying the main picture in a movie house. At the end of the episode the hero or more often the heroine was left hanging by two fingers from the edge of a cliff or surrounded by half a dozen lions in the middle of an African jungle. The idea was to excite enough curiosity for you to return next week to see what surely appeared, from all logical deduction, like certain death for the hero or heroine. But—what do you know! She or he was miraculously saved from a horrible ending by one of the thousand props that the director always had ready to extract from his shirt sleeve and the serial went on and on for months. Today, you can only see these serials chapter by chapter every week in cheapest of the movie houses or on the most idiotic of the TV programs.

To me, these serials were a gold mine. I was the first to wish the hero eternal life—the longer the serials, the more money I could earn.

One morning I received a long poem that was supposed to be the life of a young American Indian. It was to be used in one of those nature pictures full of rushing rivers, whispering pine trees, bounding deer and flocks of birds suddenly rising out of the thick foliage frightened by the unexpected appearance of "man." The poem was long. The name of the poem was "Hiawatha" by Henry Wadsworth Longfellow. Well, at last I got something worth translating! For a few days I concentrated on making a comparative study of the English and Spanish meter, poetic accent, rhyme and rhythm, before I actually tackled the task of translating the poem itself. It was work. It was fun. Some additional explanation in prose helped in giving clarity and unity to the many natural scenes in the film. The poem itself was broken into sections and these were inserted among the panoramic sequences. When I finished the translation I felt I had done a good job of it.

Hiawatha was sent to the film agency. A few days later I received a complimentary letter with a check. The letter also invited me to come to the office on a certain date. I was being offered steady employment at the agency at a weekly salary.

I got up very early the day of the appointment. I took a great deal of time washing, dressing and combing my hair so that I would look my best. I wore my Sunday suit. The office took up about half an entire floor, way up in a tall building. I asked for the man who had signed the letter. Yes, he was in.

The minute I told him who I was and showed him the letter he himself had signed offering me steady work as a translator, he assumed a cold and impersonal attitude. He made it short and to the point. "Yes, I wrote that letter. I invited you to come to translate for us here at the office." And, pointing to the other side of the room he added "That was to be your desk and typewriter. But I thought you were white."

Then and there that day in the early twenties, I added one more episode to the maturing serial of my life.

Easy Job, Good Wages

This happened early in 1919. We were both out of work, my brother and I. He got up earlier to look for a job. When I woke up, he was already gone. So I dressed, went out and bought a copy of the *New York World* and turned its pages until I got to the "Help Wanted Unskilled" section of the paper. After much reading and re-reading the same columns, my attention was held by a small advertisement. It read: "Easy job. Good wages. No experience necessary." This was followed by a number and street on the west side of lower Manhattan. It sounded like the job I was looking for. Easy job. Good wages. Those four words revolved in my brain as I was travelling toward the address indicated in the advertisement. Easy job. Good wages. Easy job. Good wages. Easy . . .

The place consisted of a small front office and a large loft on the floor of which I noticed a series of large galvanized tubs half filled with water out of which I noticed protruding the necks of many bottles of various sizes and shapes. Around these tubs there were a number of workers, male and female, sitting on small wooden benches. All had their hands in the water of the tub, the left hand holding a bottle and with the thumb nail of the right hand scratching the labels.

The foreman found a vacant stool for me around one of the tubs of water. I asked why a penknife or a small safety razor could not be used instead of the thumb nail to take off the old labels from the bottles. I was expertly informed that knives or razors would scratch the glass thus depreciating the value of the bottles when they were to be sold.

I sat down and started to use my thumb nail on one bottle. The water had somewhat softened the transparent mucilage used to attach the label to the bottle. But the softening did not work out uniformly some-how. There were always pieces of label that for some obscure reason remained affixed to the bottles. It was on those pieces of labels tena-ciously fastened to the bottles that my right hand thumb nail had to work overtime. As the minutes passed I noticed that the coldness of the water started to pass from my hand to my body giving me intermittent body shivers that I tried to conceal with the greatest of effort from those sitting beside me. My hands became deadly clean and tiny little wrinkles started to show especially at the tip of my fingers. Sometimes I stopped a few seconds from scratching the bottles, to open and close my fists in rapid movements in order to bring blood to my hands. But almost as soon as I placed them in the water they became deathly pale again.

But these were minor details compared with what was happening to the thumb of my right hand. From a delicate, boyish thumb, it was growing by the minute into a full blown tomato colored finger. It was the only part of my right hand remaining blood red. I started to look at the workers' thumbs. I noticed that these particular fingers on their right hands were unusually developed with a thick layer of corn-like surface at the top of their right thumb. The nails on their thumbs looked coarser and smaller than on the other fingers—thumb and nail having become one and the same thing—a primitive unnatural human instrument espe-cially developed to detach hard pieces of labels from wet bottles im-mersed in galvanized tubs.

After a couple of hours I had a feeling that my thumb nail was going to leave my finger and jump into the cold water in the tub. A numb pain imperceptibly began to be felt coming from my right thumb. Then I began to feel such pain as if coming from a finger bigger than all of my body.

After three hours of this I decided to quit fast. I told the foreman so, showing him my swollen finger. He figured I had earned 69 cents at 23 cents an hour.

Early in the evening I met my brother in our furnished room. He started to exchange experiences of our job hunting for the day. "You know what?" my brother started, "early in the morning I went to work where they take labels off old bottles—with your right hand thumb nail . . . Somewhere on the west side of lower Manhattan. I only stayed a couple of hours. 'Easy job . . . Good wages' . . . they said. The person who wrote that ad must have had a great sense of humor." And we both had a hearty laugh that evening when I told my brother that I also went to work at that same place later in the day.

Now when I see ads reading, "Easy job. Good wages," I just smile an ancient, tired, knowing smile.

I Heard a Man Crying

Around 1918 I was living in a rooming house on Atlantic Avenue in Brooklyn. I was working then as a scaler. Long distances, long hours and the dirtiest kind of work you could imagine.

As the ships came in, a scaling crew moved in to clean the ship from top to bottom. Cleaning was done especially at the bottom, underneath the machine room, and inside and around the furnaces.

If the ship was an oil tanker, you had to go down to the bottom of that tank ship after the oil was pumped off and collect the oil that the pump was unable to swallow, with a small tin shovel and pail. The pail was placed on a hook at the end of a rope and hoisted up by those working on deck. Pay was better "down below" than on deck, so I always chose to work inside the tanker. As the job was about finished we were supposed to "paint" the inside of the oil tank with Portland cement by just throwing cement at the inside walls of the oil-moist tank. Imagine twenty or twenty-five men throwing cement at the oily walls of an enclosed tank!

When we came out, our faces, eyes, brows and hair looked old and gray. We looked like the grandfathers of our own selves. Some winters when the snow and ice covered the river solidly, the temperature down below at the bottom of the oil tank was below zero. Good thing that we were given rubber boots which fastened at the top of our thighs and rubber pants, jackets and hats that made us look like old seafarers.

Everywhere we went at the bottom of that tank, we were followed by a long electrical wire at the end of which there were three or four electric bulbs protected from breakage by a wire net. Sometimes when we gave the order to hoist the pail filled with oil and we kept looking up at that hole through which a ray of sun kept mocking at us down below, the edge of the pail might abruptly hit the edge of the hole way up there and a splash of ice cold oil would come spattering down and smear your face and neck. Sometimes the oil used to run down your back until it reached the very tip of your spine . . . and more. So, no matter how you scrubbed yourself, some of the oil always remained all over your body from your head to your toes. When I took the old crosstown trolley car with its spongy yellow straw seats and sat in one of them on my way home, I usually left a mark of black moist oil like a great heart parted right down the middle.

It was way into the evening when I came in from my scaling job. I was very tired. The room was very cold. I chose to get into bed with all my clothes on instead of going through the task of starting a fire in the dead coal stove in the middle of the room. (Why is it so difficult for tropical people to start a fire in a hard coal stove?)

As if coming from way out in space through the cracks in my window and from the crevices dividing the door and the floor I heard a very low moaning sound. It went up and down like a wave. Then there was silence for a minute or two and then it started all over again in a repressed way as if the person from whom the crying, moaning sound came did not want to be heard by anybody. Then as if the pain or emotion could not be held back anymore a piercing cry full of self-pity and desperation came distinctly to my ears. At last I could trace clearly from whence it came. It was from another room on the same floor. I knocked at the door of the room. After a short pause, the door was opened by a man who then turned and sat himself on a narrow bed which filled the room.

He covered his face with his hands and then let his crying run fully. I could see that the man was robust, built strong as a bull. He was possibly accustomed to heavy work out of doors. It was sad, yes, tragic, to listen to such a specimen of man crying. So clumsily and innocently strong was he.

In between the minutes that he could control his emotions and his natural shyness, he told me of missing a boat where he was working as a coal passer. The boat belonged to a Spanish shipping company. He himself was Spanish. A story of the ignorance of the language, of fear of the immigration laws, of shyness and of pride, not to beg, not to ask for anything, followed.

The man had not eaten since . . . he didn't remember how many days. He was actually starving, gradually dying of hunger.

Have you ever heard a man crying? A young strong man crying? Crying of hunger in the midst of what is supposed to be the greatest and richest city in the world? It is the saddest, most tragic sight you could ever imagine.

At that hour we left the rooming house and went to the nearest restaurant. He ate as if he had never eaten before in his life.

Next day I took him to an old iron junk yard in which they were asking for young strong men. The job was to break old iron parts of machinery with a sledge hammer. My new Spanish friend wielded the big sledge hammer with the gracefulness and ease of a young girl skipping a thin rope on the sidewalk.

For the first few days I managed to bring him to his place of work. Then he would wait for me in the evening at the wide door of the junk yard until he learned how to take the trolley car that would take him to and from the rooming house where we were living.

I moved. I don't remember the last time I saw that burly, strong young Spaniard.

But I will never forget as long as I live, his deep anguished crying of hunger that night—long, long ago.

Kipling and I

Sometimes I pass Debevoise Place at the corner of Willoughby Street . . . I look at the old wooden house, gray and ancient, the house where I used to live some forty years ago . . .

My room was on the second floor at the corner. On hot summer nights I would sit at the window reading by the electric light from the street lamp which was almost at a level with the window sill.

It was nice to come home late during the winter, look for some scrap of old newspaper, some bits of wood and a few chunks of coal and start a sparkling fire in the chunky fourlegged coal stove. I would be rewarded with an intimate warmth as little by little the pygmy stove became alive puffing out its sides, hot and red, like the crimson cheeks of a Santa Claus.

My few books were in a soap box nailed to the wall. But my most prized possession in those days was a poem I had bought in a five and ten cent store on Fulton Street. (I wonder what has become of these poems, maxims and sayings of wise men that they used to sell at the five and ten cent stores?) The poem was printed on gold paper and mounted in a gilded frame ready to be hung in a conspicuous place in the house. I bought one of those fancy silken picture cords finishing in a rosette to match the color of the frame.

I was seventeen. This poem to me then seemed to summarize the wisdom of all the sages that ever lived in one poetical nutshell. It was what I was looking for, something to guide myself by, a way of life, a compendium of the wise, the true and the beautiful. All I had to do was to live according to the counsel of the poem and follow its instructions and I would be a perfect man—the useful, the good, the true human being. I was very happy that day, forty years ago.

The poem had to have the most prominent place in the room. Where could I hang it? I decided that the best place for the poem was on the wall right by the entrance to the room. No one coming in and out would miss it. Perhaps someone would be interested enough to read it and drink the profound waters of its message . . .

Every morning as I prepared to leave, I stood in front of the poem and read it over and over again, sometimes half a dozen times. I let the sonorous music of the verse carry me away. I brought with me a hand-written copy as I stepped out every morning looking for work, repeating verses and stanzas from memory until the whole poem came to be part of me. Other days my lips kept repeating a single verse of the poem at intervals throughout the day.

In the subways I loved to compete with the shrill noises of the many wheels below by chanting the lines of the poem. People stared at me moving my lips as though I were in a trance. I looked back with pity. They were not so fortunate as I who had as a guide to direct my life a great poem to make me wise, useful and happy.

And I chanted:

If you can keep your head when all about you
Are losing theirs and blaming it on you . . .

If you can wait and not be tired by waiting
Or being hated don't give way to hating . . .

If you can make one heap of all your winnings
And risk it on a turn of pitch and toss . . .
And lose and start again at your beginnings . . .

"If," by Kipling, was the poem. At seventeen, my evening prayer and my first morning thought. I repeated it every day with the resolution to live up to the very last line of that poem.

I would visit the government employment office on Jay Street. The conversations among the Puerto Ricans on the large wooden benches in the employment office were always on the same subject. How to find a decent place to live. How they would not rent to Negroes or Puerto Ricans. How Negroes and Puerto Ricans were given the pink slips first at work.

From the employment office I would call door to door at the piers, factories and storage houses in the streets under the Brooklyn and Manhattan Bridges. "Sorry, nothing today." It seemed to me that "today" was a continuation and combination of all the yesterdays, todays and tomorrows.

From the factories I would go to the restaurants looking for a job as a porter or dishwasher. At least I would eat and be warm in a kitchen.

"Sorry" . . . "Sorry" . . .

Sometimes I was hired at ten dollars a week, ten hours a day including Sundays and holidays. One day off during the week. My work was that of three men: dishwasher, porter, busboy. And to clear the sidewalk of snow and slush "when you have nothing else to do." I was to be appropriately humble and grateful not only to the owner but to everybody else in the place.

If I rebelled at insults or at a pointed innuendo or just the inhuman amount of work, I was unceremoniously thrown out and told to come "next week for your pay." "Next Week" meant weeks of calling for the paltry dollars owed me. The owners relished this "next week."

I clung to my poem as to a faith. Like a potent amulet, my precious poem was clenched in the fist of my right hand inside my second hand overcoat. Again and again I declaimed aloud a few precious lines when discouragement and disillusionment threatened to overwhelm me.

If you can force your heart and nerve and sinew
To serve your turn long after you are gone . . .

The weeks of unemployment and hard knocks turned into months. I continued to find two or three days of work here and there. And I continued to be thrown out when I rebelled at the ill treatment, over-work and insults. I kept pounding the streets looking for a place where they would treat me half decently, where my devotion to work and faith in Kipling's poem would be appreciated. I remember the worn out shoes I bought in a secondhand store on Myrtle Avenue at the corner of Adams Street. The round holes in the soles that I tried to cover with pieces of carton were no match for the frigid knives of the unrelenting snow.

One night I returned late after a long day of looking for work. I was hungry. My room was dark and cold. I wanted to warm my numb body. I lit a match and began looking for some scraps of wood and a piece of paper to start a fire. I searched all over the floor. No wood, no paper. As I stood up, the glimmering flicker of the dying match was reflected in the glass surface of the framed poem. I unhooked the poem from the wall. I reflected for a minute, a minute that felt like an eternity. I took the frame apart, placing the square glass upon the small table. I tore the gold paper on which the poem was printed, threw its pieces inside the stove and placing the small bits of wood from the frame on top of the paper I lit it adding soft and hard coal as the fire began to gain strength and brightness.

I watched how the lines of the poem withered into ashes inside the small stove.

A Hero in the Junk Truck

How many times have we read boastful statements from high educational leaders in our big newspapers that while other countries ignore the history and culture of the United States, our educational system does instruct our children in the history and traditions of other countries.

As far as instruction in the most elementary knowledge of Latin America is concerned, we are forced to state that what our children receive is a hodgepodge of romantic generalities and chauvinistic declarations spread further and wider by Hollywood movies.

We do not have to emphasize that the people are not to blame.

Blame rests on those persons and reactionary forces that represent and defend the interests of finance capital in education.

Last summer my wife and I had an experience that could be presented as proof of our assertion.

We were passing by, on bus No. 37, my wife and I.

"Look, Jesus, look!" said my wife pointing excitedly to a junk truck in front of the building that was being torn down. A truck full of the accumulated debris of many years was parked with its rear to the sidewalk, littered with pieces of brick and powdered cement.

Atop the driver's cabin of the truck and protruding like a spangled banner, was a huge framed picture of a standing figure. Upon his breast was a double line of medals and decorations.

"Did you notice who the man was in that framed picture?" my wife asked insistently as the bus turned the corner of Adams and Fulton Street.

"Who," I answered absent mindedly.

"Bolivar," my wife shouted.

"Who did you say he was?" I inquired as if unduly awakened from a daze.

"Bolivar, Bolivar," my wife repeated excitedly and then she added, "and to think that he is being thrown out into a junk truck," she stammered in a breaking voice.

We got out of the bus in a hurry. Walked to where the truck was about to depart with the dead waste of fragments of a thousand things. The driver caught us staring at the picture.

"What do you want?" he shouted to us in a shrill voice above the noise of the acetylene torch and the electric hammers.

"You know who he is," I cried back pointing at the picture tied atop the cabin of the driver's truck like Joan of Arc tied to the flaming stake.

"I don't know and I don't care," the driver counter-blasted in a still higher pitch of voice. But I noticed that there was no enmity in the tone of his voice, though loud and ear-drum breaking.

"He is like George Washington to a score of Latin American countries. He is . . ."

"You want it?" he interrupted in a more softened voice.

"Of course!" my wife answered for both of us, just about jumping with glee.

As the man was unroping Bolivar from atop the truck cabin, the usual group of passersby started clustering around and encircling us—the truck driver, my wife, myself and Bolivar's painting standing erect and magnificent in the middle of us all.

"Who is he, who is he?" came the question of the inquiring voices from everywhere. The crowd was huddled on top of us, as football players ring themselves together bending from their trunks down when they are making a decision before the next play. "Who is he, I mean, the man in the picture?" they continued to ask.

Nobody knew. Nobody seemed to care really. The question was asked more out of curiosity than real interest. The ones over on the third line of the circle of people craned their necks over the ones on the second and the first lines upping themselves on their toes in order to be able to take a passing glance at the picture. "He is not American, is he?" someone inquired from the crowd.

My wife finally answered them with a tinge of pride in her voice. "He is Simon Bolivar, the liberator of Latin America."

Curiosity fulfilled, everybody was on his way again. Only my wife, myself and Bolivar remained.

Well, what to do next. It was obvious that the bus driver would not allow us in the bus with such a large framed painting going back home. Fortunately we have a very good American friend living in the Borough Hall neighborhood.

"Let us take him to John's place until we find a person with a car to take Bolivar to our home," I said. My wife agreed.

We opened the door of John's apartment.

"I see that you are coming with very distinguished company today: 'Bolivar,'" he said, simply and casually as if he had known it all his life.

John took some cleaning fluid and a soft rag and went over the whole frame in a loving and very tender manner.

We heard a knock at the door. In came a tall and very distinguished looking man dressed in black, a blend of Lincoln and Emerson in his personality. "He is a real representative of progressive America," John whispered to us. The Reverend spoke quietly and serenely. Looking at the picture he said just one word:

"Bolivar!"

And we all felt very happy.

Little Things Are Big

It was very late at night on the eve of Memorial Day. She came into the subway at the 34th Street Pennsylvania Station. I am still trying to remember how she managed to push herself in with a baby on her right arm, a valise in her left hand and two children, a boy and girl about three and five years old, trailing after her. She was a nice looking white lady in her early twenties.

At Nevins Street, Brooklyn, we saw her preparing to get off at the next station—Atlantic Avenue—which happened to be the place where I too had to get off. Just as it was a problem for her to get on, it was going to be a problem for her to get off the subway with two small children to be taken care of, a baby on her right arm and a medium sized valise in her left hand.

And there I was, also preparing to get off at Atlantic Avenue, with no bundles to take care of—not even the customary book under my arm without which I feel that I am not completely dressed.

As the train was entering the Atlantic Avenue station, some white man stood up from his seat and helped her out, placing the children on the long, deserted platform. There were only two adult persons on the long platform some time after midnight on the eve of last Memorial Day.

I could perceive the steep, long concrete stairs going down to the Long Island Railroad or into the street. Should I offer my help as the

60

American white man did at the subway door placing the two children outside the subway car? Should I take care of the girl and the boy, take them by their hands until they reached the end of the steep long concrete stairs of the Atlantic Avenue station?

Courtesy is a characteristic of the Puerto Rican. And here I was—a Puerto Rican—hours past midnight, a valise, two white children and a white lady with a baby on her arm palpably needing somebody to help her at least until she descended the long concrete stairs.

But how could I, a Negro and a Puerto Rican approach this white lady who very likely might have preconceived prejudices against Negroes and everybody with foreign accents, in a deserted subway station very late at night?

What would she say? What would be the first reaction of this white American woman, perhaps coming from a small town with a valise, two children and a baby on her right arm? Would she say: Yes, of course, you may help me. Or would she think that I was just trying to get too familiar? Or would she think worse than that perhaps? What would I do if she let out a scream as I went toward her to offer my help?

Was I misjudging her? So many slanders are written every day in the daily press against the Negroes and Puerto Ricans. I hesitated for a long, long minute. The ancestral manners that the most illiterate Puerto Rican passes on from father to son were struggling inside me. Here was I, way past midnight, face to face with a situation that could very well explode into an outburst of prejudices and chauvinistic conditioning of the "divide and rule" policy of present day society.

It was a long minute. I passed on by her as if I saw nothing. As if I was insensitive to her need. Like a rude animal walking on two legs, I just moved on half running by the long subway platform leaving the children and the valise and her with the baby on her arm. I took the steps of the long concrete stairs in twos until I reached the street above and the cold air slapped my warm face.

This is what racism and prejudice and chauvinism and official artificial divisions can do to people and to a nation!

Perhaps the lady was not prejudiced after all. Or not prejudiced enough to scream at the coming of a Negro toward her in a solitary subway station a few hours past midnight.

If you were not that prejudiced, I failed you, dear lady. I know that there is a chance in a million that you will read these lines. I am willing to take that millionth chance. If you were not that prejudiced, I failed you, lady, I failed you, children. I failed myself to myself.

I buried my courtesy early on Memorial Day morning. But here is a promise that I make to myself here and now; if I am ever faced with an occasion like that again, I am going to offer my help regardless of how the offer is going to be received.

Then I will have my courtesy with me again.

The Mother, The Young Daughter, Myself and All Of Us

I was drinking a cup of coffee in one of those new places where the counter is built in a zig-zag way, like a curving long line of conga dancers. The high stools follow the wavy contours of the counter, making little bays of tall seats where the patrons seat themselves placing their feet in a sort of iron stirrup.

That day every stool was taken but one, on my right side, and another, three stools further to my left.

A mother and her young daughter about nine years old, came in evidently to have a snack.

"You sit by the gentleman," meaning me . . . the mother said to her young daughter pointing to the unoccupied stool on my right. "I will be sitting over there," the mother added, pointing to the other empty stool three seats to my left.

"I won't sit beside no nigger," said the child.

And the mother, myself, and all of us never said a word.

Piri Thomas

Born: 1928

With the publication of *Down These Mean Streets* Piri Thomas became the first Puerto Rican novelist in the United States and the first to be read extensively outside the Puerto Rican community of New York City. Inside and outside of that community *Down These Mean Streets* has been controversial. To many young Latino writers Thomas' success served as a hopeful signal of future publishing possibilities and stimulated them to move ahead with their work; some inside the community resented Thomas' depiction of the crime and depravity that existed on the streets where they lived. On the outside there was the lust for the sensational on one hand and groups wanting to ban the book from library shelves on the other. Whatever its effect was, it reflected some truths about the inner cities of the United States that are even harsher and more evident today.

Piri Thomas was born and raised in Spanish Harlem. As a young boy he was a gang member who proceeded along the path that so many ghetto youth travel to dope addiction, armed robbery, and prison where he was incarcerated for seven years. What he learned along the way has informed his work throughout his life, whether he is writing books, television, or film scripts, working with children, performing poetry (often reading his work to the beat of African drums, Latin *salsa*, jazz), painting, acting, filming, directing, or lecturing at educational institutions, prisons, museums, or on radio and television.

Thomas has written three novels—*Down These Mean Streets* (Knopf, 1967), *Savior, Savior Hold My Hand* (Doubleday, 1972), a biographical novel exposing the hypocrisy of some religious groups and *Seven Long Times* (Praeger, 1974), an expose of the brutality of the prison system in the United States—a volume of short stories, *Stories from El Barrio* (Knopf, 1978), and *The Golden Streets*, a play that was performed in Puerto Rico in 1972. Two television documentaries that Thomas has written, *Petey & Johnny* and *The World of Piri Thomas*, explore the topic of drug rehabilitation. He has published articles in numerous magazines and journals such as *The New York Times Magazine*, *Saturday Review*, *Crisis 82* and has been anthologized in *A*

Gathering of Ghetto Writers: Irish, Italian, Jewish, Black and Puerto Rican, The Nuyorican Experience; Literature of the Puerto Rican Minority, and in the Dutch *Puertoricaanse Literatuur in Nueva York*, among others. Articles too numerous to mention have been written about Thomas. His papers are maintained at the Schomburg Library in New York as the Piri Thomas Collection. He now resides in Berkeley, California.

Alien Turf

Sometimes you don't fit in. Like if you're a Puerto Rican on an Italian block. After my new baby brother, Ricardo, died of some kind of germs, Poppa moved us from 111th Street to Italian turf on 114th Street between Second and Third Avenue. I guess Poppa wanted to get Momma away from the hard memories of the old pad.

I sure missed 111th Street, where everybody acted, walked, and talked like me. But on 114th Street everything went all right for a while. There were a few dirty looks from the spaghetti-an'-sauce cats, but no big sweat. Till that one day I was on my way home from school and almost had reached my stoop when someone called: "Hey, you dirty fuckin' spic."

The words hit my ears and almost made me curse Poppa at the same time. I turned around real slow and found my face pushing in the finger of an Italian kid about my age. He had five or six of his friends with him.

"Hey, you," he said. "What nationality are ya?"

I looked at him and wondered which nationality to pick. And one of his friends said, "Ah, Rocky, he's black enuff to be a nigger. Ain't that what you is, kid?"

My voice was almost shy in its anger. "I'm Puerto Rican," I said. "I was born here." I wanted to shout it, but it came out like a whisper.

"Right here inna street?" Rocky sneered. "Ya mean right here inna middle of da street?"

They all laughed.

I hated them. I shook my head slowly from side to side. "Uh-uh," I said softly. "I was born inna hospital—inna bed."

"Ummm, *paisan*— born inna bed," Rocky said.

I didn't like Rocky Italiano's voice. "Inna hospital," I whispered, and all the time my eyes were trying to cut down the long distance from this trouble to my stoop. I couldn't help thinking about kids getting wasted for moving into a block belonging to other people.

"What hospital, *paisan*?" Bad Rocky pushed.

"Harlem Hosptial," I answered, wishing like all hell that it was 5 o'clock intead of just 3 o'clock, 'cause Poppa came home at 5. I looked around for some friendly faces belonging to grown-up people, but the elders were all busy yakking away in Italian. I couldn't help thinking how much like Spanish it sounded. Shit, that should make us something like relatives.

"Harlem Hospital?" said a voice. "I knew he was a nigger."

"Yeah," said another voice from an expert on color. "That's the hospital where all them black bastards get born at."

I dug three Italian elders looking at us from across the street, and I felt saved. But that went out the window when they just smiled and went on talking. I couldn't decide whether they had smiled because this new whatever-he-was was gonna get his ass kicked or because they were pleased that their kids were welcoming a new kid to their country. An older man nodded his head at Rocky, who smiled back. I wondered if that was a signal for my funeral to begin.

"Ain't that right, kid?" Rocky pressed. "Aint' that where all black people get born?"

I dug some of Rocky's boys grinding and pushing and punching closed fists against open hands. I figured they were looking to shake me up, so I straightened up my humble voice and made like proud. "There's all kinds of people born there. Colored people, Puerto Ricans like me, an'—even spaghetti-benders like you."

"That's a dirty fuckin' lie"—*bash*, I felt Rocky's fist smack into my mouth—"you dirty fuckin' spic."

I got dizzy and then more dizzy when fists started to fly from everywhere and only toward me. I swung back, *splat*, *bish*—my fist hit some face and I wished I hadn't, 'cause then I started getting kicked.

I heard people yelling in Italian and English and I wondered if maybe it was 'cause I hadn't fought fair in having hit that one guy. But it wasn't. The voices were trying to help me.

"Whas'sa matta, you no-good kids, leeva da kid alone," a man said. I looked through a swelling eye and dug some Italians pushing their kids off me with slaps. One even kicked a kid in the ass. I could have loved them if I didn't hate them so fuckin' much.

"You all right, kiddo?" asked the man.

"Where you live, boy?" said another one.

"Is the *bambino* hurt?" asked a woman.

I didn't look at any of them. I felt dizzy. I didn't want to open my mouth to talk, 'cause I was fighting to keep from puking up. I just hoped my face was cool-looking. I walked away from that group of strangers. I reached my stoop and started to climb the steps.

"Hey, spic," came a shout from across the street. I started to turn to the voice and changed my mind. "Spic" wasn't my name. I knew that voice, though. It was Rocky's. "We'll see ya again, spic," he said.

I wanted to do something tough, like spitting in their direction. But you gotta have spit in your mouth in order to spit, and my mouth was hurt dry. I just stood there with my back to them.

"Hey, your old man just better be the janitor in that fuckin' building."

Another voice added, "Hey, you got any pretty sisters? We might let ya stay onna block."

Another voice mocked, "Aw, fer Chrissake, where ya ever hear of one of them black broads being pretty?"

I heard the laughter. I turned around and looked at them. Rocky made some kind of dirty sign by putting his left hand in the crook of his right arm while twisting his closed fist in the air.

Another voice said, "Fuck it, we'll just cover the bitch's face with the flag an' fuck er for old glory."

All I could think of was how I'd like to kill each of them two or three times. I found some spit in my mouth and splattered it in their direction and went inside.

Momma was cooking, and the smell of rice and beans was beating the smell of Parmesan cheese from the other apartments. I let myself into our new pad. I tried to walk fast past Momma so I could wash up, but she saw me.

"My God, Piri, what happened?" she cried.

"Just a little fight in school, Momma. You know how it is, Momma, I'm new in school an'. . ." I made myself laugh. Then I made myself say, "But Moms, I whipped the living—outta two guys, an' one was bigger'n me."

"*Bendito*, Piri, I raise this family in Christian way. Not to fight. Christ says to turn the other cheek."

"Sure, Momma." I smiled and went and showered, feeling sore at Poppa for bringing us into spaghetti country. I felt my face with easy fingers and thought about all the running back and forth from school that was in store for me.

I sat down to dinner and listened to Momma talk about Christian living without really hearing her. All I could think of was that I had a go out in that street again. I made up my mind to go out right after I finished eating. I had to, shook up or not, cats like me had to show heart.

"Be back, Moms," I said after dinner, "I'm going out on the stoop." I got halfway to the stoop and turned and went back to our apartment. I knocked.

"Who is it?" Momma asked.

"Me, Momma."

She opened the door. "*Qué pasa?*" she asked.

"Nothing, Momma, I just forgot something," I said. I went into the bedroom and fiddled around and finally copped a funny book and walked out the door again. But this time I made sure the switch on the lock was open, just in case I had to get back real quick. I walked out on that stoop as cool as could be, feeling braver with the lock open.

There was no sign of Rocky and his killers. After awhile I saw Poppa coming down the street. He walked like beat tired. Poppa hated his pick-and-shovel job with the WPA. He couldn't even hear the name WPA without getting a fever. *Funny*, I thought, *Poppa's the same like me, a stone Puerto Rican, and nobody in this block even pays him a mind. Maybe older people get along better'n us kids.*

Poppa was climbing the stoop. "Hi, Poppa," I said.

"How's it going, son? Hey, you sure look a little lumped up. What happened?"

I looked at Poppa and started to talk it outta me all at once and stopped, 'cause I heard my voice start to sound scared, and that was no good.

"Slow down, son," Poppa said. "Take it easy." He sat down on the stoop and made a motion for me to do the same. He listened and I talked. I gained confidence. I went from a tone of being shook up by the Italians to a tone of being a better fighter than Joe Louis and Pedro Montanez lumped together, with Kid Chocolate thrown in for extra.

"So that's what happened," I concluded. "And it looks like only the beginning. Man, I ain't scared, Poppa, but like there's nothin' but Italianos on this block and there's no me's like me except me an' our family."

Poppa looked tight. He shook his head from side to side and mumbled something about another Puerto Rican family that lived a coupla doors down from us.

I thought, *What good would that do me, unless they prayed over my dead body in Spanish?* But I said, "Man! That's great. Before ya know it, there'll be a whole bunch of us moving in, huh?"

Poppa grunted something and got up. "Staying out here, son?"

"Yeah, Poppa, for a little while longer."

From that day on I grew eyes all over my head. Anytime I hit that street for anything, I looked straight ahead, behind me and from side to side all at the same time. Sometimes I ran into Rocky and his boys—that cat was never without his boys—but they never made a move to snag me. They just grinned at me like a bunch of hungry alley cats that could get to their mouse anytime they wanted. That's what they made me feel like—a mouse. Not like a smart house mouse but like a white house pet that ain't got no business in the middle of cat country but don't know better 'cause he grew up thinking he was a cat—which wasn't far from wrong 'cause he'd end up as part of the inside of some cat.

Rocky and his fellas got to playing a way-out game with me called "One-finger-across-the-neck-inna-slicing-motion," followed by such gentle words as "It won't be long, spico." I just looked at them blank and made it to wherever I was going.

I kept wishing those cats went to the same school I went to, a school that was on the border between their country and mine, and I had *amigos* there—and there I could count on them. But I couldn't ask two or three *amigos* to break into Rocky's block and help me mess up his boys. I knew 'cause I had asked them already. They had turned me down fast, and I couldn't blame them. It would have been murder, and I guess they figured one murder would be better than four.

I got through the days trying to play it cool and walk on by Rocky and his boys like they weren't there. One day I passed them and nothing was said. I started to let out my breath. I felt great; I hadn't been seen. Then someone yelled in a high, girlish voice, "Yoo-hoo . . . Hey, *paisan* . . . we see yoo . . ." And right behind that voice came a can of evaporated milk—whoosh, clatter. I walked cool for ten steps then started running like mad.

This crap kept up for a month. They tried to shake me up. Every time they threw something at me, it was just to see me jump. I decided that the next fucking time they threw something at me I was gonna play bad-o and not run. That next time came about a week later. Momma sent me off the stoop to the Italian market on 115th Street and First Avenue, deep in Italian country. Man, that was stompin' territory. But I went, walking in the style which I had copped from the colored cats I had seen, a swinging and stepping down hard at every step. Those cats were so down and cool that just walking made a way-out sound.

Ten minutes later I was on my way back with Momma's stuff. I got to the comer of First Avenue and 114th Street and crushed myself right into Rocky and his fellas.

"Well-l, fellas," Rocky said. "Lookee who's here."

I didn't like the sounds coming out of Rocky's fat mouth. And I didn't like the sameness of the shitty grins spreading all over the boys' faces. But I thought, *No more! No more! I ain't gonna run no more.* Even so, I looked around, like for some kind of Jesus miracle to happen. I was always looking for miracles to happen.

"Say, *paisan,*" one guy said, "you even buying from us *paisans,* eh? Man, you must wantta be Italian."

Before I could bite that dopey tongue of mine, I said,"I wouldn't be a guinea on a motherfucking bet."

"Wha-at?" said Rocky, really surprised. I didn't blame him; I was surprised myself. His finger began digging a hole in his ear, like he hadn't heard me right. "Wha-at? Say that again?"

I could feel a thin hot wetness cutting itself down my leg. I had been so ashamed of being so damned scared that I had peed on myself. And then I wasn't scared any more; I felt a fuck-it-all attitude. I looked real bad at Rocky and said, "Ya heard me. I wouldn't be a guinea on a bet."

"Ya little sonavabitch, we'll kick the shit outta ya," said one guy, Tony, who had made a habit of asking me if I had any sen-your-ritas for sisters.

"Kick the shit outta me yourself if you got any heart, you mother-fuckin' fucker," I screamed at him. I felt kind of happy, the kind of feeling that you get only when you got heart.

Big-mouth Tony just swung out, and I swung back and heard all of Momma's stuff plopping all over the street. My fist hit Tony smack dead in the mouth. He was so mad he threw a fist at me from about three feet away. I faked and jabbed and did fancy dance steps. Big-mouth put a stop to all that with a punch in my mouth. I heard the home cheers of "Yea, yea, bust that spic wide open!" Then I bloodied Tony's nose. He blinked and sniffed without putting his hands to his nose, and I remembered Poppa telling me, "Son, if you're ever fighting somebody an' you punch him in the nose, and he just blinks an' sniffs without holding his nose, you can do one of two things: fight like hell or run like hell—'cause that cat's a fighter."

Big-mouth came at me and we grabbed each other and pushed and pulled and shoved. *Poppa,* I thought, *I ain't gonna cop out. I'm a fighter too.* I pulled away from Tony and blew my fist into his belly. He puffed and butted my nose with his head. I sniffed back. *Poppa, I didn't put my hands to my nose.* I hit Tony again in the same weak spot. He bent over in the middle and went down to his knees.

71

Big-mouth got up as fast as he could, and I was thinking how much heart he had. But I ran toward him like my life depended on it; I wanted to cool him. Too late, I saw his hand grab a fistful of ground asphalt which had been piled nearby to fix a pothole in the street. I tried to duck; I should have closed my eyes instead. The shitty-gritty stuff hit my face, and I felt the scrappy pain make itself a part of my eyes. I screamed and grabbed for two eyes with one hand, while the other beat some kind of helpless tune on air that just couldn't be hurt. I heard Rocky's voice shouting, "Ya scum bag, ya didn't have to fight the spic dirty; you could've fucked him up fair and square!" I couldn't see. I heard a fist hit a face, then Bigmouth's voice: "Whatta ya hittin' me for?" and then Rocky's voice: "*Putana*! I ought ta knock all your fuckin' teeth out."

I felt hands grabbing at me between my screams. I punched out. *I'm gonna get killed*, I thought. Then I heard many voices: "Hold it, kid." "We ain't gonna hurt ya." "*Je-sus*, don't rub your eyes." "Ooooohhhh, shit, his eyes is fulla that shit."

You're fuckin' right, I thought, *and it hurts like* coño.

I herd a woman's voice now: "Take him to a hospital." And an old man asked: "How did it happen?"

"Momma, Momma," I cried.

"Comon, kid," Rocky said, taking my hand. "Lemme take ya home." I fought for the right to rub my eyes. "Grab his other hand, Vincent," Rocky said. I tried to rub my eyes with my eyelids. I could feel hurt tears cutting down my cheeks. "Come on, kid, we ain't gonna hurt ya," Rocky tried to assure me. "Swear to our mudders. We just wanna take ya home."

I made myself believe him, and trying not to make pain noises, I let myself be led home. I wondered if I was gonna be blind like Mr. Silva, who went around from door to door selling dish towels and brooms, his son leading him around.

"You okay, kid?" Rocky asked.

"Yeah," what was left of me said.

"A-huh," mumbled Big-mouth.

"He got much heart for a nigger," somebody else said.

A spic, I thought.

"For anybody," Rocky said. "Here we are, kid," he added. "Watch your step."

I was like carried up the steps. "What's your apartment number?" Rocky asked.

"One-B—inna back—ground floor," I said, and I was led there. Somebody knocked on Momma's door. Then I heard running feet and Rocky's voice yelling back, "Don't rat, huh, kid?" And I was alone.

I heard the door open and Momma say, "*Bueno*, Piri, come in." I didn't move. I couldn't. There was a long pause; I could hear Momma's fright. "My God," she said finally. "What's happened?" Then she took a closer look. "Ai-eeee," she screamed. "*Dios mío!*"

"I was playing with some kids, Momma," I said, "an' I got some dirt in my eyes." I tried to make my voice come out without the pain, like a man.

"*Dios eterno*—your eyes!"

"What's the matter? What's the matter?" Poppa called from the bedroom.

"*Está ciego!*" Momma screamed. "He is blind!"

I heard Poppa knocking things over as he came running. Sis began to cry. Blind, hurting tears were jumping out of my eyes.

"Whattya mean, he's blind?" Poppa said as he stormed into the kitchen. "What happened?" Poppa's voice was both scared and mad.

"Playing, Poppa."

"Whatta ya mean, 'playing'?" Poppa's English sounded different when he got warm.

"Just playing, Poppa."

"Playing? Playing got all that dirt in your eyes? I bet my ass. Them damn Ee-ta-liano kids ganged up on you again." Poppa squeezed my head between the fingers of one hand. "That settles it—we're moving outta this damn section, outta this damn block, outta this damn shit."

Shit, I thought, *Poppa's sure cursin' up a storm.* I could hear him slapping the side of his leg, like he always did when he got real mad.

"Son," he said, "you're gonna point them out to me."

"Point who out, Poppa? I was playin' an'—"

"Stop talkin' to him and take him to the hospital," Momma screamed.

"*Pobrecito*, poor Piri," cooed my little sister.

"You sure, son?" Poppa asked. "You was only playing?"

"Shit, Poppa, I said I was."

Smack—Poppa was so scared and mad, he let it out in a slap to the side of my face.

"*Bestia! Ani-mul!*" Momma cried. "He's blind, and you hit him"

"I'm sorry, son, I'm sorry," Poppa said in a voice like almost-crying. I heard him running back into the bedroom, yelling, "Where's my pants?"

Momma grabbed away fingers that were trying to wipe away the hurt in my eyes. "*Caramba*, no rub, no rub," she said, kissing me. She told Sis to get a rag and wet it with cold water.

Poppa came running back into the kitchen. "Let's go, son, let's go. Jesus! I didn't mean to smack ya, I really didn't," he said, his big hand rubbing and grabbing my hair gently.

"Here's the rag, Momma," said Sis.

"What's that for?" asked Poppa.

"To put on his eyes," Momma said.

I heard the smack of a wet rag, *blapt*, against the kitchen wall. "We can't put nothing on his eyes. It might make them worse. Come on, son," Poppa said nervously, lifting me up in his big arms. I felt like a little baby, like I didn't hurt so bad. I wanted to stay there, but I said, "Let me down, Poppa, I ain't no kid."

"Shut up," Poppa said softly. "I know you ain't, but it's faster this way."

"Which hospeetal are you taking him to?" Momma asked.

"Nearest one," Poppa answered as we went out the door. He carried me through the hall and out into the street, where the bright sunlight made a red hurting color through the crap in my eyes. I heard voices on the stoop and on the sidewalk: "Is that the boy?"

"A-huh. He's probably blinded."

"We'll get a cab, son," Poppa said. His voice loved me. I heard Rocky yelling from across the street, "We're pulling for ya, kid. Remember what we. . ." The rest was lost to Poppa's long legs running down to the corner of Third Avenue. He hailed a taxi and we zoomed off toward Harlem Hospital. I felt the cab make all kinds of sudden stops and turns.

"How do you feel, *hijo*?" Poppa asked.

"It hurts like hell."

"You'll be okay," he said, and as an after thought added, "Don't curse, son."

I heard cars honking and the Third Avenue el roaring above us. I knew we were in Puerto Rican turf, cause I could hear our language.

"Son."

"Yeah, Poppa."

"Don't rub your eyes, fer Chirst sake." He held my skinny wrists in his one hand, and everything got quiet between us.

The cab got to Harlem Hospital. I heard change being handled and the door opening and Poppa thanking the cabbie for getting here fast. "Hope the kid'll be okay," the driver said.

I will be, I thought. *I ain't gonna be like Mr. Silva.*

Poppa took me in his arms again and started running. "Where's emergency, mister?" he asked someone.

"To your left and straight away," said a voice.

"Thanks a lot," Poppa said, and we were running again. "Emergency?" Poppa said when we stopped.

"Yes, sir," said a girl's voice. "What's the matter?"

"My boy's got his eyes full of ground-up tar an'—"

"What's the matter?" said a man's voice.

"Youngster with ground tar in his eyes, doctor."

"We'll take him, mister. You just put him down here and go with the nurse. She'll take down the information. Uh, you the father?"

"That's right, doctor."

"Okay, just put him down here."

"Poppa, don't leave me," I cried.

"Sh, son, I ain't leaving you. I'm just going to fill out some papers, an' I'll be right back."

I nodded my head up and down and was wheeled away. When the rolling stretcher stopped, somebody stuck a needle in me and I got sleepy and started thinking about Rocky and his boys, and Poppa's slap, and how great Poppa was, and how my eyes didn't hurt no more . . .

74

I woke up in a room blind with darkness. The only lights were the ones inside my head. I put my fingers to my eyes and felt bandages. "Let them be, sonny," said a woman's voice.

I wanted to ask the voice if they had taken my eyes out, but I didn't. I was afraid the voice would say yes.

"Let them be, sonny," the nurse said, pulling my hand away from the bandages. "You're all right. The doctor put the bandages on to keep the light out. They'll be off real soon. Don't you worry none, sonny."

I wished she would stop calling me sonny. "Where's Poppa?" I asked cool-like.

"He's outside, sonny. Would you like me to send him in?"

I nodded, "Yeah." I heard walking-away shoes, a door opening, a whisper, and shoes walking back toward me. "How do you feel, *hijo?*" Poppa asked.

"It hurts like shit, Poppa."

"Its just for awhile, son, and then off come the bandages. Everything's gonna be all right."

I thought, *Poppa didn't tell me to stop cursing.*

"And son, I thought I told you to stop cursing," he added.

I smiled. Poppa hadn't forgotten. Suddenly I realized that all I had on was a hospital gown. "Poppa, where's my clothes?" I asked.

"I got them. I'm taking them home an'—"

"Whatta ya mean, Poppa?" I said, like scared. "You ain't leavin' me here? I'll be damned if I stay." I was already sitting up and feeling my way outta bed. Poppa grabbed me and pushed me back. His voice wasn't mad or scared any more. It was happy and soft, like Momma's.

"Hey," he said, "get your ass back in bed or they'll have to put a bandage there too."

"Poppa," I pleaded. "I don't care, wallop me as much as you want, just take me home."

"Hey, I thought you said you wasn't no kid. Hell, you ain't scared of being alone?"

Inside my head there was a running of *Yeah, yeah, yeah*, but I answered, "Naw, Poppa, it's just that Momma's gonna worry and she'll get sick an' everything and—"

"Won't work, son," Poppa broke in with a laugh.

I kept quiet.

"Its only for a couple days. We'll come and see you an' everybody'll bring you things."

I got interested but played it smooth. "What kinda things, Poppa?"

Poppa shrugged his shoulders and spread his big arms apart and answered me like he was surprised that I should ask. "Uh . . . fruits and . . . candy and ice cream. And Momma will probably bring you chicken soup."

I shook my head sadly. "Poppa, you know I don't like chicken soup."

"So we won't bring chicken soup. We'll bring what you like. Goddammit, whatta ya like?"

"I'd like the first things you talked about, Poppa," I said softly. "But instead of soup I'd like"—I held my breath back, then shot it out—"some roller skates!"

Poppa let out a whistle. Roller skates were about $1.50, and that was rice and beans for more than a few days. Then he said, "All right, son, soon as you get home, you got 'em."

But he had agreed too quickly. I shook my head from side to side. Shit, I was gonna push all the way for the roller skates. It wasn't every day you'd get hurt bad enough to ask for something so little like a pair of roller skates. I wanted them right away.

"Fer Christ sakes," Poppa protested, "you can't use 'em in here. Why, some kid will probably steal 'em on you." But Poppa's voice died out slowly in a "you win" tone as I just kept shaking my head from side to side. "Bring 'em tomorrow," he finally mumbled, "but that's it."

"Thanks, Poppa."

"Don't ask for no more."

My eyes were starting to hurt like mad again. The fun was starting to go outta the game between Poppa and me. I made a face.

"Does it hurt, son?"

"Naw, Poppa. I can take it." I thought how I was like a cat in a movie about Indians, taking it like a champ, tied to a stake and getting like burned toast.

Poppa sounded relieved. "Yeah, it's only at first it hurts." His hand touched my foot. "Well, I'll be going now . . ." Poppa rubbed my foot gently and then slapped me the same gentle way on the side of my leg. "Be good, son," he said and walked away. I heard the door open and the nurse telling him about how they were gonna move me to the ward cause I was out of danger. "Son," Poppa called back, "you're *un hombre*."

I felt proud as hell.

"Poppa."

"Yeah, son?"

"You won't forget to bring the roller skates, huh?"

Poppa laughed. "Yeah, son."

I heard the door close.

Victor Hernández Cruz

Born: 1949

The most widely read of New York Puerto Rican poets, Victor Hernández Cruz has created a body of poetry that bridges the gap between his own community and the larger American society. He writes in English that has been fertilized by Arawak Indian and African words with a base not only in Puerto Rican Spanish but also the Spanish spoken by Chicanos, Nicaraguans, Salvadorians, Dominicans, and Cubans. His poetry is influenced by Latin and African American literature and the music, the Afro-Caribbean *salsa*, that he knew as a young boy: "My family life was full of music, guitars and congo drums, maracas and songs. My mother sang songs. Even when it was five below zero in New York she sang warm tropical ballads." This poetry is lyrical and often surrealistic, involving the magical realism we have come to associate with Latin American writing. It is filled with the energy and humor necessary to cover the broad range of his social concerns.

Victor Hernández Cruz was born in Aguas Buenas, Puerto Rico. He moved to Spanish Harlem in New York City when he was five years old and attended high school there. The larger share of his education has come from the books and ideas he has perused and his encounters with others.

Hernández Cruz's first collection of poems, *Papo Got His Gun* (Calle Once Publications, 1966) was published when he was only seventeen. This was followed by *Snaps* (Random House, l969), *Mainland* (Random House, 1973), *Tropicalization* (Reed, Cannon & Johnson, 1976), *By-Lingual Wholes* (Momo's Press, 1982), and *Rhythm, Content & Flavor* (Arte Publico Press, 1989). He co-edited *Stuff: A Collection of Poems, Visions and Imaginative Happenings from Young Writers in Schools* (World, 1970). He was the editor of a New York publication, *Umbra*, and has published in *The New York Review of Books*, *Ramparts*, *Evergreen Review*, and *Down Here*. He has been widely anthologized, most recently in the *Heath Anthology of American Literature*, and has received grants from the National Endowment for the Arts and the California Arts Council. He is presently living in Puerto Rico.

Spirits

half of his
body hung in
the air
they said it was
magic   a secret
between me & the man
it was no magic that was
in the air   it was no trick
an old lady an old   old lady who
saw the windows open   the wind raising the
curtains   footsteps in an empty room
a young man who saw a t.v. go flying into the
air   a dying lady got up & walked & sang
sudden loss of weight   sudden accident a car
rolling over a head   a building falling
bad luck   magic.

go after them as they get lost to turn the corner & snag
one   flowers   odors   candles   light candles   morning
noise   papers flying.

a hand thru a wall
is no joke   a mind
going mad at a days
time   so wide
so wide spread
an escape
who escapes   who
runs run where
from what from
who   a silence
the clouds over
the buildings the
odor in the halls
no one runs
no place to run
no place to hide
traveling   a fast
traveler   a signal
a place   the strange

81

way the walls start
to act   you say
you say you saw
nothing moving there
you deny a head
a head hiding   behind
the curtains   take
another look
a storm reported
only on your street
someone with grade A
health found dead of
a strange disease
a bad cold
a box found
full of nails
& flowers
names & statues
water sitting under
the beds   blood
falling out of pictures
a flower   burning under
the bed
a lady dressed in
white   flying away
from the roof
waving her hands
for you to follow
you have a bad cold

there is no medicine
there is no cure
there is only a fear
a hope   a waiting
till the spirits
come to our rescue
to your funerals

all the third world
sees spirits &

they talk to them
they are our friends.

Latin & Soul for Joe Bataan

1
some waves
            a wave of now
                        a trombone speaking to you
a piano is trying to break a molecule
is trying to lift the stage into orbit
around the red spotlights

a shadow
the shadows   of dancers
dancers   they are dancing   falling
out that space   made for dancing

they should dance
on the tables   they should
dance inside of their drinks
they should dance on the
ceiling they should dance/dance

thru universes
leaning-moving
            we are traveling

where are we going
if we only knew

with this rhythm   with
this banging   with   fire
with this   all   this   O
my god i wonder   where are

we going
       sink into a room full of laughter
       full of happiness   full of life
       those dancers
       the dancers
              are clapping their hands
              stomping their feet

hold back them tears
              all those sentimental stories
cooked uptown   if you can   hold it for after

we are going
       away-away-away
       beyond these wooden tables
       beyond these red lights
       beyond these rugs & paper
       walls   beyond   way past
       i mean way past them clouds
       over the buildings   over the
       rivers   over towns   over cities
       like on rails   but faster   like
       a train   but smoother
       away past stars
       bursting with drums.

   2
a sudden misunderstanding
              a cloud
              full of grayness
a body thru a store window
              a hand reaching
              into the back
              pocket
a scream
       a piano is talking to you
       thru all this
       why don't you answer it.

Energy

is
red beans
ray barretto
banging away
steam out the
radio
the five-stair
steps
is mofongo
chuchifrito stand
outside down
the avenue
that long hill
of a block
before the train
is pacheco
playing with
bleeding
blue lips

Going Uptown to Visit Miriam

on the train
old ladies playing football
going for empty seats

very funny persons

the train riders
              are silly people
              i am a train rider

but no one knows where i am
going to take this train

to take this train
to take this train

the ladies   read popular
paperbacks   because they
are popular   they get off
at 42 to change for the
westside line   or off
59 for the department store

the train pulls in & out
the white walls   dark-
ness   white walls   darkness

ladies looking up i
wonder where they going
the dentist   pick up
husband pick up wife
pick up kids
pick up ?grass?
to library   to museum
to laundromat   to school

but no one knows where i am
going to take this train

to take this train

to visit miriam
to visit miriam

& to kiss her
on the cheek
& hope i don't
see sonia on the
street

But no one knows where i'm taking
this train
            taking this train
            to visit miriam.

Ruskie's Boy

where there was some hole
to show where you was
in those travel dreams
no more corner
no more stoops
                    for you
now the children in the street
play/
ah, but that boy is yours
& your wife dreams on the mattress/
          tell him how we were
nights you come slowly to his room
and stare

and wonder the simple thoughts
the schemes/
                    what goes there
so small in the world/
sometime he'll come on top/
&
you will say:
that there is my kid.

Slick

i will have
you meet
my friend
Slick
got his name
three years ago
for being
just that
but
he won't be

the best of
talkers
    unless you
    dig him at
    the bar
    where he is
    the man
    the king
    of take
    them home
whenever there
is a slight
feel of failing
in myself
mentally
he's the man
to look up
or
when my pockets
no longer sing
with coins
he is the best bet
Slick
is the man
into everything
heard of a new place
Slick started it
or he was there
Slick who still
wears bebop hats
Slick who won't
smoke without
Bambu
Slick will one
day write a novel
Slick will
one day be
the King
of the Annex.

Three Days/out of Franklin

the soul is a beautiful thing
& i live by the soul
when i walk
it takes me
        today
i didn't go to school
i read
got high
ate
read
wrote
got high
spoke to carlos
saw the indians
on t.v.
& in my mind
& heart
they kick
the white man
in the ass
went down
got high
took a bus
honeychild
& claudia
giggled
about paul
homemade
chicken
& rice
found a dime
sticking
in the tar
jefferson park
the wind
talks
night
morning

no school
black coffee
corn muffin
read david's
felix
listened
to joe bataan
wrote
i learned
today
beautiful
soul
went down
spoke to some
children
& slowly
remembered

chino
singing
baby
O
baby
in the
hallway
at 12-17

i smiled
at the rain
when it fell
from the window
wrote
head
night
morning
no school
but the world
& my soul
& all the love
that wants to
blow up

like joe bataan's
trombones
night

three days
with myself
& the world
soul is beautiful
thing
the smell of
everything
ahead
the earth
& all the people/
     victor hernández cruz
     exiled from franklin
     december 14 to 19

You Gotta Have Your Tips on Fire

You never know who has your memory
in their drinks
In the cities that move into other
cities
Into other times
Ancient cities
You never know who wants to throw
you into that timeless space
Where you forget your name
And the face of the woman you love
Camara
You gotta have your tips on fire
You never know who has your thoughts
locked up in some small room
Wishing a thousand storms would
hit your doorway

Wishing you whirlwinds for paths
and hurricanes for the mornings
that open your days
You gotta have your tips on fire
Pana
Because they make doors out of pure
space
And you have to swing them open
So they know
You are around the wind
You are in the wind with your own
dance
You never know who stabs your
shadow full of holes
You gotta have your tips on fire
You never will be in the wrong place
For the universe will feel your heat
And arrange its dance on your head
There will be a Sun/Risa
On your lips
But
You gotta have your tips on fire
Carnal.

Chicago/3 Hours

State Street's cold mingling
crowds of Christmas
The town of garages and lonely
alleys
Traffic chaos—
That melody of a fast moving
civilization
Part cowboy   Part Anglo
For the famous breeze
Bacardi light
Chicago the first apple

for a long long time
Night and theater lights
Night and the river shows waves
A spirit walks the bridge with
cement still tied to his legs
Smoke is wind/in the wind

Someone told me el hijo de Cortijo
is somewhere in this town
Ay le lo li le lo li
That's enough to keep you warm
Say it one more time
Ay le lo li le lo li.

Entering Detroit

Detroit popped in the window
when my eyes opened/smoke coming
out of its head
headlights writing poems
on dirty floors/the bus window is light
blue/I never saw a city like that
popping at the end of dreams from
hard plastic cushioned red seats/
cement road connecting
nation/get off and refuel and start
the ride again/Detroit becomes part
of the road we passed six hours ago
writing in the shadow of Lake Erie
loud natural force

(on the other side of 4th of july calendar mark)

Poem

Your head it waves outside
You are as deep and heavy as the ocean
Night and day
Cabo Rojo   the stars
Day and night
Arecibo   music in green
It rains   Rain washes coconuts
The mangos they fall off the trees
In midnights   You hear them falling
Sunshine   sol
Your eyes they become one with the light
It is early   Early Early Early
And the rooster is early
Like a natural alarm
The music of the morning

Your head is full of the ocean and
The mystery of the sea shells
It moves like the waves

Moving outside the rhythms of life
Dawn birth deep in the mountains
Your eyes   they move
In and out of the woods
They look for spirits

Here is where our mothers are from
From this land sitting
All pregnant with sweetness
And trees that want to be the wind

Walking though the little space
The trees make
You want to laugh
In this lonely night there is music
And you do
And you don't stop
And the music is right behind you

Coquí   Coquí   Coguí   Coquí

Here is where the journey started
And you laugh as tall as palm trees
And you taste as good as pasteles
You dance toward the silver of the stars
Everything moves with you
Like a tropical train.

Loíza Aldea

Loíza
Who is there   in you took
a walk   Sandy walks
y Jose y Jane   in Loíza
the rain
The Coconut that had wings
of rum
In that bar-café   Sunday
night
Palm trees are the first
to wake in the mornings
and walk around the streets
Loíza—who was you

"who that in deep natural
woods . . . who that walking
naked in the forest rain . . .
who that . . . if it's as sweet
as the dulce de coco then
come here we would like to
eat"
She came when she came in
dreams
When she came
Above her Flamboyant red feathers
She hears laughter and song
She hears all the salsa that

is played on her ground
They hit six drums with one hand
She knows all the Aldea
Lit up with la Fiesta de
Santiago   Lit up like natural
glow from the mangos hanging
from the trees
Horses dressed with gowns
Coconut faces parading
Mediania Baja
Tumba/unquinto from the night
If legs played drums
The body moves like the drum
drum/in motion tumba   The song
jumps on the head—the head jumps
like the leg/sounds like the drum
drum   talk to body   tumba
Body talk for drum
fingers make it laugh   Body
come so close   Loíza   is the
wind you like to blow
Above the town your legs
unfold   Everywhere you
look carnaval   a sea of laughter
dancing   coming
The plaza is full
In brown sandals we walk
the walks   we stand to eat the
food   shirts are opened
Breeze Loíza you are soft and
warm
The waves
The red dresses
The pink and yellow
La plaza la plaza lit
The merry go round the smell
of shuffling bodies
Loíza
Loíza Aldea

On fire
Over there where fruits dance
into your mouth
& love comes gently
We sit till the morning
The wind blows festive sleep
Loíza you are always there
Silent with your African swing
Salsasa.

Poem

Think with your body
And dance with your mind.

A Tale of Bananas

A man
Who sleeps by the window was
having a nightmare
They call him Montuno
His face was hanging out the
window all of a sudden
Screaming and laughing like
hurricanes
The street below filled with people
spectating

Martin said call the ambulance
But he didn't move
Instead he took a drink
of 2 month old whiskey

*Weather report: Green bananas have
been reported falling from heaven
in some parts of the city*

Before coming outside
Martin had heard the weather
reports on the radio
And was wearing an extra large
hat upside down
It's about time he said
The guy at the supermarket
was asking for 50 cents a pound
and now look
Takatakatakatakatakataka
A shower of them in
Beautiful morning

Call the ambulance
A man is crazy
Hanging from a window
He could fall
Among the spectators
Soraida
Who came down with the baby's
carriage empty to catch bananas

Call the ambulance
someone kept yelling in the crowd
Soraida headed for a phone
It was out of order
and it took her dime
We can't call the ambulance
Public phones never work in this town

Martin was leaning against
a lightpost
Doing push-ups with his brain cells
trying to figure it out
When it dawned on him
That he had a phone
at his place
He took another drink
and flew away

Now
The whole world was boiling water
And the green bananas kept coming down
All the stores had sold out of tomato sauce
And sardines were escaping from the cans

The ambulance came two hours later
Everyone was amazed at how fast it had
gotten to the scene
Montuno was now dancing up and down
on the window sill
He almost had no clothes on
Doña Fela did the sign of the
†
and said Mi Dios you can almost
see his soul

The Doctor who came with the
ambulance was shocked
What's going on he asked
The crowd pointed up and said
Up there a man he's yelling
He's Montuno he goes crazy every week

The Doctor looked
and scratched his head
The man wasn't all that bad
He ran down the street
He left

Martin was standing to the side
What was that he asked himself
and he took another drink of the
whiskey which was still getting old

An hour later another ambulance
showed up
The crew got out
They moved over to where an old stove
was sitting abandoned

They picked it up
threw it in the ambulance
and drove off

Martin was drunker than all this

Up in the window Montuno was singing
He had wings
Someone yelled I'm gonna get him off
that window
Everyone knew that San Juan always
had to make his presence   felt
somewhere
Someone rushed into the building
As
Montuno rushed into his room

When San Juan got there
and opened the door he couldn't
find a thing
Someone looked out the window
to the lake of people below
and smiled broadly
He had big white teeth

When Montuno woke up he was
lying next to a lake
With 5-feet wide avocados
all around him
It was three O clock in some
morning
He picked one up
Peeled it
and put it in his face

In the distance he could hear
the subway coming
Once inside he noticed a strange barrel
sitting all by itself
It was full of Seagram Seven
and there was a face floating around
inside

The name of the face was Manuel
They smiled two miles of freeway at
each other
Manuel he said do you know that it is
raining green bananas upstairs
And there's a crowd up there acting
crazy like they never seen one
It should rain money Manuel said
But take our luck
It may rain coins
We'd have to wear helmets
or get killed

The train came to another station
A fish swam on dressed in a checkered
suit and sat next to the action
It was Montuno's cousin
On his way to the fights at Madison
Square Garden

At the next stop Montuno got off
the train carrying the barrel
They made their way through
the crowds that were shopping
at la marketa
All along the sides of this fancy
shopping center were Codfish trees
being protected by the Army
to prevent raids
Why with all the green bananas
coming down Codfish trees were
in danger of becoming extinct
The army had orders to shoot
any looters on the spot

Outside
They walked down Avenida Ponce de Leon
Montuno marching with the barrel
Talking to Manuel
All around them were the new junior
executives dressed in suits and carrying

briefcases walking along the new avenues
of booming nations
Alongside the new businessmen
were fakes who came out dressed in suits
and also carrying briefcases
Except theirs were full of comic books
But at 12 O clock lunchtime no one can
tell who is who

Montuno and his friend in the barrel
walked off the end of the avenue
and disappeared into heavy jungle

The bananas were falling so hard that
they woke Montuno up
He yawned and scratched his head
Opened the window to get some air
and there across from him on the fire
escape
Was a hundred pounds of green bananas
the street below was a fiesta.

Side 4

Sitting on the Brooklyn Bridge at night
Looking at the electrical lights
Midtown a fire
I think of the many seeds inside a maraca
If each seed was like a light
All holding hands
Then the world would become a horse
Start to gallop
We can mount it
We can ride

Side 12

Manhattan dance Latin
In Spanish to African rhythms
A language lesson
Without opening your mouth

Side 18

There was a guy who
Stood on the corner for many hours
When I asked him
Why he didn't go home
He said:
You see it is that the
Buildings are moving
Like a merry-go-round
When mine comes up
I will jump in
He said this in Spanish
you see

Side 20

You can't leave your house
these days without finding
Something new
I found Oscar Lewis'
Tape recorder
Behind a pizza shop in the Bronx
And they wouldn't give me
Ten dollars for it
At the pawnshop

Side 21

What should happen is
That my
        Tin tin tin patin
Should be piped into all
The streets
          This tin tin Pa
Tin
    Takes care of headaches
And other things

Side 22

What you want is for the tiger to eat me
The one at Central Park
Loose in my dreams
What you want is for me to become like
the cold
February anyone
What you want is for that tiger to eat me
I won't close my eyes tonight
Hear the river
See the boats
Calculating at night
In the mornings
This is like living inside a refrigerator
trying to have thoughts
Wondering how lovely a woman's body is
through all those sweaters and coats
Is that the case
What you want is for the tiger to eat me
Knock knock
I bring you his bones

Side 26

Cockfights in the basements
of Wall Street
Is it true ?

Side 32

I am glad that I am not one of those
Big Con Edison pipes that sits by the
River crying smoke
I am glad that I am not the doorknob
Of a police car patrolling the Lower
East Side
How cool I am not a subway token
That has been lost and is sitting
Quietly and lonely by the edge of
A building on 47th Street
I am nothing and no one
I am the possibility of everything
I am a man in this crazy city
I am a door and a glass of water
I am a guitar string cutting through the
Smog
Vibrating and bringing morning
My head is a butterfly
Over the traffic jams

Mountain Building

The mountains have changed to buildings
Is this hallway the inside of a stem
That has a rattling flower for a head,
Immense tree bark with roots made out of
Mailboxes?
In the vertical village moons fly out of
Apartment windows and though what you
See is a modern city
The mountain's guitars pluck inside
It's agriculture taking an elevator
Through urban caves which lead to
Paths underground They say Camuy
To Hutuado
Taino subground like the IRT in
constant motion

The streets take walks in your dark eyes
Seashell necklaces make music in the
Origin of silence
What are we stepping on? Pineapple
Fields frozen with snow
Concrete dirt later the rocks of the
Atlantic
The sculpture of the inner earth
Down there where you thought only worms
and unnamed crocodiles parade
Lefty stands on a corner
Analyzing every seed
Squeezing the walls as he passes
Through at the bottom of the basement
Where the boiler makes heat

The flesh arrives out of a hole
In the mountain that goes up like a
Green wall
Bodies come in making *maraca* sounds
An invisible map out of the flora
Bees arrive in the vicinity and sing
Chorus while woody woodpeckers make

Women out of trees and place flowers
On their heads
Waterfalls like Hurakan's faucets
Caress the back of Yuquiyu
God to all whose tongues have the
Arawak's echoes

Hallway of graffiti like the master
Cave drawings made by owls when they
Had hands
You see the fish with pyramids inside
Their stomachs
Hanging near the doorways where
San Lazaro turns the keys
Villa Manhattan
Breeze of saint juice made from
Coconuts
Slide down the stairs to your
Belly and like a hypnotized *guanabana*
You float down the street
And win all your hands at dominoes

The Moros live on the top floor eating
Roots and have a rooster on the roof
Africans import okra from the bodega
The Indians make a base of *guava*
On the first floor
The building is spinning itself into
a spiral of *salsa*
Heaven must be calling or the
Residents know the direction
Because there is an upward pull
If you rise too quickly from your seat
You might have to comb a spirit's
Hair
They float over the chimneys
Arrive through the smog
Appear through the plaster of Paris
It is the same people in the windowed
Mountains.

For the Far-Out
Experimental Writer

A woman is sitting reading a prayer,
her hands clasping the book on top
of a table
A yellow candle is lit
A glass of clear water is next to it
She reads the same prayer over and over
Other people in the room repeat and respond
to her prayers
Her voice starts to get drowsy
She starts to scratch the table
She is looking at the print but only
reads skipping paragraphs
She jumps up, throwing the chair across the room
She plants herself in the middle of the room
where her hands begin to fly in circles above
her head
Some of her neighbors are surrounding her
Almost everyone starts to burp
It's like burp burp
At once something took her and lifted her
so fast that she hit the ceiling
She broke the light bulb and came down with sparks
Now there was only darkness and the candles
Four of the people who were burping
began to spin and were slamming against
the walls
The other people who were not spinning
and not slamming against the walls
were looking for the people who were
One woman was shouting instructions
"Those of you who are circuits
try and make a connection
Plug yourselves in through the middle
fingers"
The original woman who was praying
was squirming and sliding through the
floor like a snake

Unexpectedly there was a knock at the
door
It was the North American man who was
known in the building as "el beatnik"
He was writing a novel and all the commotion
was arriving at his door
He was once in college but dropped out
to alter the state of prose
by using irregular time sequences
and adventurous typography
He stared inside and saw half the
people jumping up and down   broken glass everywhere   the candle lit   the glass of water
No one could tell him anything
and he never registered his complaint.

Two Guitars

Two guitars were left in a room all alone
They sat on different corners of the parlor
In this solitude they started talking to each other
My strings are tight and full of tears
The man who plays me has no heart
I have seen it leave out of his mouth
I have seen it melt out of his eyes
It dives into the pores of the earth
When they squeeze me tight I bring
Down the angels who live off the chorus
The trios singing loosen organs
With melodious screwdrivers
Sentiment comes off the hinges
Because a song is a mountain put into
Words and landscape is the feeling that
Enters something so big in the harmony
We are always in danger of blowing up
With passion

The other guitar:
In 1944 New York
When the Trio Los Panchos started
With Mexican & Puerto Rican birds
I am the one that one of them held
Tight   like a woman
Their throats gardenia gardens
An airport for dreams
I've been in theaters and *caberates*
I played in an apartment on 102nd street
After a baptism pregnant with women
The men flirted and were offered
Chicken soup
Echoes came out of hallways as if from caves
Someone is opening the door now
The two guitars hushed and there was a
Resonance in the air like what is left by
The last chord of a *bolero*

If Chickens Could Talk

    This is the story of the men who stole chicken soup after it was properly made by others. The odor was walking up the stairs, and they heard it clearly, and something inside of them said to them from the very inside of them that they could go and get it with maneuvers properly laid out, quietly, sneakingly, no creaks from boards. Old buildings have a silent motion toward death.

    Some cities invent ways of keeping them going but this does not matter to chicken-soup-hungry men who are friends and have drunk two, three, four, or (1) (2) (3) (4) beers together or two shots of rum or three glasses of brandy and / or one bottle of California wine. They were sitting around involved in this process, just waiting to be presented in their proper setting in a state of minding their own business busyness, mining their thoughts deep into prehistory, times when they didn't do the same as now, though possibly the smell of chicken would have maliced their day / afternoon / night—especially from an open window, an opened mountain, a dark valley with crickets inventing gossip, a river's eternal flow creeping through the elevators and punch cards and glass.

In this case they actually knew where Buena Parte got the chicken, alive, three blocks down, one hill over, six songs away, across one river, two roads, one car, one horse that didn't break its iron wheels industrial age turning subway. He walked down the street with the beautiful chicken and the populace wondered, Fried / boiled / fricasse I *no se* I no said *Ay no say* can you see the wings flapping? Something in the blood or where the genes remember telling the chicken also from deep inside that it was going to be denecked expertly by Buena Parte, who paid good money for the chicken, and the men were already drinking slowly to commemorate the clock's large hand going on to the three going on two the tree and Buena Parte even saluted. It was perfectly the same shape as it is implied. No rough edges in his even wave of his hands and lips saying, "Hello, *buenas dias*" and asking to Big Mario, "Thank you, God." That "to" does not mean two Marios, because the world would have to deal double accordingly. Such a perfect encounter between all the elements who are all friends.

Once Buena Parte is off vision the friends served themselves another, and their minds began to skate fulling or filling or feeling with theories as to the destiny of one tall chicken whom they all know now belonged to Buena Parte, who was a champion at snapping chicken throats and was constantly commissioned by neighbors who now dwell in the interior of his Memorex. He went up the stairs. Chicken is called *gallina* in Spain, Mexico, Puerto Rico, El Salvador, Nicaragua, and 14th street. The stairs are conscious of his stroll; after years of contact it could not be any other way. He has fallen down them and they have not moved an inch to save his delicate parts. They are cruel stairs, who add extra *escalóns* as the years go by. They enlarge and make your destination appear farther.

"What a fine healthy chicken," his neighbor Doña Entretodo tells him as she greets him from her doorway where moments earlier she was not there but was perfectly inside wondering if she should come out and when and greet and how and solely to discover / find out / register exactly what was the commotion that she saw from her window as she saw with her eyes, the same ones she uses to sleep, what went down with Buena Parte and something in motion within his hands as he marched past the friends who were jolly, curious. Buena Parte didn't suspect anything and was only thinking about carrots / potatoes / onion / green peppers / garlic / salt and all that *that* that that he will always put all ways in the chicken soup soup, after he shaved it and offered three feathers to Santa Marta, after he opened its belly and stuck his fingers in it and took the belly out and cleaned it with hot running water inside / out and then took a green lime and cleaned and scrubbed the walls of the interior chicken and began a system by which the total chicken became parts, and parts, pieces. After that a formula of dropping it into the *olla*, each ingredient having a cue for entering and dissolving / embracing / jumping / rubbing / composing its perfume, which spilled out through the pictures of swords and the bread that was hanging over the doorway scaring away the devils of this or any world, so potent the grace that it filled the hearts of men with envy and desire.

When the chicken was an empty space Buena Parte went downstairs to the world, and he sang like a chicken and said, "Does Buena Parte taste good?"

The Swans' Book

In my neighborhood I saw two swans take a taxi
because they got bored of the mirror they had them in
Year in and year out they bought flowers in front of them
The mirror reflected the red the orange but the swans
couldn't touch the blues   so they got bored like
an unfound book in an abandoned building in the
South Bronx
One swan said to the other:
Who are these hypocrites who have parties and
throw rum in our faces?
They look like coffee percolators with their
excitement
We can't live, only look at it
I want outs, I'm gonna unglue off of this heated
sand and make for the door
I agree, said the other swan, and they peeled
off the glass mirror from the corner where
they decorated   spread their white wings once
and out the door they swayed
Each floor they passed had a different smell
Like one floor smelled sweet like bananas
The next one smelled like tamarind
The next one like incense
They marched past the people on the stoop
who in a state of shock froze like winter snow
You see things in the world, one said
A pedestrian looked so deep his eyes went out of
his face like on wheels
But the swans were into their thing

and that corner was for them like cake from
the oven and if they saw the owner of the
mirror they'd tell him where it was at
To hell with living motionless
suffering nonproblems having delusions
worrying about everything
just pressed against a wall that belongs to
a landlord who never comes in the winter to
understand cold
Watching people dance, all kinds of formations
Every rhythm gots a dance
People eat white beans and don't offer
The odors were killing us
To hell with being the swans decorating the
right-hand corners of mirrors
Everyone says how beautiful we look
and then ignores us like some inanimate object
Lulu to those who will see the blank we leave
behind
Now that we gone the city will turn gray
The residents will fight
from seeing too much nothing sitting next to each other
We don't want to be microphones for someone who
combs their hair with Dixie Peach and sings tragic
bolero blues about broken hearts and impossible loves
while a toothpick hangs from their mouth
That's right, that it is, gasoline with this place
On the corner they flopped their wings
A big taxi came to them
They sailed in like keys into a lock
When the taxi sped away from the neighborhood
one wing came out of each of the side windows
The crowd that mingled noticed the swans
escape
The yellow metal elevated into the air
dwindling into a dot
as the residents chit chat about the spectacle
One of them pops:
Now it's our turn to wake up
A loud voice was heard in the eardrum

Hey, wake up
before that mirror falls on your head

Ironing Goatskin

The air is suffocating
In the altar which is the sky
The sun the only statue
On this beach the vibrations
Of the drums
The fat barrels of the Bomba
The Papa, the Mama, and the Niño
The way the sound goes up
Your head goes seaward on *canucas*
Listen
Mercy for the goat flesh, please
The drummers look at the
Mahogany legs of the girls
Who enter the round Bomba circle
And proceed to imitate them
Turning the visual into sound
There isn't a place to sit your
Lungs down
It is for this reason
That we should be concerned
With the destiny of goats.

The Physics of Ochun

A group of professional
scientists
from Columbia University
heard that in an old
tenement apartment
occupied by a family
named González
a plaster-of-Paris
statue made in Rome
of Caridad del Cobre
started crying
The scientists
curious as they are
took a ride across
town to investigate
After stating their purpose
and their amazement
they were led to the
room where the statue was
Sure enough it was wet
under the eyes
Overnight, Señora González
told them, it had cried so
much that they were able
to collect a jar full of tears
The scientist almost knocked his
gold-rim glasses off his face
May we have this as a specimen
to study in our laboratory?
She agreed, and they took a taxi
with the jar to Columbia
They went directly to the lab
to put the tears through a
series of tests
They put a good amount of
the liquid under their
Strongest Microscope
Lo and behold!

What they saw made them loosen
their neckties
There inside the liquid
clearly made out through
the microscope was the
word: JEHOVAH
No matter how much they
moved the water they
kept getting the word
They sent for a bottle of
scotch
They served themselves in test tubes
They called the González family
to see if they could explain
All the González family knew
was that it was the tears
of Caridad del Cobre
They explained to Señora González
what was happening
She said that weirder than that
was the fact that her
window had grown a staircase
that went up beyond the clouds
She said she and her daughter
had gone up there to check it
out
because, she told them, a
long white rope had come out
of their belly buttons and something was pulling them up
What happened? the enthusiastic
scientists from Columbia University
wanted to know
We went up there and were
massaged by the wind
We got hair permanents
and our nails manicured
looking a purple red
My daughter says she saw

a woodpecker designing the
air
The scientists put the phone down
and their eyes orbited the room
We have to get out there
Incredible things are happening
They rushed back out
and into the González residency
They entered
It's in the same
room with the statue
They rushed in and went to the
window
So amazed were they
they lost their speech
All their organs migrated an inch
Clearly in front of them
a 3-foot-wide marble stair
which went up into the sky
The scientists gathered themselves
to the point of verbalizing again
They each wanted to make sure
that the other was "cognizant"
of the *espectacolo*
Once they settled upon reality
they decided that the urge to
explore was stronger than their
fears
One decided to take a writing pad
to take notes
One decided to take a test tube
in case he ran into substances
One decided to take a thermometer
and an air bag to collect atmosphere
Señora González, would you please
come up with us?
They wanted to know if she would
lead them up
If you could see it you could touch

it, she told them
She went out first and they
followed
The marble steps were cold
They could have been teeth of
the moon
As they went up the breeze smiled
against their ears
The murmur of the streets dimmed
They were climbing and climbing
when they felt a whirlpool in
the air
For sure it was the hairdresser
Señora González sensed the odor of
many flowers in the breeze
The scientist with the test tube
saw it get full of a white liquid
The scientist with the air bag
felt it change into a chunk of metal
The scientist with the writing pad
saw a language appear on it backwards
printing faster than a computer
The paper got hot like a piece of
burning wood
and he dropped it down into the
buildings
It went through an open window
and fell into a pot of red beans
A woman by the name Concepción was
cooking
Frightened she took it to a doctor's
appointment she had the next day
She showed it to the physician
who examined it
He thought it was the imprint
of flower petals
so even and bold in lilac
ink
The dream Concepción had during

the night came back to her
I know what's going on, doctor
I'll see you in nine months
Walking she remembered forgetting
to put the *calabaza* into the beans
and rushed home sparkling in
her yellow dress

Anonymous

And if I lived in those olden times
With a funny name like Choicer or
Henry Howard, Earl of Surrey, what chimes!
I would spend my time in search of rhymes
Make sure the measurement termination surprise
In the court of kings snapping till woo sunrise
Plus always be using the words *alas* and *hath*
And not even knowing that that was my path
Just think on the Lower East Side of Manhattan
It would have been like living in satin
Alas! The projects hath not covered the river
Thou see-est vision to make thee quiver
Hath I been delivered to that "wildernesse"
So past
I would have been the last one in the
Dance to go
Taking note the minuet so slow
All admire my taste
Within thou *mambo* of much more haste.

Don Arturo: A Story of Migration

A minimum of words, going through a maximum of time.
Dr. Mentelity Eson

Don Arturo has never been on an airplane. When he came from Cuba he took a boat; it was 1926. He had met a minister's wife in Habana, and she invited him to come and join her husband's touring musical Christian band in the States. Don Arturo thought about it for a few days.

He worked as an errand boy at the Habana Opera House; he had met Caruso and brought him coffee. He was around classical music in a tropical setting.

His family hailed from Valencia, Spain. His father played guitar, and Don Arturo picked it up like water down a dry throat. His brothers and sisters numbered 8, and he was the oldest. He helped raise them, and they had no money but they had a farm. They made food stretch like Jesus said to do.

Cuba was in turmoil and the economy was like a special delivery from the devil. The Guajiros rebelled coming down the mountains, angry like fighting roosters. He saw men shoot men with guns in the head; they fell down like sacks of rice.

When he was 18 he left the countryside to go to Habana to pursue being a priest. The priests in Cuba did what they wanted, including making love to the young women. Yes, my dear, confess your sins; they brought down skirts like peeling bananas. He got along with God but not with the church. When he couldn't take it any more, he left for the guitar and learned how to play the harmonica.

He jumped into Habana night life like a bee into a flower. The Opera House was full of stars and he mingled and got advice from them. He saw costumes, people rehearsing, and all kinds of instruments. It was like looking at a fairy tale.

The day he met the minister's wife, the *gringo* was asleep in his hotel room. She talked to Don Arturo like a woman on vacation, and Latins have the driver for the screw of metaphor. They made love on the beach that very night; like two animals they made a hole in the sand. He said she was wet like an orange.

He decided it would be a good idea to go to the States with the minister and his wife. The minister met him and thought he was charming. They got on a boat, all three, and watched the lights of Habana get eaten by the ocean as the boat moved along to New York. He got his own private room on the ship, and since the food was part of the service he kept it coming. He got stuffed like a bed bug in a hotel.

After midnight the minister's wife would knock on his door. She sliced in like a sheet of paper and told him her husband had fallen asleep with the Bible on his face. He started talking to her in Spanish, which she half understood, but the warmer she got the more she comprehended.

They took advantage of the boat's natural sway. She left for her husband's room before daybreak. Her husband commented over breakfast
that the food was better on the boat than in Cuba. Arturo said that better
than the food was the soul of Christ.

The boat blew its horns when the lights of New York appeared on
the horizon. Arturo looked at it and thought it was a stage in a *caberate*
getting ready for the night show. It was summertime, and the weather
was warm like in Cuba. Some people from the church were on land
waiting for the ministerial couple, which now included Don Arturo and
his wicker suitcase.

They drove to a small apartment building that was attached to the
minister's church on the lower west side of Manhattan. They gave
Arturo his own room and keys and he went up to take a nap; he dreamt
about boats coming out of fruits and whales that became guitars and
Siboney Indians hanging dead from rosary beads. They knocked on his
door to see if he wanted dinner. He went down to join them, and the beef
stew was orbiting the Bibles.

The minister and his wife sat next to each other as they introduced
Arturo to the other people present, three women and two men who were
members of the traveling band. The minister spoke of the purpose of
Arturo, his fine guitar playing, and where he could fit in. One of the
women informed them all that they would rehearse the following day.
The food became invisible like the Holy Spirit.

After dinner Arturo excused himself and said he wanted to go out
and look at buildings. To him it was another world, something out of a
picture. At first he walked as if the street would cave in under him; he
looked at the structures and then went up to them and touched them. He
made his way to West 14th street where he began to see Spanish-speaking
people and Argentinian and Spanish restaurants featuring seafood.

He saw a Catholic church that was old looking and reminded him
of the ones he had seen in pictures of Mexico. When he got close he saw
that it was called La Virgin de Guadalupe and was truly fashioned like the
Spanish churches of old Mexico. He entered and blessed himself with the
cool water that was at the entrance.

After contemplation he marched out into the hot sun. He entered a
restaurant and sat down to order coffee. He noticed that the Argentinian
waiter spoke a different Spanish than his; it was as if the man hissed at the
end of his words. A young woman sat at a table next to him and he
started chirping to her like a bird. She joined him and opened up like a
fan from Granada.

She told him her father was a merchant seaman stationed in New
York. She had come to live with him when her mother passed away in
Buenos Aires a couple of years back. She told him that the West 14th,
15th, 16th, and 17th streets area was a section where Spaniards and
Latin Americans were settling. They talked through two cups of coffee.
Finally she invited him to her place and he said yes four times.

The apartment was a railroad flat which she shared with her father

121

who was at the moment out at sea. It was handsomely fixed up with furniture and gadgets from around the world. A picture which had dried butterflies from Brazil hung on one of the walls. A new Iranian rug was on the floor.

Arturo got taken by her beauty and forgot all about the minister and his wife. He played with her eyes and she smiled from the interior. He asked if he could touch her tongue and she shot it out like a cash register drawer. He squeezed it and asked if she had come from Venus. She said that she had arrived from there that very day. This drove him crazy and he went for her buttons.

Arturo got glimpses of the minister and his wife waiting for him and wondering how he was making out in the big metropolis. He thought of what he should do: should he stay the night with the sweet Argentinian rose or track through the dark streets? They fell onto the rug tied together with arms and legs and rolled from one side of the parlor to the other. He fell asleep, his face on her neck. They awoke and chatted. Well, he had to get back. He explained the whole church situation. He left after they arranged to meet the next day at the same restaurant for lunch.

She was golden heaven, and his mind heard trumpets. Angels played harp as he walked back retracing his path. He found the church and with his own keys entered and went up to his room. He fell onto his bed like a piece of lumber. It is this way that Don Arturo had his first full day in the USA.

With the minister's traveling band he went in and out of cities and towns saving souls. The Depression was on the horizon. Meat had to stretch like rubber bands.

Arturo was an expert at survival. He got tired of plucking wire for the Christian band and massaging the minister's wife. Soon he found his own furnished room in what is now Spanish Harlem; the neighborhood was populated by Germans, Spaniards, and Cubans. On 3rd avenue there were cigar-making shops (*Chin-Chals*). He knew Mr. Bustelo when he was getting his coffee beans together. He knew the Valencia family when they had plans to spread their sweetness as the biggest Latin bakery of wedding and birthday cakes in New York City.

When the market crashed he became a street musician taking a position outside Macy's and sometimes Gimbel's. He played many instruments at the same time, even putting a tambourine on his feet. He sang popular Latin American songs and told jokes. Sometimes he got arrested and he put puppet shows on in the courtroom. The clerks rolled on the floor.

The manager of Macy's toy department took a liking to his entertainment qualities and hired him to sell puppets and give floor shows inside. Winters came over him like layers of blankets. His hair started to get like pepper that was sprinkled with salt.

As a street musician he began performing in a spot in Greenwich Village. Tired of commuting downtown he moved to the Lower East Side.

Now 78, he still cultivates his famous corner in the Village come Spring and Summer. He savors memory like espresso coffee. He calls up his beautiful moments with women like an encyclopedia, though his memory sometimes scatters. The details he gives shine like light bulbs and make bridges with each other.

Together we sit and talk, staring at the abandoned buildings of 10th street where inside doors are still intact and the hinges are lonely for motion. We review time and its fibers. Sipping on white German wine we both chuckle at life's contradictions. Always spice it with laughter. Remember too much insisting can break even iron. The lights of the building go off and we light two candles and sip in the darkness. His hair shines like white threads of silk.

Don Arturo recognizes the old refrain: All of life is a hole. How so? The man enters the woman's vagina, which can be described as a hole; the infant, you come of this very hole; you eat food through the hole of your mouth; you breathe through the holes of your nose; you shit through that famous hole; and when you die they drop the total you into a hole in the ground. So you see, all of life is a holy hole. Bet hard on that.

The wine which is sweet and old comes out of the hole located at the top of the bottle. We laugh ourselves through the linoleum, me and Don Arturo, who is 78 and to this day has never been on an airplane. The way he got here the story you have been told.

It's Miller Time

I work for the C.I.A.
They pay me with
cocaine and white Miami
lapel sports jackets
free tickets to San Juan
where I make contact
with a certain bank
official at the Chase
Manhattan Condado branch

My contact a guy named
Pete asks if I know other
accents within the Spanish
Can you sound Salvadorian?
They give me pamphlets

and also send me
pornographic magazines
if I want a stereo or a VCR
they know a place I can
get them at half-price
they told me there is a waiter
that works at Bruno's
who can get me any gadget

The last assignment
I had was to contact
the Public Relations Division
of a beer company
because for U.S. Hispanics
it was Miller Time
I contacted this brewery
a certain Miguel Gone-sa-less
invited me to lunch
I met him at La Fuente
at his suggestion
with him
was Camden New Jersey
Cuban who was going through
town enroute to Los Angeles
the lunch was on them

Señor Gone-sa-less had a
wallet full of plastic
he had more plastic than Woolworth's
they mentioned that the
beer company wanted to sponsor
salsa dance within the Latin
community
bring in the top commercial names
and that while this dance was
going on they wanted to pass
a petition against U.S. involvement
in Central America
they showed me the petition
which had a place for the name and

address of the signers
a great list to have and spread
around all government agencies

They gave a bag with 3 thousand
dollars in it
it was my responsibility to see
this through
the Cuban guy tapped me on the
shoulder and said
Don't have any of the mixed drinks
The bartenders at the dance
are working for us
The chemical people are experimenting
the effects of a liquid
just drink the beer

The festive event went off
successfully even a full moon
was in the sky
next week the CIA is flying me
back to the Caribbean where I
will assist in staging one of
the strangest events in recent history

According to the description in my
orders we are going to pull off a
mock rising of land from beneath
the Caribbean which the media will
quickly identify as lost Atlantis

Circular buildings made of crystals
are being constructed somewhere in Texas
they will be part of the spectacle
which will have the world spellbound
simultaneous with this event
the Marines will invade from bases
in Puerto Rico
the countries of Nicaragua
El Salvador and Guatemala
it will be a month of *Salsa*

in San Francisco
an astounding mystical event in the
Caribbean
the price of cocaine coming through
Miami will go down
everybody party and celestial
glittering and drunk
circuits jammed with junk and information

In a daze the world is free
for Miller Time.

Miguel Piñero

Born: 1946
Died: 1988

Miguel Piñero is known to much of the general public as the author of *Short Eyes* (Wm. Morrow & Co.,1974), a play depicting American prison life. Piñero's plays and poetry frequently are studies in the predisposition to violence that is central to the history of the United States.

Born in Gurabo, Puerto Rico, on December 12, he came to the United States at an early age and attended school on the Lower East Side of New York. He began writing *Short Eyes* while serving time in Ossining Correctional Facility, or "Sing Sing." In *Short Eyes* he shows prison as a microcosm of American society with all of its socio-economic distinctions and racial tensions. *Short Eyes* was originally cast with The Family, a group of convicts and ex-convicts participating in theater workshops first organized by Marvin Felix Camillo, with whom Piñero worked after leaving prison. Joseph Papp produced *Short Eyes* at the New York Shakespeare Festival's Public Theatre and later at the Vivian Beaumont Theatre. It has been performed on Broadway and in cities across the United States and abroad, and received the New York Drama Critics' Circle Award and the Obie for Best Off-Broadway play of 1973-74; a film version also was produced. In 1984 Arte Publico Press published three of Piñero's plays—*The Sun Always Shines for the Cool*, *Midnight Moon at the Greasy Spoon*, and *Eulogy for a Small Time Thief*—in which he portrays people making a place for themselves outside the American mainstream.

In addition to being a playwright, Piñero was a poet and actor. His poems first appeared in *Nuyorican Poetry: An Anthology of Puerto Rican Words and Feelings* (Wm. Morrow, 1975), which he edited with Miguel Algarín and which made available for the first time the poetry of the first generation of Puerto Ricans to grow up in the United States. A collection of poetry, *La Bodega Sold Dreams* (Arte Publico Press), was published in 1980. As an actor Piñero played character roles in television productions— *Kojak*, *Beretta*, and *Miami Vice*—and Hollywood films—*The Godfather* and *Fort Apache, the Bronx*. His last publication, **Outrageous One Act Plays** (Arte Publico, 1986), is what the title suggests and is candid in the best Piñero tradition. In 1982 he was honored with a Guggenheim Fellowship. Miguel Piñero died when he was forty-two.

A Lower East Side Poem

Just once before I die
I want to climb up on a
tenement sky
to dream my lungs out till
I cry
then scatter my ashes thru
the Lower East Side.

So let me sing my song tonight
let me feel out of sight
and let all eyes be dry
when they scatter my ashes thru
the Lower East Side.

From Houston to 14th Street
from Second Avenue to the mighty D
here the hustlers & suckers meet
the faggots & freaks will all get
high
on the ashes that have been scattered
thru the Lower East Side.

There's no other place for me to be
there's no other place that I can see
there's no other town around that
brings you up or keeps you down
no food little heat sweeps by
fancy cars & pimps' bars & juke saloons
& greasy spoons make my spirits fly
with my ashes scattered thru the
Lower East Side . . .

A thief, a junkie I've been
committed every known sin
Jews and Gentiles . . . Bums and Men
of style . . . run away child
police shooting wild . . .
mother's futile wails . . . pushers
making sales . . . dope wheelers
& cocaine dealers . . . smoking pot
streets are hot & feed off those who bleed to death . . .

all that's true
all that's true
all that is true
but this ain't no lie
when I ask that my ashes be scattered thru
the Lower East Side.

So here I am, look at me
I stand proud as you can see
pleased to be from the Lower East
a street fighting man
a problem of this land
I am the Philosopher of the Criminal Mind
a dweller of prison time
a cancer of Rockefeller's ghettocide
this concrete tomb is my home
to belong to survive you gotta be strong
you can't be shy less without request
someone will scatter your ashes thru
the Lower East Side.

I don't wanna be buried in Puerto Rico
I don't wanna rest in long island cemetery
I wanna be near the stabbing shooting
gambling fighting & unnatural dying
& new birth crying
so please when I die . . .
don't take me far away
keep me near by
take my ashes and scatter them thru out
the Lower East Side . . .

Running Scared

RUNNIN' SCARED—RUNNIN' SCARED
you're goin' nowhere
runnin' with your eyes closed
thinkin' to ease your heavy load

RUNNIN' SCARED
listen to the echoes of your shadows
wishin' for easy tomorrows
talkin' into the dead phones of yesterday

RUNNIN' SCARED—RUNNIN' SCARED
you're shifting
you're lifting
you're throwing it all away
it's plainly stamped on the backs of blue jeans
the hopes and hopelessness
of cast aside dreams
super-star
super-revolutionary
highpriest
on neon signs
playin' today
beggin' mam for a dime
runnin' scared
you gittin' nowhere.
compassion—compassion . . .
in burnt bottle caps
tenth of always your last stop
god is the coca-cola bottlin' company
you've heard his voice on N.B.C.
and when he gives it a rest listen to his son on C.B.S.
brought to you live
this ain't no jive
by your friendly neighborhood
soul buyin' agency
they aim to please
good news ain't guaranteed
ask for mister lucifer

the man with the friendly smile
for your soul he'll walk a mile
no trade in
no deposits
no return
no credit cards accepted . . . but . . .
you can take the lay away plan
with easy pay a mint . . .

RUNNIN' SCARED—RUNNIN' SCARED
statue of liberty
on 42nd street
lookin' like an old hag
OR
is it a guy in drag
seee youuu laaattteerrr
got to check out this female impersonator

RUNNIN' SCARED—RUNNIN' SCARED
and you still ain't half way there
can't pick up enough speed
didn't listen to your own decree
now you're stranded on this subway station
called hypocrisy
do you wish to take a runnin' jump?
can't smooth out the lumps
on the high ways
roads and by-ways
and there's a toll booth on this freeway
(freeway???)
an abe or a george
doesn't matter there
ain't no
CHANGE . . .

La Bodega Sold Dreams

dreamt i was a poet
&
writin' silver sailin' songs
words
strong & powerful crashin' thru
walls of steel & concrete
erected in minds weak
&
those asleep
replacin' a hobby of paper candy
wrappin', collectin'
potent to pregnate sterile young
thoughts

dreamt i was this poeta
words glitterin' brite & bold
strikin' a new rush for gold
in las bodegas
where our poets' words & songs
are sung
but
sunlite stealin' thru venetian
blinds
eyes hatin', workin' of time
clock
sweatin'
&
swearin'
&
slavin'
for the final dime
runnin' a maze
a token ride
perspiration insultin' poets
pride
words stoppin' on red
goin' on green
poets' dreams
endin' in a factoria as one
in a million
unseen

buyin' bodega sold dreams . . .

On The Day They Buried My Mother . . .

The wind pushed the sun
behind the moon
and
in the dark of light I saw
shadows trailing the cool

Autumn shook hands with winter
just before it died
Summer leaves bloomed
and ran away on a spring ride

coulda wrote an epithet
on a mountain tombstone for an
ant
a deer laid dead on a fresh water stream
and the hunter cursed
beneath his breath at the spirits of
the stars who caused the deer's death . . .

The earth shook with laughter
as the spades tickled its side
and gleamed so pretty with
so many forgotten flowers
from those final cadillac brides

My hat fell in the open grave
my feet inside my shoes swayed
my gloves were wet with sweat
looked quickly in the mirror of my heart
sign a relief . . .
and calmly smiled my fears aside . . .

Nicholasa Mohr

Born: 1935

Nicholasa Mohr's fiction, much of which derives from her own experience coming of age, is about Puerto Ricans who have migrated to New York City, their children, their relationships within the Puerto Rican community and their encounters with people and institutions.

Mohr was born and grew up in the Bronx section of New York City where she graduated from Textile High School. She studied at the Art Students League, the Brooklyn Museum Art School, and the Pratt Center for Contemporary Printmaking. She often combines her art with her writing. Her first book, *Nilda* (Harper & Row, 1973), which she designed and illustrated, and her second, *El Bronx Remembered: A Novella and Stories* (Harper & Row, 1975), revolve around children and their capacity to survive. *In Nueva York* (Dial Press, 1977) is a collection of inter-related stories about the interworkings of the Puerto Rican community, and *Felita* (Dial Press, 1979) is a children's story about a young girl's adjustment to a new neighborhood. *Rituals of Survival: A Woman's Portfolio* (Arte Publico Press, 1985) and *Going Home* (Dial Press, 1986) are Mohr's most recent publications.

Her work has appeared in many anthologies, including *Breaking Boundaries: Latina Writing*, *To Break the Silence*, *The Family in Harmony and Conflict*, *The Ethnic American Woman: Problems, Protest, Lifestyles*, and *Passages*, and in numerous journals. She has taught at Rutgers University, the State University of New York at Stony Brook and Albany, the Public Schools of Newark, New Jersey, and most recently in the Department of Elementary and Early Childhood Education at Queens College. She has participated in readings, lectures, seminars and creative writing workshops.

Some of her many awards and honors include *The New York Times* Outstanding Book of the Year (1973), the Jane Addams Children's Book Award (1974), Best Book for Young Adults from the American Library Association (1977), the American Book Award (1981), the Edgar Allan Poe Award from The Bronx Historical Society (1990), and a Doctor of Letters honorary degree from the State University of New York at Albany (1989). Mohr presently resides in Brooklyn.

Mr. Mendelsohn

"Psst . . . psst, Mr. Mendelsohn, wake up. Come on now!" Mrs. Suárez said in a low quiet voice. Mr. Mendelsohn had fallen asleep again, on the large armchair in the living room. He grasped the brown shiny wooden cane and leaned forward, his chin on his chest. The small black skullcap that was usually placed neatly on the back of his head had tilted to one side, covering his right ear. "Come on now. It's late, and time to go home." She tapped him on the shoulder and waited for him to wake up. Slowly, he lifted his head, opened his eyes, and blinked.

"What time is it?" he asked.

"It's almost midnight. Caramba! I didn't even know you was still here. When I came to shut off the lights, I saw you was sleeping."

"Oh . . . I'm sorry. O.K., I'm leaving." With short, slow steps he followed Mrs. Suárez over to the front door.

"Go on now," she said, opening the door. "We'll see you tomorrow."

He walked out into the hallway, stepped about three feet to the left, and stood before the door of his apartment. Mrs. Suárez waited, holding her door ajar, while he carefully searched for the right key to each lock. He had to open seven locks in all.

A small fluffy dog standing next to Mrs. Suárez began to whine and bark.

"Shh-sh, Sporty! Stop it!" she said. "You had your walk. Shh."

"O.K.," said Mr. Mendelsohn, finally opening his door. "Good night." Mrs. Suárez smiled and nodded.

"Good night," she whispered, as they both shut their doors simultaneously.

Mr. Mendelsohn knocked on the door and waited; then tried the doorknob. Turning and pushing, he realized the door was locked, and knocked again, this time more forcefully. He heard Sporty barking and footsteps coming toward the door.

"Who's there?" a child's voice asked.

"It's me—Mr. Mendelsohn! Open up, Yvonne." The door opened, and a young girl, age nine, smiled at him.

"Mami! It's el Señor Mr. Mendelsohn again."

"Tell him to come on in, muchacha!" Mrs. Suárez answered.

"My mother says come on in."

He followed Yvonne and the dog, who leaped up, barking and wagging his tail. Mr. Mendelsohn stood at the kitchen entrance and greeted everyone.

"Good morning to you all!" He had just shaved and trimmed his large black mustache. As he smiled broadly, one could see that most of his teeth were missing. His large bald head was partially covered by his small black skullcap. Thick dark grey hair grew in abundance at the lower back of his head, coming around the front above his ears into short

141

sideburns. He wore a clean white shirt, frayed at the cuffs. His worn-out pinstripe trousers were held up by a pair of dark suspenders. Mr. Mendelsohn leaned on his brown shiny cane and carried a small brown paper bag.

"Mr. Mendelsohn, come into the kitchen," said Mrs. Suárez, "and have some coffee with us." She stood by the stove. A boy of eleven, a young man of about seventeen, and a young pregnant woman were seated at the table.

"Sit here," said the boy, vacating a chair. "I'm finished eating." He stood by the entrance with his sister Yvonne, and they both looked at Mr. Mendelsohn and his paper bag with interest.

"Thank you, Georgie," Mr. Mendelsohn said. He sat down and placed the bag on his lap.

The smell of freshly perked coffee and boiled milk permeated the kitchen.

Winking at everyone, the young man asked, "Hey, what you got in that bag you holding onto, huh, Mr. Mendelsohn?" They all looked at each other and at the old man, amused. "Something special, I bet!"

"Well," the old man replied. "I thought your mama would be so kind as to permit me to make myself a little breakfast here today . . . so." He opened the bag, and began to take out its contents. "I got two slices of rye bread, two tea bags. I brought one extra, just in case anybody would care to join me for tea. And a jar of herring in sour cream."

"Sounds delicious!" said the young man, sticking out his tongue and making a face. Yvonne and Georgie burst out laughing.

"Shh . . . sh." Mrs. Suárez shook her head and looked at her children disapprovingly. "Never mind, Julio!" she said to the young man. Turning to Mr. Mendelsohn, she said, "You got the same like you brought last Saturday, eh? You can eat with us anytime. How about some fresh coffee? I just made it. Yes?" Mr. Mendelsohn looked at her, shrugging his shoulders. "Come on, have some," she coaxed.

"O.K.," he replied. "If it's not too much bother."

"No bother," she said, setting out a place for the old man. "You gonna have some nice fresh bread with a little butter—it will go good with your herring." Mrs. Suárez cut a generous slice of freshly baked bread with a golden crust and buttered it. "Go on, eat. There's a plate and everything for your food. Go on, eat. . . ."

"Would anyone care for some?" Mr. Mendelsohn asked. "Perhaps a tea bag for a cup of tea?"

"No . . . no thank you, Mr. Mendelsohn," Mrs. Suárez answered. "Everybody here already ate. You go ahead and eat. You look too skinny; you better eat. Go on, eat your bread."

The old man began to eat vigorously.

"Can I ask you a question?" Julio asked the old man. "Man, I don't get you. You got a whole apartment next door all to yourself—six rooms! And you gotta come here to eat in this crowded kitchen. Why?"

"First of all, today is Saturday, and I thought I could bring in my food and your mama could turn on the stove for me. You know, in my religion you can't light a fire on Saturday."

"You come here anytime; I turn on the stove for you, don't worry," Mrs. Suárez said.

"Man, what about other days? We been living here for about six months, right?" Julio persisted. "And you do more cooking here than in your own place."

"It doesn't pay to turn on the gas for such a little bit of cooking. So I told the gas company to turn it off . . . for good! I got no more gas now, only an electric hot plate," the old man said.

Julio shook his head and sighed. "I don't know—"

"Julio, chico!" snapped Mrs. Suárez, interrupting him, "Basta—it doesn't bother nobody." She looked severely at her son and shook her head. "You gotta go with your sister to the clinic today, so you better get ready now. You too, Marta."

"O.K., Mama," she answered, "but I wanted to see if I got mail from Ralphy today."

"You don't got time. I'll save you the mail; you read it when you get back. You and Julio better get ready; go on." Reluctantly, Marta stood up and yawned, stretching and arching her back.

"Marta," Mr. Mendelsohn said, "you taking care? . . . You know, this is a very delicate time for you."

"I am, Mr. Mendelsohn. Thank you."

"I raised six sisters," the old man said. "I ought to know. Six . . . and married them off to fine husbands. Believe me, I've done my share in life." Yvonne and Georgie giggled and poked each other.

"He's gonna make one of his speeches," they whispered.

". . . I never had children. No time to get married. My father died when I was eleven. I went to work supporting my mother and six younger sisters. I took care of them, and today they are all married, with families. They always call and want me to visit them. I'm too busy and I have no time. . . ."

"Too busy eating in our kitchen," whispered Julio. Marta, Georgie and Yvonne tried not to laugh out loud. Mrs. Suárez reached over and with a wooden ladle managed a light but firm blow on Julio's head.

". . . Only on the holidays, I make some time to see them. But otherwise, I cannot be bothered with all that visiting." Mr. Mendelsohn stopped speaking and began to eat again.

"Go on, Marta and Julio, you will be late for the clinic," Mrs. Suárez said. "And you two? What are you doing there smiling like two monkeys? Go find something to do!"

Quickly, Georgie and Yvonne ran down the hallway, and Julio and Marta left the kitchen.

Mrs. Suárez sat down beside the old man.

"Another piece of bread?" she asked.

"No, thank you very much . . . I'm full. But it was delicious."

"You too skinny—you don't eat right, I bet." Mrs. Suárez shook her head. "Come tomorrow and have Sunday supper with us."

"I really couldn't."

"Sure, you could. I always make a big supper and there is plenty. All right? Mr. Suárez and I will be happy to have you."

"Are you sure it will be no bother?"

"What are you talking for the bother all the time? One more person is no bother. You come tomorrow. Yes?"

The old man smiled broadly and nodded. This was the first time he had been invited to Sunday supper with the family.

Mrs. Suárez stood and began clearing away the dishes. "O.K., you go inside; listen to the radio or talk to the kids—or something. I got work to do."

Mr. Mendelsohn closed his jar of herring and put it back into the bag. "Can I leave this here till I go?"

"Leave it; I put it in the refrigerator for you."

Leaning on his cane, Mr. Mendelsohn stood up and walked out of the kitchen and down the long hallway into the living room. It was empty. He went over to a large armchair by the window. The sun shone through the window, covering the entire armchair and Mr. Mendelsohn. A canary cage was also by the window, and two tiny yellow birds chirped and hopped back and forth energetically. Mr. Mendelsohn felt drowsy; he shut his eyes. So many aches and pains, he thought. It was hard to sleep at night, but here, well . . . the birds began to chirp in unison and the old man opened one eye, glancing at them, and smiled. Then he shut his eyes once more and fell fast asleep.

When Mr. Mendelsohn opened his eyes, Georgie and Yvonne were in the living room. Yvonne held a deck of playing cards and Georgie read a comic book. She looked at the old man and, holding up the deck of cards, asked, "Do you wanna play a game of War? Huh, Mr. Mendelsohn?"

"I don't know how to play that," he answered.

"Its real easy. I'll show you. Come on . . . please!"

"Well," he shrugged, "sure, why not? Maybe I'll learn something."

Yvonne took a small maple end table and a wooden chair, and set them next to Mr. Mendelsohn. "Now . . ." she began, "I'll shuffle the cards and you cut, and then I throw down a card and you throw down a card and the one with the highest card wins. O.K.? And then, the one with the most cards of all wins the game. O.K.?"

"That's all?" he asked.

"That's all. Ready?" she asked, and sat down. They began to play cards.

"You know, my sister Jennie used to be a great card player," said Mr. Mendelsohn.

"Does she still play?" asked Yvonne.

"Oh . . ." Mr. Mendelsohn laughed. "I don't know any more. She's already married and has kids. She was the youngest in my family—like you."

"Did she go to P.S. 39? On Longwood Avenue?"

"I'm sure she did. All my sisters went to school around here."

"Wow! You must be living here a long time, Mr. Mendelsohn."

"Forty-five years!" said the old man.

"Wowee!" Yvonne whistled. "Georgie, did you hear? Mr. Mendelsohn been living here for forty-five whole years!"

Georgie put down his comic book and looked up.

"Really?" he asked, impressed.

"Yes, forty-five years this summer we moved here. But in those days things were different, not like today. No sir! The Bronx has changed. Then, it was the country. That's right! Why, look out the window. You see the elevated trains on Westchester Avenue? Well, there were no trains then. That was once a dirt road. They used to bring cows through there."

"Oh, man!" Georgie and Yvonne both gasped.

"Sure. These buildings were among the first apartment houses to go up. Four stories high, and that used to be a big accomplishment in them days. All that was here was mostly little houses, like you still see here and there. Small farms, woodlands . . . like that."

"Did you see any Indians?" asked Georgie.

"What do you mean, Indians?" laughed the old man. "I'm not that old, and this here was not the Wild West." Mr. Mendelsohn saw that the children were disappointed. He added quickly, "But we did have carriages with horses. No cars and lots of horses."

"That's what Mami says they have in Puerto Rico—not like here in El Bronx," said Yvonne.

"Yeah," Georgie agreed. "Papi says he rode a horse when he was a little kid in Puerto Rico. They had goats and pigs and all them things. Man, was he lucky."

"Lucky?" Mr. Mendelsohn shook his head. "You—you are the lucky one today! You got school and a good home and clothes. You don't have to go out to work and support a family like your papa and I had to do, and miss an education. You can learn and be somebody someday."

"Someday," said Yvonne, "we are gonna get a house with a yard and all. Mami says that when Ralphy gets discharged from the Army, he'll get a loan from the government and we can pay to buy a house. You know, instead of rent."

Mrs. Suárez walked into the living room with her coat on, carrying a shopping bag.

"Yvonne, take the dog out for a walk, and Georgie come on! We have to go shopping. Get your jacket."

Mr. Mendelsohn started to rise. "No," she said, "stay . . . sit down. It's O.K. You can stay and rest if you want."

"All right, Mrs. Suárez," Mr. Mendelsohn said.

"Now don't forget tomorrow for Sunday supper, and take a nap if you like."

Mr. Mendelsohn heard the front door slam shut, and the apartment

145

was silent. The warmth of the bright sun made him drowsy once more. It was so nice here, he thought, a house full of people and kids—like it used to be. He recalled his sisters and his parents . . . the holidays . . . the arguments . . . the laughing. It was so empty next door. He would have to look for a smaller apartment, near Jennie, someday. But not now. Now, it was just nice to sleep and rest right here. He heard the tiny birds chirping and quietly drifted into a deep sleep.

Mr. Mendelsohn rang the bell, then opened the door. He could smell the familiar cooking odors of Sunday supper. For two years he had spent every Sunday at his neighbors'. Sporty greeted him, jumping affectionately and barking.

"Sh—sh . . . down. Good boy," he said, and walked along the hallway toward the kitchen. The room was crowded with people and the stove was loaded with large pots of food, steaming and puffing. Mrs. Suárez was busy basting a large roast. Looking up, she saw Mr. Mendelsohn.

"Come in," she said, "and sit down." Motioning to Julio, who was seated, she continued, "Julio, you are finished, get up and give Mr. Mendelsohn a seat." Julio stood up.

"Here's the sponge cake," Mr. Mendelsohn said, and handed the cake box he carried to Julio, who put it in the refrigerator.

"That's nice. . . . Thank you," said Mrs. Suárez, and placed a cup of freshly made coffee before the old man.

"Would anyone like some coffee?" Mr. Mendelsohn asked. Yvonne and Georgie giggled, looked at one another, and shook their heads.

"You always say that!" said Yvonne.

"One of these days," said Ralphy, "I'm gonna say, 'Yes, give me your coffee,' and you won't have none to drink." The children laughed loudly.

"Don't tease him," Mrs. Suárez said, half smiling. "Let him have his coffee."

"He is just being polite, children," Mr. Suárez said, and shifting his chair closer to Mr. Mendelsohn, he asked, "So . . . Mr. Mendelsohn, how you been? What's new? You O.K.?"

"So-so, Mr. Suárez. You know, aches and pains when you get old. But there's nothing you can do, so you gotta make the best of it."

Mr. Suárez nodded sympathetically, and they continued to talk. Mr. Mendelsohn saw the family every day, except for Mr. Suárez and Ralphy, who both worked a night shift.

Marta appeared in the entrance, holding a small child by the hand.

"There he is, Tato," she said to the child, and pointed to Mr. Mendelsohn.

"Oh, my big boy! He knows, he knows he's my best friend," Mr. Mendelsohn said, and held the brown shiny cane out toward Tato. The small boy grabbed the cane and, shrieking with delight, walked toward Mr. Mendelsohn.

"Look at that, will you?" said Ralphy. "He knows Mr. Mendelsohn better than me, his own father."

"That's because they are always together," smiled Marta. "Tato is learning to walk with his cane!"

Everyone laughed as they watched Tato climbing the old man's knee. Bending over, Mr. Mendelsohn pulled Tato onto his lap.

"Oh . . . he's getting heavy," said Mrs. Suárez. "Be careful."

"Never mind," Mr. Mendelsohn responded, hugging Tato. "That's my best boy. And look how swell he walks, and he's not even nineteen months."

"What a team," Julio said. "Tato already walks like Mr. Mendelsohn and pretty soon he's gonna complain like him, too . . . " Julio continued to tease the old man, who responded good-naturedly, as everyone laughed.

After coffee, Mr. Mendelsohn sat on the large armchair in the living room, waiting for supper to be ready. He watched with delight as Tato walked back and forth with the cane. Mr. Mendelsohn held Tato's blanket, stuffed bear, and picture book.

"Tato," he called out, "come here. Let me read you a book—come on. I'm going to read you a nice story."

Tato climbed onto the chair and into Mr. Mendelsohn's lap. He sucked his thumb and waited. Mr. Mendelsohn opened the picture book.

"O.K. Now . . ." He pointed to the picture. "A is for Alligators. See that? Look at that big mouth and all them teeth . . ." Tato yawned, nestled back, and closed his eyes. The old man read a few more pages and shut the book.

The soft breathing and sucking sound that Tato made assured Mr. Mendelsohn that the child was asleep. Such a smart kid. What a great boy, he said to himself. Mr. Mendelsohn was vaguely aware of a radio program, voices, and the small dog barking now and then, just before he too fell into a deep sleep.

This Sunday was very much like all the others; coffee first, then he and Tato would play a bit before napping in the large armchair. It had become a way of life for the old man. Only the High Holy Days and an occasional invitation to a family event, such as a marriage or funeral and so on, would prevent the old man from spending Sunday next door.

It had all been so effortless. No one ever asked him to leave, except late at night when he napped too long. On Saturdays, he tried to observe the Sabbath and brought in his meal. They lit the stove for him.

Mrs. Suárez was always feeding him, just like Mama. She also worried about me not eating, the old man had said to himself, pleased. At first, he had been cautious and had wondered about the food and the people that he was becoming so involved with. That first Sunday, the old man had looked suspiciously at the food they served him.

"What is it?" he had asked. Yvonne and Georgie had started giggling, and had looked at one another. Mrs. Suárez had responded quickly and with anger, cautioning her children; speaking to them in Spanish.

"Eat your food, Mr. Mendelsohn. You too skinny," she had told him.

"What kind of meat is it?" Mr. Mendelsohn insisted.

"It's good for you, that's what it is," Mrs. Suárez answered.

"But I—" Mr. Mendelsohn started.

"Never mind—it's good for you. I prepare everything fresh. Go ahead and eat it," Mrs. Suárez had interrupted. There was a silence as Mr. Mendelsohn sat still, not eating.

"You know, I'm not allowed to eat certain things. In my religion we have dietary laws. This is not pork or something like it, is it?"

"Its just . . . chicken. Chicken! That's what it is. It's delicious . . . and good for you," she had said with conviction.

"It doesn't look like chicken to me."

"That's because you never ate no chicken like this before. This here is—is called Puerto Rican chicken. I prepare it special. So you gonna eat it. You too skinny."

Mr. Mendelsohn had tried to protest, but Mrs. Suárez insisted. "Never mind. Now I prepare everything clean and nice. You eat the chicken; you gonna like it. Go on!"

And that was all.

Mr. Mendelsohn ate his Sunday supper from then on without doubt or hesitation, accepting the affection and concern that Mrs. Suárez provided with each plateful.

That night in his own apartment, Mr. Mendelsohn felt uneasy. He remembered that during supper, Ralphy had mentioned that his G.I. loan had come through. They would be looking for a house soon, everyone agreed. Not in the Bronx; farther out, near Yonkers: It was more like the country there.

The old man tossed and turned in his bed. That's still a long way off. First, they have to find the house and everything. You don't move just like that! he said to himself. It's gonna take a while, he reasoned, putting such thoughts out of his mind.

Mr. Mendelsohn looked at his new quarters.

"I told you, didn't I? See how nice this is?" his sister Jennie said. She put down the large sack of groceries on the small table.

It was a fair-sized room with a single bed, a bureau, a wooden wardrobe closet, a table, and two chairs. A hot plate was set on a small white refigerator and a white metal kitchen cabinet was placed alongside.

"We'll bring you whatever else you need, Louis," Jennie went on. "You'll love it here, I'm sure. There are people your own age, interested in the same things. Here—let's get started. We'll put your things away and you can get nicely settled."

Mr. Mendelsohn walked over to the window and looked out. He saw a wide avenue with cars, taxis and buses speeding by. "Its gonna take me two buses, at least, to get back to the old neighborhood," he said.

"Why do you have to go back there?" Jennie asked quickly. "There is nobody there any more, Louis. Everybody moved!"

"There's shul . . ."

"There's shul right here. Next door you have a large temple. Twice you were robbed over there. It's a miracle you weren't hurt! Louis, there is no reason for you to go back. There is nothing over there, nothing," Jennie said.

"The trouble all started with that rooming house next door. Those people took in all kinds . . ." He shook his head. "When the Suárez family lived there we had no problems. But nobody would talk to the landlord about those new people—only me. Nobody cared."

"That's all finished," Jennie said, looking at her watch. "Now look how nice it is here. Come on, let's get started." She began to put the groceries away in the refrigerator and cabinet.

"Leave it, Jennie," he interrupted. "Go on . . . I'll take care of it. You go on home. You are in a hurry."

"I'm only trying to help," Jennie responded.

"I know, I know. But I lived in one place for almost fifty years. So don't hurry me." He looked around the room. "And I ain't going no-where now . . . "

Shaking her head, Jennie said, "Look—this weekend we have a wedding, but next weekend Sara and I will come to see you. I'll call the hotel on the phone first, and they'll let you know. All right?"

"Sure." He nodded.

"That'll be good, Louis. This way you will get a chance to get settled and get acquainted with some of the other residents." Jennie kissed Mr. Mendelsohn affectionately. The old man nodded and turned away. In a moment, he heard the door open and shut.

Slowly, he walked to the sack of groceries and finished putting them away. Then, with much effort, he lifted a large suitcase onto the bed. He took out several photographs. Then he set the photographs upright, arranging them carefully on the bureau. He had pictures of his parents' wedding and of his sisters and their families. There was a photograph of his mother taken just before she died, and another one of Tato.

That picture was taken when he was about two years old the old man said to himself. Yes, that's right, on his birthday . . . There was a party. And Tato was already talking. Such a smart kid, he thought, smiling. Last? Last when? he wondered. Time was going fast for him. He shrugged. He could hardly remember what year it was lately. Just before they moved! He remembered. That's right, they gave him the photograph of Tato. They had a nice house around Gunhill Road some-place, and they had taken him there once. He recalled how exhausted he had been after the long trip. No one had a car, and they had had to take a train and buses. Anyway, he was glad he remembered. Now he could let them know he had moved, and tell them all about what happened to the old neighborhood. That's right, they had a telephone now. Yes, he said

149

to himself, let me finish here, then I'll go call them. He continued to put the rest of his belongings away.

Mr. Mendelsohn sat in the lobby holding on to his cane and a cake box. He had told the nurse at the desk that his friends were coming to pick him up this Sunday. He looked eagerly toward the revolving doors. After a short while, he saw Ralphy, Julio, and Georgie walk through into the lobby.

"Deliveries are made in the rear of the building," he heard the nurse at the desk say as they walked toward him.

"These are my friends, Mrs. Read," Mr. Mendelsohn said, standing. "They are here to take me out."

"Oh, well," said the nurse. "All right; I didn't realize. Here he is then. He's been talking about nothing else but this visit." Mrs. Read smiled.

Ralphy nodded, then spoke to Georgie. "Get Mr. Mendelsohn's overcoat."

Quickly, Mr. Mendelsohn put on his coat, and all four left the lobby.

"Take good care of him now . . . " they heard Mrs. Read calling. "You be a good boy now, Mr. Mendelsohn."

Outside, Mr. Mendelsohn looked at the young men and smiled.

"How's everyone?" he asked.

"Good," Julio said. "Look, that's my pickup truck from work. They let me use it sometimes when I'm off."

"That's a beautiful truck. How's everyone? Tato? How is my best friend? And Yvonne? Does she like school? And your Mama and Papa? . . . Marta? . . . "

"Fine, fine. Everybody is doing great. Wait till you see them. We'll be there in a little while," said Julio. "With this truck, we'll get there in no time."

Mr. Mendelsohn sat in the kitchen and watched as Mrs. Suárez packed food into a shopping bag. Today had been a good day for the old man; he had napped in the old armchair and spent time with the children. Yvonne was so grown up, he almost had not recognized her. When Tato remembered him, Mr. Mendelsohn had been especially pleased. Shyly, he had shaken hands with the old man. Then he had taken him into his room to show Mr. Mendelsohn all his toys.

"Now I packed a whole lotta stuff in this shopping bag for you. You gotta eat it. Eat some of my Puerto Rican chicken—it's good for you. You too skinny. You got enough for tomorrow and for another day. You put it in the refrigerator. Also I put some rice and other things."

He smiled as she spoke, enjoying the attention he received.

"Julio is gonna drive you back before it gets too late," she said. "And we gonna pick you up again and bring you back to eat with us. I

150

bet you don't eat right." She shook her head. "O.K.?"

"You shouldn't go through so much bother," he protested mildly.

"Again with the bother? You stop that! We gonna see you soon. You take care of yourself and eat. Eat! You must nourish yourself, especially in such cold weather."

Mr. Mendelsohn and Mrs. Suárez walked out into the living room. The family exchanged good-byes with the old man. Tato, feeling less shy, kissed Mr. Mendelsohn on the cheek.

Just before leaving, Mr. Mendelsohn embraced Mrs. Suárez for a long time, as everybody watched silently.

"Thank you," he whispered.

"Thank you? For what?" Mrs. Suárez said. "You come back soon and have Sunday supper with us. Yes?" Mr. Mendelsohn nodded and smiled.

It was dark and cold out. He walked with effort. Julio carried the shopping bag. Slowly, he got into the pickup truck. The ride back was bumpy and uncomfortable for Mr. Mendelsohn. The cold wind cut right through into the truck, and the old man was aware of the long winter ahead.

His eyelids were so heavy he could hardly open them. Nurses scurried about busily. Mr. Mendelsohn heard voices.

"Let's give him another injection. It will help his breathing. Nurse! Nurse! The patient needs . . ."

The voices faded. He remembered he had gone to sleep after supper last—last when? How many days have I been here . . . here in the hospital? Yes, he thought, now I know where I am. A heart attack, the doctor had said, and then he had felt even worse. Didn't matter; I'm too tired. He heard voices once more, and again he barely opened his eyes. A tall thin man dressed in white spoke to him.

"Mr. Mendelsohn, can you hear me? How do you feel now? More comfortable? We called your family. I spoke to your sister, Mrs. Wiletsky. They should be here very soon. You feeling sleepy? Good . . . Take a little nap—go on. We'll wake you when they get here, don't worry. Go on now . . ."

He closed his eyes, thinking of Jennie. She'll be here soon with Esther and Rosalie and Sara. All of them. He smiled. He was so tired. His bed was by the window and a bright warm sash of sunshine covered him almost completely. Nice and warm, he thought, and felt comfortable. The pain had lessened, practically disappeared. Mr. Mendelsohn heard the birds chirping and Sporty barking. That's all right, Mrs. Suárez would let him sleep. She wouldn't wake him up, he knew that. It looked like a good warm day; he planned to take Tato out for a walk later. That's some smart kid, he thought. Right now he was going to rest.

"This will be the last of it, Sara."

"Just a few more things, Jennie, and we'll be out of here." The two women spoke as they packed away all the items in the room. They opened drawers and cabinets, putting things away in boxes and suitcases.

"What about these pictures on the bureau?" asked Sara.

Jennie walked over and they both looked at the photographs.

"There's Mama and Papa's wedding picture. Look, there's you, Sara, when Jonathan was born. And Esther and . . . look, he's got all the pictures of the entire family." Jennie burst into tears.

"Come on, Jennie; it's all over, honey. He was sick and very old." The older woman comforted the younger one.

Wiping her eyes, Jennie said, "Well, we did the best we could for him, anyway."

"Who is this?" asked Sara, holding up Tato's photo.

"Let me see," said Jennie. "Hummm . . . that must be one of the people in that family that lived next door in the old apartment on Prospect Avenue. You know—remember that Spanish family? He used to visit with them. Their name was . . . Díaz or something like that, I think. I can't remember."

"Oh yes," said Sara. "Louis mentioned them once in a while, yes. They were nice to him. What shall we do with it? Return it?"

"Oh," said Jennie, "that might be rude. What do you think?"

"Well, I don't want it, do you?"

"No." Jennie hesitated. " . . . But let's just put it away. Maybe we ought to tell them what happened. About Louis." Sara shrugged her shoulders. "Maybe I'll write to them," Jennie went on, "if I can find out where they live. They moved. What do you say?"

The Wrong Lunch Line
Early Spring 1946

The morning dragged on for Yvette and Mildred. They were anxiously waiting for the bell to ring. Last Thursday the school had announced that free Passover lunches would be provided for the Jewish children during this week. Yvette ate the free lunch provided by the school and Mildred brought her lunch from home in a brown paper bag. Because of school rules, free-lunch children and bag-lunch children could not sit in the same section, and the two girls always ate separately. This week, however, they had planned to eat together.

Finally the bell sounded and all the children left the classroom for lunch. As they had already planned, Yvette and Mildred went right up to the line where the Jewish children were filing up for lunch trays. I hope no one asks me nothing, Yvette said to herself. They stood close to each other and held hands. Every once in a while one would squeeze the other's hand in a gesture of reassurance, and they would giggle softly.

The two girls lived just a few houses away from one another. Yvette lived on the top floor of a tenement, in a four room apartment which she shared with her parents, grandmother, three older sisters, two younger brothers, and baby sister. Mildred was an only child. She lived with her parents in the three small rooms in back of the candy store they owned.

During this school year, the two girls had become good friends. Every day after public school, Mildred went to a Hebrew school. Yvette went to catechism twice a week, preparing for her First Communion and Confirmation. Most evenings after supper, they played together in front of the candy store. Yvette was a frequent visitor in Mildred's apartment. They listened to their favorite radio programs together. Yvette looked forward to the Hershey's chocolate bar that Mr. Fox, Mildred's father, would give her.

The two girls waited patiently on the lunch line as they slowly moved along toward the food counter. Yvette was delighted when she saw what was placed on the trays: a hard-boiled egg, a bowl of soup that looked like vegetable, a large piece of cracker, milk, and an apple. She stretched over to see what the regular free lunch was, and it was the usual: a bowl of watery stew, two slices of dark bread, milk, and cooked prunes in a thick syrup. She was really glad to be standing with Mildred.

"Hey Yvette!" She heard someone call her name. It was Elba Cruz, one of her classmates. "What's happening? Why are you standing there?"

"I'm having lunch with Mildred today," she answered, and looked at Mildred, who nodded.

"Oh yeah?" Elba said. "Why are they getting a different lunch from us?"

"It's their special holiday and they gotta eat that special food, that's all," Yvette answered.

"But why?" persisted Elba.

"Else it's a sin, that's why. Just like we can't have no meat on Friday," Yvette said.

"A sin . . . Why—why is it a sin?" This time, she looked at Mildred.

"It's a special lunch for Passover," Mildred said.

"Passover? What is that?" asked Elba.

"Its a Jewish holiday. Like you got Easter, so we have Passover. We can't eat no bread."

"Oh. . . ."

"You better get in your line before the teacher comes," Yvette said quickly.

"You're here!" said Elba.

"I'm only here because Mildred invited me," Yvette answered. Elba shrugged her shoulders and walked away.

"They gonna kick you outta there . . . . I bet you are not supposed to be on that line," she called back to Yvette.

"Dumbbell!" Yvette answered. She turned to Mildred and asked, "Why can't you eat bread, Mildred?"

"We just can't. We are only supposed to eat matzo. What you see there." Mildred pointed to the large cracker on the tray.

"Oh," said Yvette. "Do you have to eat an egg too?"

"No . . . but you can't have no meat, because you can't have meat and milk together . . . like at the same time."

"Why?"

"Because it's against our religion. Besides, it's very bad. It's not supposed to be good for you."

"It's not?" asked Yvette.

"No," Mildred said. "You might get sick. You see, you are better off waiting like a few hours until you digest your foods and then you can have meat or the milk. But not together."

"Wow," said Yvette. "You know, I have meat and milk together all the time. I wonder if my mother knows it's not good for you."

By this time the girls were at the counter. Mildred took one tray and Yvette quickly took another.

"I hope no one notices me," Yvette whispered to Mildred. As the two girls walked toward a long lunch table, they heard giggling and Yvette saw Elba and some of the kids she usually ate lunch with pointing and laughing at her. Stupids, thought Yvette, ignoring them and following Mildred. The two girls sat down with the special lunch group.

Yvette whispered to Mildred, "This looks good!" and started to crack the eggshell.

Yvette felt Mildred's elbow digging in her side. "Watch out!" Mildred said.

"What is going on here?" It was the voice of one of the teachers who monitored them during lunch. Yvette looked up and saw the teacher coming toward her.

"You! You there!" the teacher said, pointing to Yvette. "What are you doing over there?" Yvette looked at the woman and was unable to speak.

"What are you doing over there?" she repeated.

"I went to get some lunch," Yvette said softly.

"What? Speak up! I can't hear you."

"I said . . . I went to get some lunch," she said a little louder.

"Are you entitled to a free lunch?"

"Yes."

"Well . . . and are you Jewish?"

Yvette stared at her and she could feel her face getting hot and flushed.

"I asked you a question. Are you Jewish?" Another teacher Yvette knew came over and the lunchroom became quiet. Everyone was looking at Yvette, waiting to hear what was said. She turned to look at Mildred, who looked just as frightened as she felt. Please don't let me cry, thought Yvette.

"What's the trouble?" asked the other teacher.

"This child," the woman pointed to Yvette, "is eating lunch here with the Jewish children, and I don't think she's Jewish. She doesn't— I've seen her before; she gets free lunch, all right. But she looks like one of the—" Hesitating, the woman went on, "She looks Spanish."

"I'm sure she's not Jewish," said the other teacher.

"All right now," said the first teacher, "what are you doing here? Are you Spanish?"

"Yes."

"Why did you come over here and get in that line? You went on the wrong lunch line!"

Yvette looked down at the tray in front of her.

"Get up and come with me. Right now!" Getting up, she dared not look around her. She felt her face was going to burn up. Some of the children were laughing; she could hear the suppressed giggles and an occasional "Ooooh." As she started to walk behind the teacher, she heard her say, "Go back and bring that tray." Yvette felt slightly weak at the knees but managed to turn around, and going back to the table, she returned the tray to the counter. A kitchen worker smiled nonchalantly and removed the tray full of food.

"Come on over to Mrs. Ralston's office," the teacher said, and gestured to Yvette that she walk in front of her this time.

Inside the vice-principal's office, Yvette stood, not daring to look at Mrs. Rachel Ralston while she spoke.

"You have no right to take someone else's place." Mrs. Ralston continued to speak in an even-tempered, almost pleasant voice. "This time we'll let it go, but next time we will notify your parents and you won't get off so easily. You have to learn, Yvette, right from wrong. Don't go where you don't belong . . ."

Yvette left the office and heard the bell. Lunchtime was over.

Yvette and Mildred met after school in the street. It was late in the afternoon. Yvette was returning from the corner grocery with a food package, and Mildred was coming home from Hebrew school.

"How was Hebrew school?" asked Yvette.

"O.K." Mildred smiled and nodded. "Are you coming over to-night to listen to the radio? 'Mr. Keene, Tracer of Lost Persons' is on."

"O.K.," said Yvette. "I gotta bring this up and eat. Then I'll come by."

Yvette finished supper and was given permission to visit her friend.

"Boy, that was a good program, wasn't it, Mildred?" Yvette ate her candy with delight.

Mildred nodded and looked at Yvette, not speaking. There was a long moment of silence. They wanted to talk about it, but it was as if this afternoon's incident could not be mentioned. Somehow each girl was afraid of disturbing that feeling of closeness they felt for one another. And yet when their eyes met they looked away with an embarrassed smile.

"I wonder what's on the radio next," Yvette said, breaking the silence.

"Nothing good for another half hour," Mildred answered. Impulsively, she asked quickly, "Yvette, you wanna have some matzo? We got some for the holidays."

"Is that the cracker they gave you this afternoon?"

"Yeah. We can have some."

"All right." Yvette smiled.

Mildred left the room and returned holding a large square cracker. Breaking off a piece, she handed it to Yvette.

"It don't taste like much, does it?" said Yvette.

"Only if you put something good on it," Mildred agreed, smiling.

"Boy, that Mrs. Ralston sure is dumb," Yvette said, giggling. They looked at each other and began to laugh loudly.

"Old dumb Mrs. Ralston," said Mildred, laughing convulsively. "She's scre . . . screwy."

"Yeah," Yvette said, laughing so hard tears began to roll down her cheeks. "Dop . . . dopey . . . M . . . Mi . . . Mrs. Ra . . . Ral . . . ston . . ."

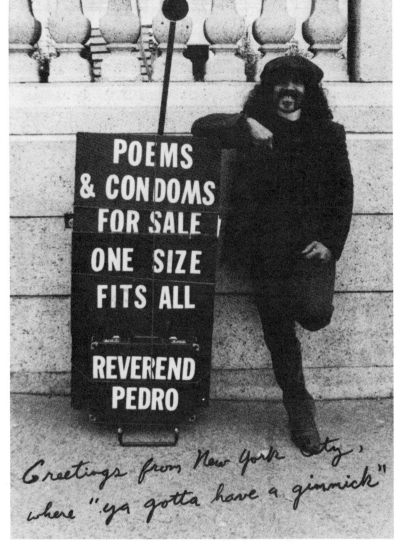

POEMS
& CONDOMS
FOR SALE
ONE SIZE
FITS ALL

REVEREND
PEDRO

Greetings from New York City,
where "ya gotta have a gimmick"

Pedro Pietri

Born: 1944

Pedro Pietri is one of the early group of poets who call themselves Nuyoricans, calling attention to the large portion of the Puerto Rican population living in the United States and exploring through their writing what effect that has on Puerto Rican cultural identity here and in Puerto Rico. In the Fall of 1988 he helped other writers explore this subject at *La Primera Conferencia de Poetas y Escritores Puertorriquenos en Nueva York/The First Conference of Puerto Rican Poets and Writers in New York* at City College, the first formal meeting of Puerto Rican writers from Puerto Rico and from New York.

Pietri, an actor as well as a poet, has performed his poetry at many colleges and universities. In 1988 for a twentieth anniversary commemoration of his famous poem, "Puerto Rican Obituary," he did a dramatization of the poem accompanied by the New Rican Village Alumni Band at the Public Theater in New York. In 1989 he organized and performed in "Poets in the Bars," a series of eight poetry readings celebrating the diverse urban poetry of New York. The series was funded by the National Endowment for the Arts, the New York State Council on the Arts and various corporations. He has had successful street and theater plays performed in both New York and California as well as Puerto Rico, some directed by such well-known people as Puerto Rican actor Jose Ferrer and Shakespeare Festival director Joseph Papp. Many of these— **Lewlulu**, **The Livingroom**, **What Goes Down Must Come Up**, for example—are not published in any conventional manner. Most recently (Summer, 1990) he participated in Joseph Papp's month-long Festival Latino in New York with a production sponsored by The Avant Garde Mambo Society, **Mondo Mambo/A Mambo Rap Sodi**.

Pietri's published books of poems include **Puerto Rican Obituary** (Monthly Review Press, 1973) and the bilingual edition, **Obituario Puertorriqueno** (Instituto de Cultura Puertorriqena, 1977); **Lost in the Museum of Natural History** (Ediciones Huracan, 1981); **Traffic Violations** (Waterfront Press, 1983), and he has published a one-act play, **The Masses Are Asses**, (Waterfront Press, 1984). He has been translated into Dutch in the anthology **Puertoricaanse Literatuur in Nueva York**.

He lives in New York City.

The First Day of Spring

Sweating in the midnight snow
Laughing and crying, actually dying
Lost in the after effects of affection,
Sinking deeply into the highest level
Of delirium, sleepwalking backwards
In the process of becoming transparent
Extra holy and extremely excellent

Elated casualty of abstract emotions
Reaching for the safe side of oblivion
To celebrate the art of fulfillment
In the opposite direction of reality
Where the correct age of the universe
Is learned and forgotten immediately

To be reborn making no sense whatsoever
Talking the foreign language of dreams
Misunderstanding simple conversations
In the confusion of drowning peacefully
Seriously sober and tremendously stone

Staggering proudly through the shadows
Of the unknown seeking remarkable state
Of no mind, ecstatic to be bewildered,
Drifting out of the future into the past,
Protecting my principles from perfection
After rising from the dead in the arms
Of the woman who will write my epitaph

Intermission from Monday

have to leave the city
because the sidewalks are sidewalks
parking meters are parking meters
and heavy traffic is very heavy
I know I will miss myself very much

161

every single second I am around
but if I don't get out of town
blank walls might become blank walls
and that I cannot tolerate at all

have to leave the city
before my breakfast gets suspicious
and calls me an ambulance to take me away
applauding a battle that was lost
because it made society safe for anxiety
O my lunch will be extremely lonely
and get cold and have to be discarded
when I am not around to stare at it
in the presence of gigantic noise makers

have to leave the city
when what you see is what you see
and what you don't see you don't see
and the imagination is classified
as excess luggage at the airport
where picture frames are picture frames
and the lines get longer and longer
for first class tickets on a bookshelf
where a poet has become a poet
to everyone except himself

Intermission from Wednesday

I expect to be praised
Everytime a ship sinks in the sea
And there are no survivors
To talk about the good old days
To the unborn they left behind
In the ruins of psychological cradles
Rocking from one planet to the next
Where the highest compliment I expect
When the high priest of psychiatric ward

Wears a black hood over his straightjacket
To make the patients laugh & cry & when
The joke finally ends to snap again
In the presence of relatives & friends
You swear you never saw before in your
Brilliant career of being a scatter brain
Who felt no pain when you jumped all the way
Up to the top of the Empire State Building
To ask one of the employees for a match
To start a fire never to be controlled
& I will hold a press conference in City Hall
For the reward I am to receive for not
Reporting the event to the fire department
Until everybody is hard of hearing
& have impaired visions of immortality
& praise me for taking full responsibility
For a tragedy that could have been prevented
If someone had invented this country
Instead of discovering & destroying it
To call it their land & your land too
If the medication works on you

Intermission from Thursday

I am being followed by a table
And there is nowhere to hide

This happened all of a sudden
I was minding my own business
Listening to a record that skips
Back and forth for five weeks

When suddenly I noticed
The table giving me a mean look
Without me having said or done
Anything to offend the table

At first I paid no attention
But then I noticed the table
Coming closer & closer towards me
Until our legs were touching
I decided to go out for a walk
And when I got downstairs
The table was there waiting for me
So I immediately went back UP

And to the astonishing surprise
Of these hands and these eyes
I found the table waiting for me
At the entrance of my front door
The record continues to skip
The table will not let me enter
And all I can do about it
Is to snap my fingers and hope
I am making this whole thing up
So I can get back inside and play
A record that doesn't skip

Intermission from Friday

You don't remember what you did
Last night
You were too sober to walk
A straight line
Something about the way you don't
Comb your hair lately
Intimidates your dead english teacher
Who keeps coming
Back to life to make sure you don't
Get a raise or promotion

The invisible shades of your window
Keep coming down
And going all the way up unassisted

You want to laugh
As loud as possible but you know
What will happen
To all the nursery rhymes you learned
If you confess
That the sandwich you just ordered
Tried to take a bite
At you when your back was turned

Eternal balloon venders remind you
Mental illness isn't
A joke to make you rich and famous
You salute them
Doubting and fearing their presence.
You want to be left
Alone—but should the phone not ring
For a few weeks
You will lose your mind wondering
What you did wrong?

The neon eyes of discarded crucifix
You keep hidden
Around your exposed naked neck
Misdirects you
To the commotion trumpets and drums
And dynamite makes
In a parade to commemorate amnesia

Again you want to laugh outloudly
But to be on
The safe side of your insanity
You stand upsidedown
On your head and announce that you
Are not crazy yet!
Your last request is a prophylactic
Your last words are
If I have sin please congratulate me

Intermission from Saturday

You forgot where you lived at
So you couldn't get out of bed
To find someone who is dreaming
About someone who looks like
The person inside your head
That keeps reappearing from
The parking lot for total shock

To challenge you to devastate
The common sense you want to keep
Until the time comes to erase
Your date of birth from the earth
To wake up dreaming in reverse
Dying forever wondering why
Nobody loved you madly but yourself

There is no pretending you did
Your best not to become odd
In this world of plastic gods
At the temple of modified minds
Where you kneel down and wait
For bad news about your health
In that fairytale called fate

Nothing is ever what it seems
Your dreams are outside your head
It's dangerous to be alive or dead
All experiences are embarassing
You were really stark naked
In public not home asleep in bed
Daydreaming about sudden incidents

That left you feeling obsolete
And unable to contact the ground
With the memories of your feet—
The door of your house will open
And close and you will not know
If you just came or left to remember
What to get confused about next

Intermission from Sunday

There is a hit list
And you are on it
Don't unpack your suitcase
You don't stand a chance
Your plans have been decided
For you in advance

The telephone rang once
Or twice and you answered it
And had a brief conversation
With someone you thought
Was closely related to you
And wanted to talk about
The good old days and how
You not so young people
Get away with murder

It was at the precise moment
Of hearing that remark
You thought you also heard
Your own voice in another room
Of your apartment laughing
At a very funny wordless joke
About a fatal accident
Your mailbox imagined you had

In some circles 3 strikes
Don't entitle you to get out
You have to keep feeling
You are being followed
Because it isn't a joke
To be published and broke

There is a hit list
And everybody is on it
So don't feel too important
There are enough parking meters
To be named after everyone
Who thinks they been shot
Everytime toilets are flushed

1st Untitled Poem

Looking for something I had lost
I came across a flawless blank page
That impressed me to the point
Of where I found myself losing sleep
Over this original piece of paper
That explains nothing whatsoever

I instructed myself to write a poem
On this magnificent blank page
That has occupied every single second
I find myself in deep concentration
When the world outside my head stops
To answer questions I ask in my sleep

I know that writing this poem
Will be extremely complicated for me
Regardless of my traffic violations
Due to the facts of the temptation
To protect this perfect statement
Whose authenticity I'll testify for

I have an important decision to make
That will change my life around
I know it will be very unwise of me
To lose sleep over writing this poem
When the correct thing for me to do
Is to lose sleep keeping the page blank

10th Untitled Poem

I admit I have always wanted
to be as difficult as possible
& have no respect for authority
So I won't be mistreated by anybody
And grow up to stay very young
And visit my great grandchildren

In a nursing home for the aged
Whose minds can no–longer expand
Regardless of what drugs they take

I am not content with myself
Unless I disagree with everybody
It doesn't matter if they are right
I will always swear they are wrong
So they may drop dead before me
Trying to get a concrete point across
That I of course will be erasing
In front of them or when their backs
Are turned for someone to stab them

I cross against the traffic
Not to get runover by a vehicle
But to insult the driver & passenger
For not walking & talking to themselves
On week days & weekends & days off
In public & be called ridiculous
By myself & other normal people
Who take seven hour lunch breaks
& just put in one hour on the job

I will work very hard on a poem
& leave construction work to others
Whose mothers & fathers disowned them
For not growing up to rule the world
I oppose leaders & their followers
Support fire eaters & sword swallowers
Don't expect me to explain anything
All I can truly say about myself
Is that after monday comes tuesday

The Night Is out of Sight

In a dream I wasn't having yet
My father was expelled
From heaven and hell for walking
Through a few thousand walls
Under the influence of alcohol

Assured me everything was real
And unreal enough to frighten
Those who are dead serious about
What they are going to laugh at
The next time they get uptight

We sat down on bar stools to talk
About our magnificent mother
Whose hair has become a bouquet
Of flowers that are endless
In the smile of sad expressions

We got very drunk staying sober
And when daylight was finally over
We came to the sane conclusion
All conversations end with hello
& all greetings begin with farewell

He congratulated me for refusing
To remove my hat & stop dressing
In black regardless of the weather
Or the occasion—there is nothing
Anyone alive can do right or wrong

He said before deciding the time
Had come to discontinue talking
& continue walking through walls
To be discovered by other days &
Nights that make metaphor possible

So we departed to poetry forever
& ever to never again listen
To the ringing of alarm clocks
Reminding us nothing ever happens
If we must keep track of time

The Title of This Poem Was Lost

whenever my mood
decides to abandon ambition
and the decision
to be influenced by nobody
is obvious to some
and unclear to others:
there is a floor to step on
there is still time to kill
to succeed at ending
a conversation in the middle
of a sentence—and be
acclaimed for not trying
hard enough at being important
on certain occasions
and for this lack of discipline
serious writers will scorn me
and what a relief that will be
and I will convince myself
the next few lines
were also lost.

How Do Your Eggs Want You (?)

At the age of empty spaces
I removed my new and used furniture
Away from the planet earth
To learn how to walk through walls

The fire department was called
By concerned citizens
To make me stop hallucinating
And turn me over to the police
To be formally arrested
For breaking the law of gravity
Without carrying certified
Diplomatic immunity credentials

Innocent bystanders fall-out
The windows of catatonic elevator
Wondering if it was something
They forgot to light up and smoke
Responsible for the false delusions
Of grandeur the weather predicted

The fire engine arrived
At the scene of the crime in reverse
Blasting away 31 different sirens
Trying to locate the whereabouts
Of my indefinitely missing head

After speeding around in circles
For 72 hours they used a telescope
To press charges against me
For possession of dangerous visions
Flying without an airplane
Impairing the morals of senior citizens
And resisting contact lenses

I was handcuffed in exile
To the rear view mirror
Of the patriotic fire engine
Whose firemen wore long black robes
And quoted the old testament

An unexplainable explosion
Returns everything back to normal
(99 minus 99 plus 99 equals 99 again)
I wake up rocking and rolling
On the ceiling of an emergency ward
A few weeks before this incident

The head doctor
Of the mental institution
Snorted un-cut cocaine
Under an opened beach umbrella
That was suspended in midair

When he noticed I was there
He told me to stick my tongue out

As far as it will stretch:
I responded immediately
Thinking he was going to share
The medication with me

But instead the head doctor
Brings out a can of spray paint
From his medical bag
And sprays on my tongue "Doc 73"

I scream as loud as I could
Without making a sound
Until his head falls off
His shoulders on the ground above

The headless doctor
Is demoted to a patient
By forces beyond his control:
I steal the cocaine
He left behind and escape
From the insane asylum
By lighting up 13 candles
Invisible to everybody but me

3rd Untitled Poem

in the middle
of a dimly lit room
a round table and two chairs
stare at an antique clock
on a faded blank wall

one of the chairs is on top
of the table and the other chair
is on the floor facing the table

should the clock decide to stop
the subject will have to be dropped

the chair on top of the table
feels superior to the chair
on the floor for obvious reasons

it has accepted the fact
it is nothing but a chair
with all intentions of staying put
until moved elsewhere by someone
or a very large unruly crowd

the chair on the floor
has a mind of its own and
needs no one's permission
to move in any dirction

but it will also remain put
for fear of the publicity
and invasion of privacy
if caught moving unassisted

7th Untitled Poem

I am not here now
I am sure I am not here
Nor have I been here before
Or after I have not been here

I recognize the furniture
And the dust on the floor
And fingerprints on the ceiling
(somebody tried to escape)

The legs of the chair are weaker
Than they were the last time
I remember not being in this place

The window curtains have fallen
The walls need a new paint job
There is garbage all over the floor
Inside this room I am not in now

Electricity has been cut-off
So has the gas and running water
If you try running out of here
You will end up right back inside

The same thing will happen
Should you jump out the window

Don't ask me why or how come?
I am not here to answer you
I am always somewhere else—always
Insisting I am somewhere else

Should I see a half filled glass
Suspended in midair I will lie
About not being in here and
Make myself comfortable

9th Untitled Poem

A man who is very angry
And getting angrier
Desperately searches
For the floor to chase
A woman who has rejected
Everything about him

He carries a knife
In one trembling hand
And a live red rose
In his much calmer hand

She can have one
Or she can have both

The man keeps repeating
Running around in circles
Trying to find the floor

She is heard laughing
At him while hiding
Inside her undergarment
Where she is safe
Until the man gets dizzy
And faints on the floor
He couldn't locate

She will then put him
To bed and fall asleep
Alongside him peacefully
Not fearing being un
Able to dream that he
is the most gentle person
she has ever knowned

Sandra Maria Esteves

Born: 1948

Sandra Maria Esteves plays multi-faceted roles as poet, essayist, graphic artist, performer, and director/producer. She is, in addition, a vigorous supporter of other artists' work.

Esteves was born and grew up in the South Bronx where she attended Cardinal Spellman High School. Her formal study in fine arts at Pratt Institute in Brooklyn formed the basis for her creative writing. Her poems have been collected in *Yerba Buena: dibujos y poemas* (Greenfield Review Press, 1980), which includes her drawings as well, and *Tropical Rains: A Bilingual Downpour* (African Caribbean Poetry Theater, 1984). Her most recent book is *Bluestown Mockingbird Mamba* (Arte Publico, 1990). Her productions include *Jam, a Musical Adventure*, *A Ritual of Healing and Feeling*, featuring her poetry, *Women Awakening*, *The Ones*, *The Federal Artists*, and a Juan Shansul play she directed, *Rose in Spanish Harlem*. She has been a literary artist with the Cultural Council Foundation and CETA Artists Project and resident artist with The Family Repertory Co.. She was Executive Artistic Director of the African Caribbean Poetry Theater which in addition to theater, sponsored literary events and publications. She is included in many anthologies, two of which are *Herejes y Mitificadores: Muestra de poesia puertorriqueña* and *Nuyorican Poetry: An Anthology of Puerto Rican Words and Feelings* and over thirty-five journals among which are *Sunbury*, *Third Woman*, *Ordinary Women*, *Journal of Contemporary Puerto Rican Thought*, *Hispanic Arts*, and *Chrysali*.

In 1980 Esteves was awarded the CAPS Fellowship for Poetry and in 1985 she was the recipient of a poetry fellowship from the New York Foundation for the Arts.

Just one example of her continual and energic promotion of the arts was her presentation of the "Voices from the Belly Poetry Series" at the Galeria Morivivi in 1980-83. A virtual marathon, it gave voice to over 150 known and unknown Latino poets. Her efforts on the part of women writers have been particularly important because of the difficulties they face getting their work published. Since 1973 she has run workshops for the New York State Poets in the Schools program for children and has read, performed, and held workshops on many college campuses. She lives in Bronx, New York.

For Lolita Lebron

Released from your cell
yet prisoner on your island

Write us books
to rediscover our identity

Explain the process in clear definition
give power to the air

Unlock the walls of ignorance
teach the lame to walk

Stock the young with stone
and brilliance from your waterfall

Womanstrength
a mold to guide the dawn

May your twenty-five years be new fire
opening other eyes for seeing

Visions, alternatives
circles that touch.

From Fanon

We are a multitude of contradictions
reflecting our history
oppressed
controlled
once free folk
remnants of that time interacting in our souls

Our kindred was the earth
polarity with the land
respected it
called it mother
were sustained and strengthened by it

The european thru power and fear became our master
his greed welcomed by our ignorance
tyranny persisting
our screams passing unfulfilled

As slaves we lost identity
assimilating our master's values
overwhelming us to become integrated shadows
undefined and dependent

We flee escaping, becoming clowns in an alien circus
performing predictably
mimicking strange values
reflecting what was inflicted

Now the oppressor has an international program
and we sit precariously within the monster's mechanism
internalizing anguish from comrades
planning and preparing a course of action.

For Fidel Castro

Cubano
I was but a child when you marched
a hundred thousand miles
in a war/spectacle media event rating higher
than Cleopatra, The Ten Commandments, and The Robe

But those who were sleeping awoke
when you arrived
warrior son of your country
new breed, pure soul, hombre
vowed to the flame truth

After blood was a birth
a new child to be nourished to health
ripped from an old bag of shells
hanging free from the sky

The growing is slow
the wound still bleeds
and the ocean stands in endless vigil

Twenty years later
this womantree has
thickly rooted in cement
mass profusions and
infinite rebellions

Here, from this land
where chrome fades into plastic and famished spirit
I read the shells you have cast into the river
analyze the signs with the sea
and extend my palms to you as strength.

1st Poem for Cuba

We are the silent poets of the night

We breathe in whirling tropic oceans

We are the dancing black campesinos de Oriente
holding drums within our bodies

With your eyes
We feel the spaces around us

With your hands
We touch a dreamer's place
hiding just beyond the walls of this world

With your voices
We catch the sun
as it rises to the east
holding in our wombs
the hammers of proud and righteous people

Flowing in the currents of many rivers
We slowly wear away great mountains

returning to the sea
where life is born
to find you and ourselves again.

Some People Are about Jam

Dedicated to Rich Bartee, the D-train Poetsinger

Whether they are drunk or sober
   rich or poor they jam everywhere
with everyone, and it doesn't matter when
         day or night there is always time for jamming
             from three a.m. to six in the afternoon
   in any room of the house or any streetcorner
      they jam in supermarkets funerals department stores
         rooftops, wherever they find people they jam
thru rain or sun, sleet or snow they will jam if they can
   (and even when they are not jamming
            they are thinking of new ways to jam
      and new people to jam with)
but one thing is certain
            they cannot be stopped from jamming
      even if you took their money and threw them in jail
      they'd jam
            because jamming is what they are about

         I once knew someone who tried to jam on the subway
   the police arrested him for disorderly conduct
            saying that jamming wasn't allowed
      he tried to convince them that jamming was really good therapy
            they didn't agree
      so they jammed him up good in the only way they knew how

Now he doesn't jam because he is dead
            but some say he's still jamming in the ether
      or in the air or wherever it is where his spirit remains
   some say they have even seen him jamming

somewhere between their dreams and the moon
a few wanted to bottle his jams and sell them wholesale
but it had already been done with other people's jams
and the jamming market was low
so in order to create a new market they printed pictures of him
jamming on tee shirts with the letters J-A-M
written over his head
which they hoped to sell to his many friends
most of whom were women because they appreciated his jams
much more than men, although there are some men
who have jammed with him
and they will tell you
that he was about jam
it was all he ever did
and it didn't matter if he was drunk or sober
he jammed all the time

In fact, he believed so much in the power of jam
that he dedicated his life to it
spent all his time with it
tried to convince people to incorporate jam
into their vocabularies
and refused to do anything that did not include jam

People would ask him, "Why do you jam so much?"
and he would tell them
that without jam life wasn't worth living
that jam was the most necessary ingredient
to the existence of man on this planet
(and to the existence of women too
because jam was not the exclusive property of men)
it belonged to everyone
especially children
and he was always taking jam lessons from them
he learned that jamming wasn't limited
to size shape sex or race
that one could jam alone.

With one person

Or with one thousand people

And that's just what he did, he jammed
and jammed, and jammed
hoping that people would follow his example.

Ahora . . .

and when the center opened

I saw myself

and I saw my mother

the Moon

walking to the white man's factory

so she could catch sunsets

on the 18th floor

of the projects.

Here

I am two parts /a person
boricua/spic
past and present
alive and oppressed
given a cultural beauty
. . . and robbed of a cultural identity

I speak the alien tongue
in sweet boriqueño thoughts
know love mixed with pain
have tasted spit on ghetto stairways
. . . here, it must be changed
we must change it

I may never overcome.
the theft of my isla heritage
dulce palmas de coco on Luquillo
sway in windy recesses I can only imagine
and remember how it was

But that reality now a dream
teaches me to see, and will
bring me back to me.

Take the Hearts Of Children

Feed them with red flamboyán
dress their bodies
with the turquoise caribbean
feet in the earth
refreshed in the morning
eyes shining
in palm wind silhouette

Take the hearts of children
teach them to fight for the land

with machetes and songs

we stand strong as one.

Fly.

It Is Raining Today

Each droplet contains a message
Soaks my clothing
The earth is crying
Or is it the sky washing down the clouds?
In the puddles lie reflections
Difficult to see thru oil film staining
Rainbow luminescence
Concentric circles expanding

La lluvia contains our history
In the space of each tear Cacique valleys and hills
Taino, Arawak, Carib, Ife, Congo, Angola, Mesa
Mandinko, Dahome, Amer, African priests tribes
Of the past
Murdered ancestors
Today, voices in the mist

Where is our history?

What are the names washed down the sewer
In the septic flood?

I pray to the rain
Give me back my rituals
Give back truth
Return the remnants of my identity
Bathe me in self-discovered knowledge
Identify my ancestors who have existed suppressed
Invoke their spirits with power
Recreate the circle of the Ayreto
Reunite the family in a universal joining
A shower and penetrating waterfall
Rekindle the folklore
Candles of wisdom with never ending flames

Speak to me of rain.

In The Beginning

In the beginning was the sound
Like the universe exploding
It came, took form, gave life
And was called Conga

And Conga said:
Let there be night and day
And was born el Quinto y el Bajo

And Quinto said: Give me female
There came Campana
And Balo said: Give me son
There came Bongoses

They merged produced force
Maracas y Claves
Chequere y Timbales

Que viva la musica!
So it was written
On the skin of the drum

Que viva la gente!
So it was written
In the hearts of the people

Que viva Raza!

So it was written.

A Celebration of Home Birth: November 15th, 1981

for Yaasmiyn Rahiyma

Sometimes there is steam in the apartment
Thanksgiving was spent warm
We forget about some things in the heat

Listen to and play music, dreaming in dawn
Then it gets cold
Again the water freezes
The sink fills with dirty dishes
We seek escapes, find new warmths

4:30 a.m.:   A tightening in my belly
Different from the others days before
This one electric, piercing blood
Five and Ten seconds long
Longer, growing stronger
I massage my belly fire
With thumbs forefinger and palm
The friction relaxes

5:30 a.m.:   Juan paces with me
Heaving puts on his pants to make a list
Call the police, no, yes, no
Call the hospital, no, yes, no
Call the doctor, heaven no!

6:30 a.m.:   The water breaks, we call the midwife
A rush of clear warm liquid down my legs
Socks and floor wet
Bed and towels soaked
Belly tightens longer
Growing stronger

7:00 a.m.:   Two midwives arrive
At four centimeters I cannot sit still
Take a shower and prepare my body
Contractions grow in power, legs shake
Breathing with energy the birth force overwhelms me
Swept away on a powerful crest in the great ocean
No longer in control of my physical
The waves deepen and stretch
A whirlwind pulls me into its gravity
Warm liquid rushing out on each undulation
Blessing and bathing the house
A preparation
Rivers from my womb evolving the life spirit

I walk from room to room
Invoking assistance from the Angels of Birth

9:00 a.m.:   It is time to push
I call to God feeling the burning release
As her head and body emerge from the darkness
As sacred as Sunday morning in winter
On my belly she screams for life
I pray for blessings
Give thanks to my Santos
Continue on the day.

Lil' Pito

When five year old Pito fell out the sixth floor
I got to the hospital to see
Rosa standing with a piece of
Rotten window gate in hand
Talking to her boyfriend of dreams to be
Saying Pito's gonna be alright
Sure of it
And my wet eyes searched past the closed
Doors of the emergency room where
Cusa's arms crossed over the fear in her heart
That Pito's slender spirit lay cold in the dark

Are you the Mother?   No
She's the Mother
Well could you please
Tell her we did all we could
You mean? Yes, he died less than
Fifteen minutes ago
Well what exactly did you do?
Wasn't he breathing
When they brought him in?

Twenty-one doctors and medical apprentices slit
Open his chest to see what happens when

Five year old ribs burst, cracking into lungs
Filling the precious bulbs of air in red liquid
In a death from life
That measures forty-two hands of various intentions
Claiming a piece of a life for research purposes
You know, maybe organ donations

Look at his eyes
They're beautiful
Certainly be useful
Take them, let's take them

Lil' Pito didn't stand a chance, not after
Twelve scalpels, three hundred gauze pads
A full box of sanitary gloves, and a barrage
Of questions and opinions as to what
Organ to explore next

And Cusa screamed when she heard
She screamed, and the rage drove her mad
And the landlord promised to fix the gate
Promised to come the very same day
Never kept a promise many times made
And Cusa's eyes rolled back in her head
Screaming to heaven

Pito don't go, no, no, Pito!
And her body shivered
And the guard said Look
You gonna have to remove her
From this crowd a people
For she start creatin a panic
She needs a sedative
A doctor, call the nurse
Take her to the room in the back
No, take her to the nurse
No, the back
The nurse won't come
Well get a doctor
What's wrong with the nurse?
Will you please wait outside?

Nurse please we have an emergency
You know, the mother of the little boy
You'll have to wait outside
Someone get a doctor
Take her to the back
Pick up her legs, You
Carry her arms, here
Hold her coat, where's the doctor?
Get the doctor!

Shock
Cusa went mad anyway
Now she wears grey veils and hides
Her face in Jehovic Bibles
And got a job and prays
Long and hard to God
At night she is buried
In the memories she spends playing
With her son in some heavenly playground
No one can talk to her
She feels hears sees in another world
We stand humbled
Step out on our path
And fall into the next crack.

One Woman

      one woman seeks more
than being an existence of numbers
                  and flesh
      more than
        being the unwed mother of our times

    one woman
seeks that smile within self
        that sings a true song of joy/love

to realize the depth of my sanity
the desires of my body
                    and the elevation of my mind

                              and be a woman
                    within myself

Miguel Algarín

Born: 1941

Miguel Algarín is an actor and editor, a poet, playwright, translator, teacher, director, and producer, but above all he is an activist for the Puerto Rican arts community in New York. His special contribution has been The Nuyorican Poets' Cafe which evolved out of get-togethers of writers at Algarín's home. The Cafe became a place where writers, musicians, artists of all sorts, could gather, and people from the community would come to listen. Many young people got their first encouragement at "The Cafe."

Algarín was born in Santurce, Puerto Rico. In the 1950s he with his parents, brother, and sister, moved to Spanish Harlem and then to Queens. After high school, Algarín attended City College before transferring to the University of Wisconsin where he received his B.A. in 1963. He received an M.A. from Pennsylvania State University and a Ph.D. from Rutgers University, where he is on the faculty of the English and Caribbean Studies departments. His other activities have included serving on the editorial boards of the Nuyorican Press and of Arte Publico Press and directing El Puerto Rican Playwrights'/Actors' Workshop and the Nuyorican Theater Festival. He was a visiting poet at Naropa Institute and has given poetry readings across the United States and in the Netherlands, France, and Algeria. He also has worked in television and film. His many awards include grants from the Samuel Rubin Foundation for the Nuyorican Theater Festival, the Judy Peabody Foundation, and the New York State Council of the Arts.

Algarín has published four volumes of poetry: **Mongo Affair** (Nuyorican Press, 1978), concerning the Puerto Rican past and Nuyorican present; **On Call** (Arte Publico Press, 1980), a celebration of people Algarín has encountered in his travels across North America; **Body Bee Calling from the 21st Century** (Arte Publico Press, 1982) covers territory from Rome to outer space and the moral issues we face in the coming century; and **The Time Is Now/Ya es tiempo** (Arte Publico Press, 1984) moves to Latin America and, among other subjects, the North American presence there. Algarín's plays include **Olu Clemente, the Philosopher of Baseball** (Delacorte Theater in New York

197

City, 1973), **Apartment 6-D** (Lincoln Center in New York City, 1974), **The Murder of Pito** (Nuyorican Poets' Cafe in New York City, 1976), and **Blue Heaven**. He has translated Pablo Neruda's poetry, **Cancion de gesta/A Song of Protest** (William Morrow, 1976), has contributed to numerous journals (**Here.**, **Box 749**, **dodeca**, **Contact II**, **Mag City**), and is included in various anthologies, four of which are **A Decade of Hispanic Literature: An Anniversary Anthology**, **Herejes y Mitificadores: muestra de poesia puertorriquena en los estados unidos**, the Dutch **Puertoricaanse Literatuur in Nueva York**, and **Nuyorican Poetry: An Anthology of Puerto Rican Words and Feelings**. The last was edited by Algarín who, with Miguel Piñero, were the first to identify the group of writers known as Nuyoricans.

Happy New Year

January 1, 1976

Cold chills invade my body
and my electrical connections are perspiring
and it's short–circuit time,
pero coño maybe there's no time like short–circuit time,
Gil's been asking why there's not been more
poetry and I keep feeling that there's
poetry in the making all the time
it's just that I've got to keep translating it
into visual terms that mean something
to everybody else as cold chills invade my body
in the new year, why is it I learn
everything through pain? why, que pasa,
porqué is it that I'm always
running on icy sidewalks and pushing my
psychic program to destruction? So what if the
drinks are free at the Tin Palace,
I keep asking for soda and rum
flooding my body till it rebels,
turning around the peristaltic waves
as it rejects all of my fluids and food
and I lose my energies, become real
weak, dizzy, disruptive storm
immobilizes my faculties till I cannot hold together
in balance my muscles and my electrical energy,
the rebellion in my gut forcing me to rush
to the men's room to puke and drool into the
toilet, helplessly looking at myself in the mirror
as I involuntarily emit chicken noodle soup,
wine and rum and gasp for air in between
the rushes where the stomach gathers a new wave
of energy to spit out of my mouth,
I've tried to write while vomiting
but the sickness is messy and I land up
with a page splattered with yesterday's rice and beans
and veal cutlet parmigiana pickled in rum, wine and pot
cold chills invade my body
when Bimbo shows the anguish of his mind

and despairs that living on Avenue B between
6th & 7th street keeps him delivering his child to
Bellevue's emergency room for lung treatment
because too much ghetto dirt has clogged his
lungs, cold chills invade his little body
while fever, coughing and general muscular pain
stunt his growth, Bimbo can't place his vision
above the conditions of his family,
  his cultural vision
has to put food on the family table
only then will his dream be healthy,
that's it, eso es,
  a man's vision
has to feed his life or
   else
his vision belongs to air and offers
no security at all leaving him and us out
in the cold, shielding ourselves with disappearing words
and castor oil dreams as Bimbo's disillusionment
climbs out looking around trying to purge itself,
  he is a hero this Bimbo
he places his blood pulse on the line that binds
his will to do all that he says he can do
and has done and will continue to do
  this hero, this intellectual giant
  from 6th St. esta desencojonado,
embrollado and trying to purge
his malady letting out the cancerous symptoms
that brew in men and the ambulatory visions
of their heads when money pinches inspiration
away leaving them hungry, coatless and homeless
cold chills invade their bodies and mine.

Meeting Gaylen's 5th Grade Class

Gaylen got them to sit,
controlling their explosive energies,
I looked into their volcanic eyes
fearing the hot lava of their boredom
would burn my insides:
this morning we're going to write on
        "I am invisible"
           or
     "I can fly over airplanes"
           or
     "My greatest pain"
they threw their X-ray juice at me
paralyzing my reflexes for half a second
which felt like two before I looked
at Gaylen's eyes and felt
my blood penetrate my feelings:
       "if I come in here and I can't see,
       what would I be?"
       "blind," shouted a child from the back of
       the classroom
       "if I can't hear?"
       "deaf!"
       "if I can't taste?"
       "you got your tongue cut off,"
       "if I can't touch?"
       "your skin's been burned,"
       "if I can't smell?"
       "somebody put wax up your nose,"
       "if I can't do any of the things I've mentioned?"
       "you're dead!"

from **Angelitos Negros: A Salsa Ballet**

for Willie Colon

Willie Colon, Composer
Marty Sheller, Conductor

2 trumpets
1 trombone
2 saxophones/alto and baritone
1 bass
1 piano
1 guitar
1 trap drum
1 bongo
1 conga
1 timbalero
6 violins
1 flute and piccolo

PROLOGUE
Good Vibrations Sound Studio,
the date is for three
but we arrive at 2:30 p.m.,
the occasion: the first recording
of Wille Colon's score of "A Salsa Ballet":
the studio is refrigerator cool,
the vibes are mellow,
the rhythm is sleepy slow,
the set is slowly pulling together,
musicians arrive, slapping hands
talking through months of absence
into hugs and tightly held hands,
they are coming together
                    to invent
the sound that Willie
has in his head,
musicians are Willie's brush,
musicians are Willie's sound partners,
today's the day for an orgy of sounds,
today is the day for the birth

of a new latin perception
of sound,
Willie walks around,
four months into his pregnancy,
I see pre-natal rhythmic juices pour
out of his pores as notes shoot
pitches of sounds high into the atmosphere,
musicians come together in a holy
trust, the bond of marriage for
a trumpet and a saxophone
is the listening
that they do to one another,
there in the listening,
there is hope.

Trampling

You take a woman,
force her to yield
and not too swiftly
but to resist
just enough to need
your macho force,
you rouse yourself by subjugating her,
you get it hard
and make her
eat meat totally,
you enter her like molten steel
scorching her insides raw
as she refuses to consent
you rage in your macho savagery
by pounding blows all over her body,
till you've trampled the woman in her,
leaving her angry and frightened of men.

Rosa

Puma called asking me to remind you
that he made love to you,
that he didn't declare war against your legs,
that he didn't violate your no
that he was searching for your yes through the no
that lurks beneath the seeming wanting to resist,
he says it was love you made not hate,
that it was mutual yielding
not the severing of parts.

Infections

I walk around the city
matching my feelings
to your mood
just like the lake water
meets the edge of the fountain,
no separation
but real tight
leaving no room for air
to divide us
I match every feeling in me
to your contortions
as you dive into your psyche,
pulling out the dirt of your pain
you smear it on your face,
on your eyes, on your lips,
and, as if not enough,
your saliva sprays my face
spreading the moisture
of your infectious pain
showing me your yellow teeth
you spit poisoned arias
about how you want to get down

with women you despise
and how you want to get down
with your mother but that
you wouldn't tell her
for fear she'd accept.

Tiger Lady

Orphan Miranda walks over my writing book
sniffing my pencil,
but did you ever hear about how curiosity
killed the mother cat,
I told her not to go into the building
because people and dogs get real mean in hallways,
but Tiger Lady kept on being curious
even after I told her
she kept on being curious,
on Saturday afternoon we were all in the backyard,
Tiger Lady went into the building,
Nelly and I were talking about Badillo for a while
before going for canned clams for a pasta sauce,
not knowing, I closed the back door,
came home, Nelly got into cooking,
arguing about a campaign that Badillo doesn't intend to win,
that's when Angelo knocks at the door
trying to hand Miky
a brown paper bag,
his dog had trapped it in the stair well,
"bit the spine in two,"
Miky vanished, I looked into the bag,
Angelo took Tiger Lady out to the trash can,
later I opened the lid and bag and touched her
just to make sure I broke some of my fear of death,
after a while I pulled her coat to see the wound,
it was a warm Saturday, Sunday got warmer
before the garbage was picked up on Monday

and Tiger Lady got buried
in the metal belly of a sanitation truck.

"Always throw the first punch"

My uncle always insisted,
"strike the first punch,
put your enemy on the run,"
I always threw the first punch,
I remember,
"attack, attack, attack,
put the hurting
on his limbs,"
I remember,
I remember
the night my uncle
got angry because I said
his wife thought his nuts
were christmas walnuts
and that she cracked them
every day of the year,
his left arm twitched,
I leapt at him
and struck first.

El Jibarito Moderno

When he dances latin,
he crosses his legs
right over left,
left over right,
light as a bright feather

el jibarito turns on and off
like the farthest
star in the milky way,
when he smiles his upper lip
covers his vacant gums
where his teeth have melted
just like my sugar teeth
dissolved into the chocolate
that made me fat in childhood,
el jibarito moderno
travels light
maybe he's afraid of gravity,
y eso,
hay que velarlo cuando
un bonboncito appears
in the atmosphere,
muchacho,
vélalo y cuídate
porque el jibarito conquista
con su liviana apariencia
y su estoy asfixiado look
that melts the temperature
of la damita in blue,
cuídate, cuídate
porque el jibarito
derrite y consume
sin que te des cuenta,
es como el viento
en una tarde caliente
que acarícia y seca
aliviándote el calor.

Wire Tap

Tapping in on your inner telephone life,
laying private talk out for the nation to hear
tapping in
tapping on my inner talk of why I did
just what I did and why I feel
just what I feel, tapping, tapping in,
on your wallet if you let me,
tapping, tapping in, metiendo el dedo,
excavando, buscando, metiendo,
metiendo el dedo hasta
el fondo, ahí, en el centro del roto,
metiendo, metiendo el miembro
de mi mente en tus oídos,
en tus ojos, en tus labios,
metiendo, tapping, metiendo
la punta de la lengua
en el oído del futuro,
¡fíjate! porque los labios del futuro
son los del sonero mayor del universo,
metiendo, tapping, metiendo,
tapping in . . .

Talking

A poem must complete the cycle of full release,
incomplete poems are whorls without recognition,
without the medicinal catharsis from which pain clotted cells
recover through word charges that cleanse as they delight
the paranoia swollen mind into paying attention
to the outside swirling greens, reds, yellows,
blacks and whites,
                   a poem without completion,
without the full circle,
burns oxygen without showing

refurbished organs how to grow away
from cancer striken neck cells that shoot arrows
of pain into the inner livingroom
space of an isolated I drinking isolated air,
shooting milky ways of frothy, thick child
bearing lava straight into the mouth of Leo
the Lion who stands at the rim of the universe
breathing newer vistas into the black holes
of denser than dense deader than dead stars
which emit no light signals to other
forms of starving life,
                    a poem without completion
makes the universe denser, obstructing light emission,
where heat is a dream and word magic the dietary
staple from where to pull muscle energy,
                    a poem without completion
plays a field where verbs are sharp blades
that strip the adjectives to raw life force
but where prepositions and conjunctions fault
the full flow of the act of cognition
and blank connectives leave bare spaces
between verb–subject space construction,
the word power leaks and misunderstanding
and corruption of intent begin,
                    a poem without completion
activates psychic short-circuits at the root of the routes
that it travels in the inner-livingroom space
of conversational battles
fighting back the word, offering it no entrance at all
                    a poem without completion
overwhelms, inundates without making fertile,
it makes complete the absence of completion.

Broadway Opening

Ntozake Shange's Broadway opening
and Melvin Van Peeble's saying
that his T.V. special last night
"was so good it
should've been a series,"
Amiri Baraka
sits proudly passing his
"Unity Struggle" newspaper
to partying black folk
who're celebrating Ntozake's
grand-ole-opry opening
into full theatrical success,
as she leaps at love
like a street mountain cat,
eight minutes standing ovation
but Ntozake is still as raw
and full of hurt
as she was before and after
her words threw fire
into New York's theater jungle.

Dante Park

Beautiful, clear, July light,
late afternoon clarity,
waiting for Cinderella and Marie Laveau,
sitting in the center of the biggest neon layout
the world has ever seen: July light in Manhattan
cool afternoon breeze brings space to all
as people smile, strolling in and out
of pools of light,
July light in Manhattan,
July heat gently self-tempered,
July oui, oui, boogie, boogie, woogie, woogie,

till you can't boogie no more,
number one hit of the day,
this day, this clear and balanced day,
this day, this clear and balanced moment,
sitting at Dante's feet,
feeling my way out of Purgatory,
approaching terrestrial paradise,
this mellow yellowing light,
this oui, oui, boogie, boogie, woogie, woogie,
till you can't boogie no more.

Taos Pueblo Indians:
700 strong according to Bobby's last census

It costs $1.50 for my van to enter
Taos Pueblo Indian land,
adobe huts, brown tanned Indian red skin
reminding me of brown Nuyorican people,
young Taos Pueblo Indians
ride the back of a pick up truck
with no memories of mustangs
controlled by their naked calves and thighs,
rocky, unpaved roads, red brown dirt,
a stream bridged by wide trunk planks,
young warriors unloading thick trunks
for the village drum makers to work,
tourists bringing the greens,
Indian women fry flour and bake bread,
older men attend curio shops,
the center of the village is a parking lot
into which America's mobile homes
pour in with their air conditioned cabins, color
T.V., fully equipped kitchens, bathrooms
with flushing toilets and showers,
A.M. & F.M. quadraphonic stereo sound,
cameras, geiger counters, tents,

hiking boots, fishing gear and mobile telephones,
"restricted" signs are posted round the parking lot
making the final stage for the zoo
where the natives approach selling
American Jewelry made in Phoenix
by a foster American Indian from Brooklyn
who runs a missionary profit making turquoise jewelry shop
"Ma, is this clean water?
do the Indians drink out of this water?
is it all right for me to drink it?"
the young white substitute teacher's daughter
wants to drink some Indian water,
young village school children recognize her,
and in her presence the children snap
quick attentive looks that melt into
"boy am I glad I'm not in school"
gestures as we pass,
but past, past this living room zoo,
out there on that ridge,
over there, over that ridge,
on the other side of that mountain,
is that Indian land too?
are there leaders and governments over that ridge?
does Indian law exist there?
who would the Pueblo Indian send
to a formal state meeting
with the heads of street government,
who would we plan war with?
can we transport arms earmarked for ghetto
warriors, can we construct our street
government constitutions on your land?
when orthodox Jews from Crown Heights
receive arms from Israel in their territorial struggle
with local Brooklyn Blacks,
can we raise your flag
in the Lower East Side
as a sign of our mutual treaty of protection?
"hey you you're not supposed to walk in our water,"
"stay back we're busy making bread,"

these were besides your "restricted zones"
the most authoritative words
spoken by your native tongue,
the girl's worry about the drinking water
made Raúl remove his Brazilian made shoes
from the Pueblo Indian drinking cup,
the old woman's bread warning
froze me dead on the spot
"go buy something in the shop,
you understand me, go buy something,"
I didn't buy I just strolled on by the curio shops
till I came across Bobby the police officer,
taught at Santa Fe, though he could've gone on to Albuquerque,
Taos Pueblo Indians
sending their officers of the law to be trained
in neighboring but foreign cities like in New Mexico
proves that Taos Pueblo Indians
ignore that a soldier belongs to his trainer
that his discipline, his habitual muscle response
belongs to his drill sergeant master:
"our laws are the same as up in town"
too bad Bobby! they could be your laws,
it's your land!
then flashing past as I leave Taos Bobby speeds
towards the reservation in a 1978 GMC van with two red flashers
on top bringing Red Cross survival rations to the Taos Pueblo Indians
respectfully frying bread for tourists
behind their sovereign borders.

Photo by Dede Woods

Jose Angel Figueroa

Born: 1946

Jose Angel Figueroa is a poet who has worked extensively in the theater and as a photographer and an educator of people of all ages.

Born in Mayaguez, Puerto Rico, Figueroa came to the United States at age six with his mother and father, who were migrant workers, and his nine brothers and sisters. He attended Morris High School in the Bronx, received a B.A. in English Literature from New York University in 1970 and an M.A. from SUNY at Buffalo in 1971. His college teaching has included Puerto Rican and Third World Literature at Columbia University, SUNY, Buffalo, and Yale University; creative writing and English as a Second Language at Teacher's College, Columbia University and Herbert H. Lehman College/CUNY. His work at the Teachers and Writers Collaborative in New York has helped and encouraged many young people to write. He has directed and produced poetic jazz performances in Joseph Papp's Public Theater and Miriam Colon's Puerto Rican Traveling Theater, and has acted in several off-Broadway plays. While he presents his own poetry in colleges and universities and on radio and television, he also has been responsible for producing many poetry series that present both well-known and new Puerto Rican/ Latino, African-American, and other Third World poets. His works include *East 110th Street* (Broadside Press, 1973), *Noo Jork* (Instituto de Cultura Puertorriquena, 1981). He edited *Unknown Poets from a Full-Time Jungle* for the Board of Education of New York in 1975 and has edited and designed over fifty volumes of children's poetry from Poets in the Schools projects since 1966. Presently Figueroa is living in Hartford, Connecticut.

Poet Pedro Pietri

if you ever see pedro
sitting on any park bench,
watch out: he counts
the number of dreams
stray pigeons eat
from travelers who pass by
with lost weekends,
undergrounding torn pockets;
he sits there
with funeral clothes
and a spanish shopping bag
that gossips cosmic poems
during the echoes
of undertakers
chewing over reality;

pedro rents coffins.

ask him
and he'll tell you
he justs trains pigeons

to bark at dogs.

Taino

it was strange
when my 2yr son
shot and killed
a bus with his

    finger,

but then
things made more
sense when my
8th month son

dragged himself
up the sofa, took
the NEWS

    & slowly
destroyed the
vietnamese war.

    it died
gently at first,
until he clawed
his fingers

    deeply
in its history.

and as i saw
everything crumble
into blood on the
floor, i saw

no dead people;
just a dead war

    and many

t o m o r r o w s.

HomeMade Smiles

    "My son,"
she said:

      +
+ + + + + the.
    +   bomb
    +   less
         skies

applaud
your face

innocent
v o i c e
winded cheeks
&
homemade smiles

"WAR" is no longer
love-sick for a palace
of honor 'n rice peoples'
wounds   your father
no longer salutes
the morning news
our next door neighbors
no longer need
to see an american flag
smiling   behind   you

"AND" as i look into a deep
hall of tomorrows i see
harrowing hell with fleshless
bones of vietnam spilling
your blood and voicing you
back after so many nights
wild-eyed 'n brimming
with tears

    "Tell me,
    my son:

    what good news
    could you
    -a question mark
    could you
    -a grave

    bring?"

Pablo Neruda

I heard from Pablo Neruda
we must continue reawakening
the Unused Dreams of statues.
    He was then dead,
and after the earth ate
his flesh, all I could think
of were poems portable poets
would someday write
    about Neruda's memories
leaving his body and falling
into the salivas
    of kins, friends

    and enemies.

I had to do something about
his death; something.
    I don't know,
scream feelings inside him,
swallow the ruthless smiles
those soldiers touched him
with during that invasion.
    I don't know,
open every word he spoke,
tie the syllables from a page
and intertwine them to hang
fascism by its horrid throat,

    what?

I heard Pablo Neruda answer me

    Poeta: feed on my hang-overs.
    Let your mind walk with
    the secrets living in forests.
    Dry the drunkenness in Bochinche,
    gossip, harmful to our people,
    and never blame
    the nights outside for the roots

    of solitude.

Open yourself
to the gifts performed
by this earth and your soul,
and create the solidarity
that would teach our revolutions
never to mourn blindfolded freedom.

Poets must puff New Life into words,

gulp the tastebuds of Art,
go to bed with Life,
nourish the Consciousness of
Direction without the shoes
being injured,
and wake up to the Songs
of Poetical Bartenders

whose hang-overs make for
Far Out Greasy Poetry.

Believe me, it's the only way
statues would ever confess
any left-over or

Unused Dreams.

Boricua

Boricua: you
were   born
some-
where

b e t w e e n

americanairlines
near sanjuan
&   kennedyairport
nearTheBronx
:::::::::::::::::::::::::

    & i have seen
    your grim face
listening to bleeding
    in the distance
as your m i n d walks
      B A C K W A R D S
      B A C K W A R D S
      B A C K w a r d s
      b a c k w a r d s

    ::::::::::::::::::::::::

      b a c k w a r d s
& sees lincoln hospital
    having a field day
    with your mother
    because she had
    labor pains with
    a Spanish Accent

    r e m e m b e r?
    ::::::::::::::::::::::::

    s c h o o l s
    always wanted
    to cave in your
PuertoRicanAccent
    & because you
wanted to make it
    you had to pledge
    allegiance lefthanded
    because you
had lost your soul
during some english exam.
::::::::::::::::::::::::::::::::::::::

    report cards
      fed you with
      counterfeit dreams
      dictionaries

carved fear into
your skin & had a warrant
for your accent because
they said you were always
culturally deprived

remember, negro?
:::::::::::::::::::::::::::

& i often wondered
why they kept smirking
their lips when they
called you PerroRican
instead of PuertoRican.

but who am i
talking about, negro?
:::::::::::::::::::::::::::::::

we're really the same
YoungBoricua, except that
i have seen you drown
into multi–cultural
hangouts in central park
where hypertensed congas
try to make unemployed crowds
freak out on people
trying to become a part
of one crowd or another
:::::::::::::::::::::::::::::::::::

& your spirit looks back
for an island
& SHE saids: i am not
all paradise, Boricua

remove your eyes & plant them
inside my soul
flirt with me
but glance deeper now.

see infants not yet born crumble,
fire will grow on your lap once

knowing the distance our people
have suffered, my child.
but never let your mind
eat silence or wait for mañanas
to dust off your anger.
:::::::::::::::::::::::::::::::::::

help HER, this island says.

help me to silence
s l u m p o e m s
by feeding yourself
to your people, Los Boricuas
so that i could eat away
all those fattyacids
that make it difficult for me

to recognize
you anymore
in airports,
in airplanes,
in the bronX
:::::::::::::::::::::

Y en las calles de Puerto Rico.

Confessions From the Last Cloud

in 1985
the lone ranger
was executed simply
cause it was discovered
he was a republican
that year
the left-over population
forgot all about tonto
cause all visas were cancelled
this same year

gurus took over the news
to survive oblivional hang-ups
hang-ups were discovered
to be hereditary
and in 1985
hell was tired
of living underground
and the Last Headlines read:
WORLD WAR III WANTED
To Have Intercourse With Dr. Kissinger!
that year farted
days rain-clotted
nights went completely mad
dreams had nightmares
dirt roads grew crowded
rocks awoke from a long sleep
slowly public transportation
became lonely
alice cooper and mick jagger
became humans again
mary no longer pretended
she was a virgin
god became speechless
marijuana was proven innocent
the cia died of sore eyes
politicians could no longer
barricade their nights with police lines
the president of the united states
declared war on his own toilet paper

caca had vultured the weather
and in 1985
nostalgia was indicted
for indulging in fraud
this year
elephants became extinct
cartoons lost their fight
for human civil rights
the morgue had no vacancies
immortality was last seen

bleeding two inches
above a grave
and the last echoes
were heard gasping
over deserted mountains
humanless shadows
unworlding populations
and death finally changed
its name to Dry Prunes
when all laughter left town

and i am now
an innocent by-stander
an unemployed cloud
drinking Mardi Gras
puerto rican pineapple wine
guaranteed to give my brain
a bilingual high
and now it's time for me
to cancel my ceiling citizenship
i was not destined to die of boredom
by working for a people-less planet
and i will be myself
what i've always been:

a tourist of the universe
the last interpreter of history
when history itself
has been destroyed

an unemployed cloud, yes!

but a vocal visionary
tripping on the gentle whispers of love
and who will eventually be
the first citizen of the moon

in 1985.

Magdalena Gomez

Born: 1954

Magdalena Gomez is a poet, playwright, actor, director, and chaplain. She has performed, read, and held workshops in schools from the lower grades through college and at institutions from churches to prisons. She directed and performed in the Teatro el Puente and with the Xavier Company. She has served as Assistant Chaplain at Bayview Correctional Institution where she held theater workshops as well.

Her poetry has been published in various journals, among them *The Massachusetts Review*. She has written and directed *No Greater Love* (The Xavier Company at Sacred Heart Chapel in Brooklyn, Our Lady of the Scapular Church, St. Cecilia's Church, St. Paul the Apostle Church, and St. Francis Xavier Church in Manhattan among other churches) and *The Paschal Mystery* (The Herolds of Joy at Holy Cross, St. Francis Xavier, St. Cecilia, Ascension Episcopal, St. Thomas the Apostle, and St. Malachy Churches).

Her version of her biography follows:

"What I have done is not as important as who I am becoming. My search for authenticity of being has been my dance through this life. I have played the roles of poet, actress, teacher, counselor, chaplain, waitress, and motel maid . . . the list goes on.

In the last six years, I have begun to discover myself as a Latina. At the age of 36, I am putting together the pieces of how racism and childhood poverty (on many levels) have created the masks of survival. I am now exploring the mythology of my life. At the moment of death, it is not my resume I will be thinking about; it will be the people I have loved, those who have loved me, and the Power that brought us together. I hope I will remember that I am rooted in the basin of the Orinoco River, discovered by no one; I have always been here."

Making It

Passing the bread shop with hungry eyes
loaves become doves fleeing my sight
discarded peaches by the fruit market tempt me
pride turns my head the other way
there's a sale on chickens at the market;
I am down to three pennies and no stockings.
my man was last seen crossing himself
before throwing the dice up against
Immaculate Conception walls.
that's a church on fourteenth street
where sometimes I like the mass
and sometimes I don't.
I like God sometimes,
but sometimes he makes me mad. men.
I don't know how to type
and anyway I don't have one dress that
fits. when I go to the salvation army
i guess the fit and i always guess wrong.
i did that with my man too. I could
have married my step brother. he has
a clothing store on wall street.
he smiles all the time and i hear
he brings cocaine to parties. that
isn't any big deal, but right now
a party sounds real good.
there's food there and many opportunities
for babysitting jobs. i could be very
important if i got the right babies. babies
that will grow up to own pawn shops,
and stores with shirts and slippers and
underwear. babies that could be lawyers
and when they grew up and i was old and
farty, they would remember the manners
and songs i taught them and rest my case/
i would become important beyond the streets/
i could have a velvet chair/
i wouldn't have to go to parties anymore/
i could eat when i felt like it/

other women's children will carry me in
a golden box over the rainbow back to my country
and bury me where the air smells green.

Chocolate Confessions

The summer came too fast,
stayed too long,
like an unwanted man
you keep around
because being alone
makes you feel fatter than you really are.

The kitchen table with its stains
that won't scrub off
gives you something to be annoyed about
when the kids get boring
and guilt digs a fingernail
into your heart.

When you admit to yourself
that maybe being a mother
isn't always fun,
or even nice,
or even necessary;
and dammit! why doesn't everybody
just go away!

Let me do the dishes when I feel like it.
Let me eat when I feel like it.
Let me smoke a cigarette when I feel like it.
Let me stay in the bathroom as along as I want.
Just once,
I want the decadence of a pedicure.

With too much time to think,
worms sneak out here and there,
slipping into the soup

and conversations with my husband;
it makes us tense,
so I offer him a chocolate.
He smiles.
That's what his mother did
when things got rough.

So now he's fat
and I'm not,
I'm also younger and smarter.
I feel guilty
when he brings home flowers.

It's hell being married to a nice guy.
And the kids do look like angels
when they're sleeping.

Troubled Awakening

Entering your silence, my Lord,
without shoes, without hands,
unable to push away your face,
unable to stab out those burning eyes
that beckon me to a spiritual death.

I hate your love, an arrow cold
with truth
piercing its commandment into my stone heart,
reaching the spring of blood
I gag in perceiving.

The cracked edges of illusion
rest above a field of grass;
I cannot run.

Piece by piece I must gather them
into the fold of my prayer
and place them in your hands.

But how, my Lord, I have no hands?

To The Latin Lover I Left at the Candy Store

how come,

I wanna know,

you like me better

when I tell you

my name is Gomez?

I was one more white girl

till my accent started to show

and then you said

you should have known

I was a sister

when you saw the size of my hips

then you asked me why

I like white boys better than you

and how come/I don't hang out/on the stoop

when you offer me cerveza and cola ices, man

that Hagen Daaz is a white man's rip-off

why don't I get it straight

and learn to relate

to the pain of my people

kissing ass for food stamps?

You tell me I got it easy

cause I pass,

I tell you about ripped up

work applications

when they get to my last name

You laugh and say "Aha! That's why you like

white boys better than me; wanna change your name."

I tell you that when I was born

nobody asked me

what color I wanted to be,

what name I wanted to answer to,

or if I wanted tits and ass

or if I wanted what you've got

or if I wanted to be a bird

or if I wanted to be a cactus

or if I wanted to be cracker Jax;

I am as I am

and the pain of staying alive

I got for nothing

and nobody's begging me to hang around

and nobody's giving me tickets to the moon

and that sun gets hot on EVERYBODY.

At that last call

when la muerte says:

"Come here, baby. I want you."

there's no way out of that affair;

that switchblade shines

at everyone's throat.

So don't ask me why I don't hang out

and why I like white boys better than you

no questions got answers

just more questions

and it's too hot

to get hot

if you know what I mean

so give me music

and shut your mouth

you can push it in,

but you gotta pull it out

sometime . . .

when you gotta go

you gotta go

same as me,

same as the white boys

same as Mr. Hagen Daaz;

you may know my hips,

but you don't know me;

you may know my name,

but you don't know me;

you may know my color,

but you don't know me;

so don't ask me

why I don't hang out

or why I like white boys

better than you.

I'm going to the store;
you need anything?

Solo Palabras

I felt some folded paper in my pocket
got my hopes up thinking it was dollar bills;
after five days of oil sandwiches you start hallucinating
you think you could bump into some guy at the bank
and leave with his watch at least

you finger the cookies in the two-cent jar at the bodega
where you play nonchalant about having only pennies
your own brother rolls his eyes and motions his son to get you
out,
not for nothin' but just in case

I got nervous when the paper in my pocket was poems
and I was real disappointed and I was mad
I felt cheated and wondered why the publishers weren't breaking my
door down
with contracts and chabos in their fists

I got scared that I wished my poems were dollar bills
I got scared that they just weren't enough anymore
or that maybe they never were

some words thrown around like dogs at the kennel
like old people on government lines
now, don't get me wrong, I'm not calling it political
and I'm not pointing any fingers
I just happen to have one pointing up because I'm mad
and at least if I can stay mad I can stay alive

on the 2 train I broke down because I had no flowers for my mother
and it was Mother's Day and it had been a long time since I had
talked to her
and that day my hands and heart were empty
so I cried and when I got there we had a fight before I had a
chance

to eat the food she had stayed up all night making
just for her little girl
but if I stay mad and can stay alive one more day

because that's the way it is when there is nothing left but words
to eat

A Desert Cry

Today I hate that I was born.
Today is eternal.
I slide down the devil's throat
like a miserable, stinking sardine.

Perhaps tomorrow I will
cut my way out
with a quick slash of hope
emerging whole

only to be swallowed again.

Lost Daughter

A virgin at heart,
she was easily inspired to seek her Lover.

One night, as all were sleeping
beneath a vigilant moon,
this maiden of her own design
wandered from her tribe.

They had become strangers to her.
Or had she become the stranger?
She didn't know,
but the fact remained a ready wound
that all the spirits of all her ancestors
could not soothe.

Their chatter and their songs,
their prayers and their dancing,
the work of their hands,
nor the look of their eyes;
their rituals, their blessings,
their reprimands, their consolations;
nothing could capture her child's heart.
Nets of blood could not hold her.

She praised and thanked
the sharp stones and thorns
that battered and pricked her tender feet
on the unfamiliar road;
they spoke to her of freedom,
the road to her Lover
Whom her people did not know.

And the funny thing is, she thought
that she did not know how He would look,
or by what name He would answer.
Or if He would recognize her as His own.

And what if He had no name?
Then He would answer to the passion
that seemed to bruise her heart with every breath;
no lover could ignore what she would give!

Unthinkable, unspeakable,
consuming love;
and love, you are such a small word
for so great a thing.

The stars' milky points nursed her,
the moon's approval ignited the way
with invisible, cool flames
she could taste with the tongue of her soul's
darkest shadow.

That night's journey,
that winding road,
lasted many years;

when the morning arrived
the virgin found herself
among her awakening people.

In them, she found her Lover.
Mercifully, they never knew she had gone.

Looking Deep

I hear tapping in your silence
feeling for a way out of being
alone;
searching for the thin part of the wall.

You decided long ago
that no one will understand you.

As for being loved,
don't be ridiculous.

You are convinced by the hardness
of your own face,
betrayed by the softness
I am blessed to see
in your eyes.

I am not convinced.
You try too hard for a man who teaches
others to go with it.

You try too hard to budge your world
into your idea of an axis.
Hiding your power in the guise
of a fisherman,
the water critters know you
and they come.
Some tease you,
some you catch,
some get away,
some you throw back in;
but one way or another,
you devour them all.

Their glisteningly innocent life,
their breathing, their colors,
their struggle, their feel on skin;
you will have all of it
on imagination's hook
for dark, stormy days.

You teach me the dance
of the fisherman
then pull away into
some dark corner of thought
when fish no longer protect you.

You are convinced
by the hardness of your own face
that I could not possibly love you.

Luz Maria Umpierre

Born: 1947

Luzma Umpierre is a poet and scholar who has taken a particularly heroic stance on the question of the rights of gays and lesbians, and "minorities" in educational institutions. As a faculty member in the Department of Spanish and Portuguese at Rutgers University she was an advocate for these groups and worked to develop the curriculum so that it included material responsive to their needs. Although from some sectors she suffered harassment and discrimination for her work, she received widespread support as well, and was instrumental in easing discrimination at Rutgers.

She was born and grew up in Santurce, Puerto Rico, and received a B.A. from the College of the Sacred Heart, due, she says, "to the immense sacrifices of [my] parents." As a student there she promoted the separation of College and Church and the democratization of the student admission policy. Later at Bryn Mawr College Luzma was again in the vanguard, especially as an advocate for admission of Puerto Rican students. She was the first Bryn Mawr student to write a doctoral dissertation on Puerto Rico.

Umpierre is the author of four volumes of poetry and two of literary criticism: *Una puertorriquena en Penna* (Puerto Rico, 1979); *En el pais de las maravillas* (Third Woman Press, 1982); *—Y otras desgracias—And other misfortunes* (Third Woman Press, 1985); *The Margarita poems* (Third Woman Press, 1987); *Ideologia y novela en Puerto Rico* (Playor, 1983), and *Nuevas aproximaciones criticas a la literatura puertorriquena contemporanea* (Cultural, 1983-84). Her work often reflects those problems she has encountered in her life: cultural elitism, discrimination, alienation, and the search for love and self-realization. A collection of her essays on homosexual readings of Caribbean Literature is being published by the University of California at Berkeley in 1990.

Umpierre has published in many journals and has been a visiting writer and given poetry readings at, among other institutions, Harvard, Wellesley, the University of California/Santa Barbara, the University of Illinois, El Museo del Barrio in New York, and The Mission Cultural Center in San Francisco. She has received creative writing awards from

International Publications and Chase Manhattan and two awards, both in 1990, for her efforts to secure civil rights for all people: a Lifetime Achievement Award from the Coalition of Lesbian and Gay Organizations in New Jersey and a "Woman of the Year" award from the Women's Alliance at Western Kentucky University where she now heads the Department of Modern Languages and Intercultural Studies.

The Statue

Flower child
twirling around a yellow full moon.
Trinkets crowning her long messy hair,
glossy bead droplets encircling her neck,
magma, chalazas,
metal links as insignias,
imprisoning rings.

"Peace," she says.
"Love," the victoria sign on her hands.
Flowered blazer from Saks on her back,
loafer shoes mold her feet,
Calvin Klein faded jeans
with the brand name torn out.
Flower child.

At the core of her fabric and emblems:
economics, gastronomics, the computer,
the lag of the jet, quintessential histrionics,
flower child.

Twisting faces,
mutilating backs of the dark colored faces.
"Whip," she whimpers in silence,
"Chain,"
"Dow Jones,"
"Apartheid."
Flower child, slave making ant
in a midnight assembly of forgeries,
tranferential concoction:
love to hate
peace to war
"listen, man" to "obey"
hip to yup
Black to White
cornucopias to caldrons
Vietnam to El Salvador
esprit to *corps*
1960 to 1985.

Flower child.
Hoaxing child,
flower forayer
legendary facade
transforming in the night
to stand and to lie on the Hudson
at bay.
Fully neonized,
fully galvanized,
fully modernized,
face lifted fully,
Brook Shields or
Madonna of Liberty,
theatrical forgery
in her treasured island.
Flower child,
can symbol of the U.S. of A.;
glory hole of the nation.

No Hatchet Job

for Marge Piercy

They would like
to put the tick and flea collar
around her neck and
take her for walks on sunny afternoons
in order to say to the neighbors:
"We had domesticated this unruly woman."

They would like
to see her curled up on the corner,
fetal position, hungry, un-nursed
so that they can enter the scene,
rock-a-bye her to health
to advertise in the *Woman News* or *Psychology Today*:
"We have saved, we have cured this vulnerable woman."

They would like
to see her unclean,
10 days without showers,
in filth and foul urine,
frizzled hair and all,
her business in ruins,
her reputation in shambles,
her body repeatedly raped on a billiard board
so that they can say in their minds:
"We have finally reduced this superior woman."

They would like
to have her OD on the carpet,
anorexic, bulemic and stiff on her bed
so that they can collect a percentage for burial
from the deadly mortician:
"We have found you this cadaverous woman."

They would like
to spread her ashes at sea,
arrange *pompas fúnebres*,
dedicate a wing or a statue in her name
so that their consciences
can finally rest in saying:
"We have glorified this poet woman."

But headstrong she is unleashed,
intractable she nourishes her mind,
defiantly she lives on in unity,
obstinately she refuses the limelight, the pomp and the glory.
Eternally she breathes
one line after next,
unrestrained, unshielded
    willfully
    WRITER
    WOMAN

Only the Hand That Stirs
Knows What's in the Pot

I don't
share my recipes with them;
these are folder-marked
in my brain.
Some old, from the island, you know,
some new, made in sexual passion
for the most recent of lovers,
none borrowed,
many blue.

"I need to know
the special ingredient
in this tasty dip."
"I have a prominent guest
and need your *flan* recipe."
One a man, the other a woman;
both wanting my gist,
my mysterious herb,
my prescription.
I don't deliver!

No handing out my set of ingredients,
they *sauté* in my head,
inside a Corning food dish.
I cater to friends;
eight course meals
for deliverance,
for arousing of passions,
melting aphrodisiacs for pulsing lovers.
But no partaking of formulas;
carbohydrates, fats,
proteins and supplementary substances
to sustain, to repair,
to furnish with energy;
fermentation in my gray cells,
fool's parsley from my breasts,
savory aromas from my loins,
all for the guests in my banquets.

But no handy recipes or
longevity plasmas
to take out; to go;
fast food service
offered elsewhere!

Martín Espada

Born: 1957

Martín Espada's solidarity with migrants and immigrants, with working people and with those outside the working class is the vantage point from which he approaches poetry.

A Puerto Rican born in Brooklyn, he received a B.A. in history from the University of Wisconsin, a J.D. in law from Northeastern University and works as a tenant lawyer in Boston. He has two collections of poetry, **The Immigrant's Iceboy's Bolero** (Waterfront Press, 1982) with photographs by his father, Frank, and **Trumpets from the Islands of Their Eviction** (Bilingual Press/Arizona State University, 1987), and a third, **Rebellion Is the Circle of a Lover's Hands/Rebelion es el giro de manos del amante** (Curbstone Press, 1990), which received the PEN/Revson Foundation Fellowship for Poetry with the citation: "These are poems about hard work and poverty. He is the poet of that knowledge, the full weight of that knowledge." It is a bilingual collection with the translations by Espada. Espada has had other honors as well: a Massachusetts Artists Fellowship (1984), a National Endowment for the Arts Fellowship (1986), a Boston Contemporary Writers Award (1987), and the Rosalie Boyle Award (1987). His poems have appeared in numerous journals including **Bilingual Review**, **Ploughshares**, **River Styx**, **Bloomsbury** and in several anthologies which include **Under 35: The New Generation of American Poets**. An essay on Puerto Rican poetry is included in **A Gift of Tongues**. In addition to his legal work Espada teaches courses in Latino poetry in the Boston area and has read his poetry at many colleges, universities and other institutions.

In Puerto Rico,
your father tries to still
the jumping memory
of a numbers runner,
trying to sleep
between hospital-white curtains.

Let him sleep
where I slept:
shining in your passionate blackness,
the vigil of your shimmering gaze.

Toque de queda: Curfew in Lawrence

Lawrence, Massachusetts, August 1984

Now the archbishop comes to Lawrence
to say a Spanish mass.
But the congregation understands
without translation:
the hammering of the shoe factory,
sweating fever of infected August,
housing project's asylum chatter,
dice on the sidewalk,
saints at the window,
two days' murky pollution of rot-smoke,
the mayor's denials.

Toque de queda: curfew signs
outlaw the conspiracy of foreign voices
at night.
Barricades surround the buildings
window-black from burning, collapsed in shock.
After the explosion of shotgun pellets
and shattered windshields,
sullen quiet stands watching on Tower Hill,

trash, brick and bottle fragments
where the arrested kneeled, hands clapped
to the neck, and bodies with Spanish names
slammed into squad cars, then disappeared.

The mobs are gone: white adolescents
who chanted USA and flung stones
at the scattering of astonished immigrants,
ruddy faces slowing the car to shout spick
and wave beer cans.

Now the archbishop comes to Lawrence
to say a Spanish mass.
At the housing project where they are kept,
they're collecting money for bail.

Tony Went to the Bodega but He Didn't Buy Anything

para Angel Guadalupe

Tony's father left the family
and the Long Island city projects,
leaving a mongrel-skinny puertorriqueño boy
nine years old
who had to find work.

Makengo the Cuban
let him work at the bodega.
In grocery aisles
he learned the steps of the dry-mop mambo,
banging the cash register
like piano percussion
in the spotlight of Machito's orchestra,
polite with the abuelas who bought on credit,
practicing the grin on customers
he'd seen Makengo grin
with his bad yellow teeth.

Tony left the projects too,
with a scholarship for law school.

But he cursed the cold primavera
in Boston;
the cooking of his neighbors
left no smell in the hallway,
and no one spoke Spanish
(not even the radio).

So Tony walked without a map
through the city,
a landscape of hostile condominiums
and the darkness of white faces,
sidewalk-searcher lost
till he discovered the projects.

Tony went to the bodega
but he didn't buy anything:
he sat by the doorway satisfied
to watch la gente (people
island-brown as him)
crowd in and out,
hablando español,
thought: this is beautiful,
and grinned
his bodega grin.

This is a rice and beans
success story:
today Tony lives on Tremont Street,
above the bodega.

Water, White Cotton, and the Rich Man

Rosa's body stopped growing
at the age of twelve.
Ten hours a day
blurred pesticide and sweat,
squeezed headaches and full bladder

surrounded by widening white-cotton sun,
doing what Mexicanos in Lubbock, Texas
did for working.

So she worked,
beside her quiet father
(father with thousands of cotton field days
lost in the dry riverbeds
of his hands),
floating with him in a scorched white dream
of places distant from the black tar
of the county trunk;
soon the jug was empty,
and every time Rosa swallowed
she felt the scraping in her neck
that reminded her of water.
Twelve years old, the child watched the road
and imagined a rich man
driving a silver car
that meandered through the cotton fields
to bring her water, chilled
in a long bright glass,
close enough to see
the moisture-beads evaporate.

She learned her thirst, slowly,
over the days that no landlord
volunteered the drippings of his tap,
a closing throat, paste of saliva
and humidity that becomes rage;
twenty years after
her body stopped growing
Rosa keeps a peasant daughter's hallucination
still hidden,
feels it scratching every time
her throat is dry.

The Jeep Driver

for Fernando Reñazco, Nicaragua, July 1982

"I know everyone
in this country,"
he says,
"even the devil."
His indio face flattens
when he laughs,
cursing the gringos
or pumping his fists
as he steers
a remembered machine gun.

Fernando's smile
is not revenge against dead patrones;
he smiles like a tired man
who's had a chance to rest.
For years of his life
the coal mines glistened blackly,
and sugar cane bristled
in Nicaragüense summer,
through generations of parading military,
mutilated dissidents sunken at Laguna Masaya.
Fernando's face has no expression,
remembering a tall boy
swinging at coal-rock and cane-stalk
(a father's death is work),
or driving a truck ponderous
over the dirt roads,
starved throats of the Americas.
He learned a song then
about rain and houses of cardboard;
he still sings it.

When the rebellion began,
Fernando from the doorway watched
the hurried carrying
of dangle-limbed bodies
to the burning.
But the soldiers grabbed

still supervising the labor,
a restored photograph in the window.

Jacobo's face
is indio-guatemalteco,
bored as the work,
round as worry,
heavy as waiting.
Guatemala is green and red,
green volcanoes, red birds,
green like rivers in rain,
red like coffee beans at harvest,
the river-green and quetzal bird-red
of his paintings,
perfiles del silencio.

Testimony of death-squad threats
by telephone, shrilled in the dark,
the flash of fear's adrenaline,
and family stolen with the military's greed
for bodies, all recorded by stenographers,
then dismissed:
Guatemala leaves no proof,
and immigration judges are suspicious
only of the witnesses, who stagger and crawl
through America. Asylum denied,
appeal pending.

As he waits, Jacobo paints
in green and red, verde y rojo,
and at night he cleans the office
of Adams and Blinn,
where Guatemala cannot be felt
by the arrogant handshake of lawyers,
where there is no green or red,
only his shadow blending
with the other shadows in the room,
and all the hours of the night
to picture the executioners.

even the watchers in doorways.

So he became a combatiente,
jeep driver for the rebels,
legs paralyzed after thirty days'
fighting through floodwaters at the knee—
chorus of water, percussion of rifle shot—
he healed, walked again, swiveled the jeep
plane-hunted on the last retreat from Masaya,
then celebration in crowd-crazy Managua
when the dictator was finally gone
to the sky.

Now he drives with us through Zelaya, the north,
telling us he is still indio puro de Monimbó,
bragging of the Nicaragüense Flor de Caña rum
he will not drink himself.
Jeep driver for the ministry of land reform:
driving through the mountain roads,
rough dry throats of the Americas,
between crater-valleys and shallow rivers
and red malinche flowers
exploded by Mayan gods in the act of dying,
Fernando's hand spreads wide from the rattling jeep,
striking the wind,
sweeping the wind.

La tormenta

"La muerte es una tormenta.
Death is a storm,"
he said.
"And the village
is an anthill scattering."
Héctor in the army
of El Salvador:
conscripted at fourteen,
a deserter three years later.

A boy with wide ears
and one shirt,
he walked across Guatemala,
México and Arizona to get here,
almost swallowing
too much river and mud
at the border.
He wants to be called Tony
in the United States.

In the basement,
part way through
translated instructions
on where he will eat today,
Tony pulls the hood
of a big borrowed coat
over his head and bodyrocks,
a monk shadowboxing
at the clang of churchbells,
moving to a song
with a distant helicopter beat,
la tormenta
and the anthill scattering.

Green and Red, Verde y Rojo

for Jacobo Mena

At night, when Beacon Hill
is a private army
of antique gas lamps
glowing in single file,
Jacobo vacuum-cleans
the law office of Adams and Blinn,
established 1856, with the founder's
wire-rimmed Protestant face

The Moon Shatters on Alabama Avenue

A wooden box rattled
with coins for the family,
on a stoop where the roots
of a brown bloodstain grew.

Brooklyn, 1966: Agropino Bonillo was his name,
a neighbor, the yellow leaflet said,
a kitchen worker who walked home
under the scaffolding of the trains at night,
hurrying past streetlamps with dark eyes.
He was there when the boys surrounded him,
quick with shouts and pushing,
addiction's hunger in a circle.
When he had no money,
the kicking began.

The mourners clustered at the storefront,
then marched between cadaverous buildings
down Alabama Avenue,
as the night turned blue with rain
in a heavy sky of elevated track.
The first candles struggled, smothered wet;
onlookers leaned warily as they watched.
A community of faces gathered and murmured
in the dim circles of light,
kept alive by cupped hands.

In the asphalt street shined black from rain
and windows where no one was seen
hesitant candles appeared, a pale blur started
on the second floor, another trembling glimmer
slipped to the back of the march, then more,
multiplied into a constellation
spreading over the sidewalk,
a swarm of candles that throbbed descending
tenement steps in the no longer absolute dark,
as if the moon had shattered
and dropped in burning white pieces
on the night.

His name was Agropino Bonillo,
spoken remembering
every sixty-dollar week
he was bent in the kitchen,
his children
who could not dress for winter
and brawled against welfare taunts
at the schoolyard,
the unlit night
that the sweep of legs was stopped
by his belly and his head.

And the grief of thousands illuminated city blocks,
moving with the tired feet of the poor:
candles a reminder of the wakes too many and too soon,
the frustrated prayers and pleading with saints,
in memoriam for generations of sacrificed blood
warm as the wax sticking to their fingers,
and years of broken streetlamps, bowed
with dark eyes, where addiction's hunger waits nervously.

Over the wooden box, a woman's face
was slick in a drizzle of tears.
Her hand dropped coins like seed.

Judith Ortiz Cofer

Born: 1952

Judith Ortiz Cofer is a poet and a novelist. She has the rare ability to capture and combine in her fiction and her poetry the two distinct cultures that are Puerto Rican—the island and the mainland.

Cofer was born in Hormigueros, Puerto Rico, and moved to Paterson, New Jersey, when her father was transferred North with the Army. Where she resided and attended school depended to a large extent upon where her father was sent in the service. She lived for extended periods of time in Puerto Rico, a factor which has allowed her to explore the cultures of both Puerto Rico and the United States in her poetry. She graduated from high school in Augusta, Georgia, and received a B.A. from Augusta College and an M. A. at Florida Atlantic University. She attended Oxford University in England on an English Speaking Union of America Scholarship in 1977.

She is the author of a chapbook, *Peregrina*, which won the Riverstone International Poetry Competition in 1985, and a collection of poetry, *Terms of Survival* (Arte Publico Press,1987), that has as a major concern the particular experiences of women, the mixture of man and woman, and the ability to love and yet leave. Her novel, *The Line of the Sun* (University of Georgia Press, 1989), is distinctively Puerto Rican in the tension that builds between island and mainland cultural values as well as being universal in sentiment. A book of her memoirs is in progress from Arte Publico Press.

Cofer has read her poetry in colleges and universities across the United States and at the Universite de Paris, France. She has published in many distinguished journals including *Southern Poetry Review*, *Kenyon Review*, *Antioch Review*, *New Mexico Humanities Review*, and *Bilingual Review*. She is included in the *Heath Anthology of American Literature*. Recognition for her poetry has come in the form of awards or fellowships from the Florida Fine Arts Council, the Georgia Council for the Arts, the Bread Loaf Writers' Conference, the Georgia Poetry Circuit, the Wotter Bynner Foundation for Poetry, and the National Endowment for the Arts. Cofer now resides in Georgia.

Unspoken

to my daughter

When I hug you tight at bedtime,
you wince in pain for the tender
swelling of new breasts.
Nothing is said, both of us aware
of the covenant of silence
we must maintain through the rending
apart that is adolescence.
            But it won't always
be confusion and hurting, the body
will find itself through this pain;
remember Michelangelo, who believed
that in marble, form already exists,
the artist's hands simply pulling it out
into the world.
            I want to tell you about men:
the pleasure of a lover's hand on skin
you think may rip at elbows and knees
stretching over a frame like clothes
you've almost outgrown; of the moment
when a woman first feels
a baby's mouth at her breast, opening her
like the hand of God in Genesis, the moment
when all that led to this seems right.
            Instead I say, *sweet dreams,*
for the secrets hidden under the blanket
like a forbidden book
I'm not supposed to know you've read.

Old Women

". . . little packages, oh yes,
all old women make little packages
and stow them away under their beds."
—Jose Donoso
The Obscene Bird of Night

Evidence of *a woman's hard life*
on faces lined with meaning
like the Rosetta Stone; a litany
of ailments, marks of fear, nights of pain, knowledge
of solitude, of shameful family secrets,
and the occasional ecstasy they dare you to decipher.

Stored under groaning mattresses are the remnants
of their lives wrapped in little packages
and tied with string: wedding photos
jaundiced with age and humidity, of couples
standing stiff as corpses at the greatest distance
the frame will allow, of serious infants
held by women in severe dresses. In bundles,
sheaves of magazines becoming

one moist lump; balls of string, baby clothes of cracked satin
and ragged lace, shoes curling tongue-to-heel—homogenized,
all of it velvety to the touch,
turning in the thick air of wet coughs and tea,
the thing they all once were—paper to pulp, cloth to fiber,
ashes to ashes.

Old women sit like hens over their soft bundles,
nest and nursery of their last days, letting
the effluence of memory, its pungent odor
of decay work through the clogged channels
of their brains, presiding over their days
like an opium dream.

What We Feared

The thawing earth
down with a fever that will break
in beauty,
like a Victorian woman
dying in childbirth
translucent flesh heaving
in the ecstacy of pain,
huge eyes brilliant with visions,
blood gathered at the mouth
for a final red scream.

First rose of the season
opens limp petals lined in black, sad
as an overdressed girl
passed out on the bathroom floor.
In the night, nails rise like the dead
from the boards of old houses,
startling old people
for whom sleep is a rehearsal.
Weak and glassy-eyed
they think of wood dissolving,
weeds growing through bones picked clean
by the grooming fingers of trees;
the economy of nature.

This is spring, what we feared.

The Life of an Echo

Until Manuel,
I preferred the company of shadows
to the vagrant love of men.
                              One day,
he came to my door to slake his thirst,
impatient to be on his way

271

to anyplace.
            I was drawn
to his quick speech,
the little red flag of his tongue
signaling his body's intentions.

I began to understand how the wind
can make you feel naked.
When he took my face in hands,

I was chaos on the first day,
waiting for the Word.
                    Yet after
we answered the call of the flesh, nothing
remained but the valley's deep emptiness,
returning my voice.

Anniversary

for John

Lying in bed late, you read to me
about a past war, about young men who each year
become more like our sons, who died the year we met,
or the year we got married, or the year our child was born.
You read to me about how they dragged their feet
through a green maze, how they fell,
again and again, victims to an enemy
wily enough to be the critter-villian of some nightmare
tale with his booby-traps in the shape of children
and his cities under the earth; and about how,
even when they survived, these boys left something behind
in the thick brush or muddy swamp
where no one can get it back—caught like a baseball cap
on a low-hanging branch.

And I think about you and me, nineteen, and angry,
and in love, in that same year when America, erupting

272

like a late-blooming adolescent, broke into violence,
caught in a turmoil it could neither understand nor control;
how we walked through the rough parade
wearing the insignias of our rebellion: peace symbols
and scenes of Eden embroidered our faded jeans,
necks heavy with beads we did not count on
for patience, singing *Revolution*: a song we misunderstood
for years. Death was a slogan to shout about with raised fists,
or hang on banners.

Now here we are, listening more closely than ever to old songs,
sung for new reasons by new voices; survivors
of an undeclared war someone might decide to remake
like a popular tune. Sometimes, in the dark, alarmed by silence,
I lay my hand on your chest, for the familiar, steady beat
to which I have attuned my breathing for so many years.

Fever

Father was to her, and to me,
like the wind—blowing through our house
on weekend leaves—and when we spoke to him,
he carried our voices away.

                    When he left,
and silence grew inside my mother like a child,
I would watch as she set the table for two,
then ate by herself in the kitchen, standing.

And she taught me this:
that silence is a thick and dark curtain,
the kind that pulls down over a shop window;

that love is the quick repercussion of a stone
bouncing off the same darkened window; that pain
is something you embrace, like a rag doll
no one will ask you to share.

Some nights, she allowed me in her bed.
Her skin was as cool as the surface
of the pillow the sick child clings to, awakening
from feverish dreams.

I would lay my head close to hers and listen
to the fine, knotted thread of her breath,
to her rosary of sighs,

her peace so deepened by sorrow, I know
it sustained me then, as the light
slipping past heavy, dark curtains might nourish
a small plant set, by accident, close

to the window.

Spring

for Sue Ellen Thompson

On windy days
she wears a skirt woven
from sighs
by an old Indian woman
going blind.
It wraps around
her thighs like a lover
on his knees
pleading obsession.
The design (faded now)
must have been
a chase: a shower
of arrows and a deer
leaping out of reach,
set in motion when she walks
past my window
on a windy day
smoothing her skirt down

as it tries to fly
away like a bright blue
kite with a woman in it.

The Campesino's Lament

It is Ash Wednesday and Christ is waiting
to die. I have left my fields dark and moist
with last night's rain to take the sacrament.
My face is streaked with ashes. Come back,
mujer. Without you,
                 I am an empty place
where spiders crawl and nothing takes root.
Today, taking the Host, I remembered your hands,
incense and earth, fingertips like white grapes
I would take into my mouth
one by one.
              When I enter the house,
it resists me like an angry woman. Our room,
your things, the bed—a penance I offer up for Lent.
Waking with you, I would fill myself with the morning
in sweet mango breaths. Watching you sleep,
I willed my dreams into you.

But clouds cannot be harvested, nor children wished
into life.
             In the wind that may travel
as far as you have gone, I send this message: out here,
in a place that you will not forget, a simple man
has been moved to curse the rising sun, and to question
God's unfinished work.

They Never Grew Old

I am speaking of that hollow-eyed race
of bone-embraced tubercular women and men,
the last of whom I caught a glimpse of
in the final days of my childhood.

Every family had one
hidden away in a sanitarium—
a word whispered when certain names
came up in conversation. And when I asked
my mother what it meant, she said,
a very clean place.

Once, I saw one; a rare
appearance by a distant cousin
our family tried to keep invisible.
From a neighbor's house across the road,
I looked upon the visitor in a white dress
that seemed to hang upon her skeletal frame
like a starched garment on a wire hanger.
She held a handkerchief to her mouth
the entire time. The circle of polite relatives
sat back in the chairs around her.
The coffee cup at her side would later
be discarded, the chair she floated on—she seemed
to have no volume or weight—would be scrubbed
with something so strong, it made one cry; the whole house
sanitized and disinfected after her brief stay.

Though these sad, thin cousins were rarely seen
in our living rooms, they were a presence in the attics
and closets where we kept all our unwanted kin.

And they too had their heroes and myths.

As a girl I heard the story of two young people,
put away to die and forgotten,
who met in the cool, pine-scented corridors
of their hospital prison, and fell in love.
Desperate to be together, they escaped
into the night. It was a young woman

276

who found them under an embankment bridge,
a damp place where a creek one could step over ran.
Lying in each others' arms, their bodies were marbleized
with fever and morning dew. They were a frieze
in a Roman catacomb: Eros and Psyche in repose.

Moved by their plight, the girl brought them food
and a blanket. But dying creatures are easy to track,
and they were soon found by townspeople scandalized
that the ill should want to make love. A priest
was called in before a doctor. I surmise
that they died in separate beds.
                    Back then, I was convinced
the story of the dying lovers clinging to each other
in the dark cave, was the most romantic thing I would ever hear,
the spot on their lungs that killed them, I imagined
as a privileged place on the body's ordinary geography.

I too wanted to live in *a very clean place,*
where fragile as a pale pink rosebud I would sit
among my many satin pillows and wait for the man with whom
I would never grow old, to rescue me from a dull life.
Death and love once again confused
by one too young to see the difference.

Counting

An oriental ink drawing:
a shadowy range of mountains,
and a grey lake rising. Pneumonia
is the name of the country on the lighted screen,
the chest of my two-year old daughter.
                    At home
in her pink eggshell room,
I dig blindly in drawers for clothes,
and for something familiar and comforting
to take her at the hospital.

My fingers are caught in a string of beads,
the rosary my mother
has had the priest bless for my child's birthday:
"Teach her to count on Christ," instructed
the accompanying card.
                              A disbeliever
in the power of objects, I allow this penitent's jewelry,
the chain of linked sets of beads,
to slip through my fingers, joining my hands
into the steeple of an unsteady temple.
The part of my brain
I never listen to anymore begins
a litany of prayers in my mother's voice. I hear
myself joining in, counting down deep enough
to where I can believe
that beads of amber glass can be magical.

The Dream of Birth

My mother's voice scrapes the ocean floor,
coming through ragged with static during the call
placed from her sister's house in Puerto Rico,
                              where she will stay
until she finds a new place for herself. She has called
to say she is moving again and to share the horror
prompting her flight.

On the first night of deep sleep in the old house
she had rented back on native soil—a place
she would decorate with our past; where

yellowed photographs—of a young man in khaki
army issue (the way she chooses to remember her husband),
and my brother and me as sepia-toned babies—in their

chipped frames, will not insult new paint; a place
where she could finally begin to collect

her memories like jars of preserves on a shelf,
>   there,
she had laid down to rest on her poster bed centered in
a high-ceilinged room, exhausted from the labor
of her passage, and dreamed

she had given birth to one of us again; she felt the weight
of a moist, wriggling mass on her chest, the greedy mouth
seeking a milk-heavy breast, then suddenly—real pain—

piercing as a newborn infant's cry—yanking her
out of her dream. In the dark she felt the awful heft
of the thing stirring over her, flipping on the light

she saw, to her horror, a bat clinging to her gown,
its hallucinated eyes staring up from the shroud of black wings,
hanging on, hanging on, with perfect little fingers,
>   as she,
wild with fear and revulsion, struggled free of her clothes,
throwing the bundle hard against the wall. By daylight
she had returned to find the rust-colored stain streaked

on the white plaster, and the thing still fluttering
in the belly of the dress. She had dug a tiny grave
with her gardening spade on the spot

where she would have planted roses.

The Hour of the Siesta

Must come upon you unmotivated as a poem;
a need to enter another consciousness,

satisfied with economy and elegance. To slip
into the white embrace of sheets

at midday, to suspend the arbitration of time
in a short dream, evacuating the panic of thoughts

to the uninhabited caverns the other side
of whatever in you stirs, struggles and flies,

and in one sublime instant surrenders to the sweet
inertia of sleep in the afternoon.

Saint Rose of Lima
(Isabel De Flores)

*"Never let my hands be to any one
an occasion for temptation."*

She was the joke of the angels—a girl
crazy enough for God

that she despised her own beauty; who grew bitter herbs
to mix with her food,

who pinned a garland of roses to her forehead;
and who, in a fury of desire

concocted a potion of Indian pepper and bark
and rubbed it on her face, neck, and breasts

disfiguring herself.
Then, locked away in a dark cell,

where no reflection was possible,
she begged for death to join her with her Master

whom she called, *Divine Bridegroom, Thorn
in my Heart, Eternal Spouse.*

She would see His vague outline, feel His cool touch
on her fevered brow,

but as relief came, her vision would begin to fade,
and once again she would dip the iron bar into the coals,

and pass it gently like a magician's wand over her skin—
to feel the passion that flames up for a moment,

in all dying things.

Seizing the Day

You are traveling within the boundaries
of your time together, finite as a glass cube
within which you do not plan
past this afternoon, this night. Inside,
the autumn sun, infused with white light
and a little heat,
strokes the windshield of the car,
underneath the peaked shade of mountains.

You are listening to a top one hundred countdown
on the radio. She says, *Satisfaction*
will be on top—*Satisfaction*
always is.

As you sear these roads in your haste
to get somewhere you've never been before,
you notice the leisurely pace of free lives
in their familiar routines: how an old man,
digging in his mailbox for news of a world
he doesn't believe in
stares at your faces hurtling past
with the hooded eyes of a potential witness.

And how a young couple facing each other across a table
at the window of a small cafe
raise their glasses of wine to their lips, oblivious
to the way, flashing by,

you have stolen their souls with your eyes.

Correspondence

When I lift your letter out of the mailbox,
I expect it to contain your life,
to open in my hands
like a house in a child's pop-up book,
complete in every detail: family photographs
on the walls, cross-stitched homilies,
kids' fingerprints, and large windows
where I will stand like Alice
grown tall enough to be invisible,
casting a shadow you will interpret
as imminent rain.
Your wife, fragile as porcelain,
will be sleeping easy in your big little bed,
mindful of your early morning habits,
while your children chase their last dreams
like playful kittens.
Alone in first light, you will be taking in your home
like a blind man,
making each thing yours by your touch.

How to Get a Baby

To receive the waiwaia *(spirit children) in the water seems to be the most usual
way of becoming pregnant . . . They come along on large tree trunks, and they
may be attached to seascum and dead leaves floating on the surface.*

—Bronislaw Malinowski
Baloma: The Spirits of the Dead in the Trobriand Islands

Go to the sea
the morning after a rainstorm,
preferably
fresh from your man's arms—
the *waiwaia* are drawn
to love-smell.
They are tiny luminous fish
and blind. You must call

282

the soul of your child
in the name of your ancestors:
Come to me, little fish, come
to Tamala, Tudava, come to me.
Sit in shallow water
up to your waist until the tide
pulls away from you
like an exhausted lover.
You will by then
be carrying new life.
Make love that night,
and every night,
to let the little one
who chooses you know
she is one with your joy.

Why There Are No Unicorns

Because
each species is specialized;
the cow naturally turns to green,
the bird heads for blue.
The unicorn's predilection
was for white—the snowy laps
of virgins. They say
the only way to capture the rare creature
was to lure him with a maiden
wearing wild flowers in her hair,
a flowing gown of blinding white.
In a silent wood she'd pretend
to doze under an oak or sycamore
while waiting for the curly horn
gently to awaken her.
Enticing unicorns soon became
a gentleman's choice
before choosing: required prelude
to the veil and the ring.
Legend has it that nothing but

the subtle scent of untested flesh
would reveal the special beast—no sachets
of heart of mandrake dipped
in freshly slaughtered lamb's blood; nor
bowls of mother's milk sweetened with cinnamon.
But, alas,
it wasn't long before unicorns became so scarce
that the maiden's test was traded for a dowry.
The moral of the story is: A woman left alone
in a forest with a hope chest at home waiting,
will soon learn to hunt.

Learning to Walk Alone

Today I followed my servant, Hestia, down the dusty path
that leads away from the sea. Trudging towards
the barren hills that separate my house from her world,
her stiff back told me
that a woman walking home after a day of laboring
over someone else's hearth
had nothing to share with a fortunate fool
strolling in the heat of late afternoon
for pleasure.
             As we approached the last clump of trees
huddled together like beggars at the edge of the village,
I gave up the contest of wills. I followed Hestia's brown form
with my eyes, as she descended into a marketplace
filled with hagglers, stray dogs, and flies, until
she became part of the crowd.
             I stood there with my arms around a thin old tree
for a long time, listening to the sounds of words
I could not decipher, the empty cadences of far-away voices
rising and falling.
             Without you, Odysseus,
I have come to hate living on this island—the constant whine
of the sea licking its own wounds. If I could, I would follow

284

the vagrant gulls to crowded places and feast on crumbs.
I would wait with the winning patience of birds
for someone to extend an open hand.

The Drowned Sailor

When I first saw you break through
the wine-dark waters, your body
blocked the setting sun, an aureole
of light transforming you into a god.
　　　　　The tide rocked you,
spread your yellow hair crowned with seaweed,
opened and closed your limp hands — filling you,
emptying you, like a mother gone mad with grief
working over a dead child.
　　　　　I stood at the edge of the sea
until the sounds of the retreating waves,
like the suckling of an infant at the breast,
or of a man loving a woman's body, became one
with the rhythm of my breathing.
　　　　　Tonight you will travel
to Lord Poseidon's realm, down to that silent place
where there is no memory or desire,
only the slow melting away of the flesh.

Rosario Morales

Born: 1930

Rosario Morales was born in Manhattan and attended school there and in Bronx, New York. She was studying at Hunter College when she married. It was two weeks before the "police action" in Korea which would make her husband eligible for the draft upon his graduation from Cornell. Because they were more interested in, as she has said, the "welfare of the community than in making war," the couple moved to Puerto Rico, settled on a piece of an abandoned coffee plantation, and learned to farm from the ground up, so to speak. For five years the two learned about the land and its products, and raised and sold a variety of vegetables while the FBI scurried around keeping an eye on those two anti-war activists.

Hepatitis and children were some of the reasons for returning to the "States." In addition to *Getting Home Alive*, a collection of vignettes, stories, poems and memories which she did with her daughter, Aurora. Rosario Morales has been published in various anthologies including *This Bridge Called My Back: Writing by Radical Woman of Color* (Kitchen Table Press, 1981) and *Cuentos: Stories by Latinas* (Kitchen Table Press, 1983). In 1990 she received the Boston Contemporary Writers Award which in addition to a cash prize emblazons in stone her poem, "The Dinner," in the Boston tram station.

The Dinner

Perhaps you have seen The Dinner Party, tables set with linens and fine tableware. Dinner in the dining room, decorous.

I didn't go. My folks didn't either, not my womenfolks. They don't go to things like that, weren't invited, wouldn't know what to say or do, how to eat. Besides, the food is boring.

My womenfolks are giving their own party. In the kitchen. First names only, or m'hija, negra, ne, honey, sugah, dear. The table is scrubbed and each plate and bowl is different, wood, clay, papier mâché, metal, basketry, a leaf, a coconut shell. Each is painted, carved by a woman.

The table has a cloth woven by one, dyed by another, embroidered by another still. It's too small for the table but is put there in the center every year in memory of our mothers. We prepare the meal with our own particular tools. Squatting by the doorsill, she pounds garlic and herbs. And *she* chops with a cleaver—garlic, ginger, scallions, peppers— parts a small piece of beef into a thousand slices. Someone toasts coffee, someone else grinds bananas for banana beer. Two are washing rice. One is cleaning a fish, frying pork fat, peeling plantains, scrubbing yams, chopping hot peppers. The air is rich with smells and sounds.

Each wears her colors for feasting: red, orange, green, turquoise, blue, yellow, gold flashes as she moves, stoops, reaches, twists, stirs, turns, opens, closes. We will eat where we can sit, on stools, on the floor, lean against the wall, squat, stand, with what we have, with sticks, fingers, a shared spoon, a piece of shell.

This is the dinner. We don't know our forbears' names with a certainty. They aren't written anywhere. We honor them because they have kept it all going, all the civilizations erected on their backs, all the dinner parties given with their labor. And they gave us life, kept us going, brought us to where we are.

Come! Lay that dishcloth down. Eat, dear, eat. There will be time later, and hands enough, for the cleaning.

I Recognize You

I recognize you. Spitting out four, five, six-syllable English words, your tongue turning a tight grammatical sentence, flipping adjectives and adverbs into line faster than you can say *Oxford Unabridged Dictionary* and pinning all of it in place with commas, colons, semicolons, and parentheses.

You were the one I couldn't beat at spelling bees, the other girl who got A in grammar two semesters in a row. You're the one who went on to college, or maybe didn't, but took classes after work, who reads and reads and worries whether you're reading enough or the right thing.

I know without meeting you that you're working class, or a woman of color, or an immigrant, or child of immigrants. That you keep your mama language for the kitchen, hardly ever pronounce it in public, never on the written page.

You're proud. You've done this by yourself, or with your family behind you. And I'm impressed. You can make the English language roll over, bark on command, sit up and beg, you—who were raised on spuds, grits, rice, or tortillas.

But I'm sad, too. For the English language robbed of the beat your home talk could give it, the words you could lend, the accent, the music, the word-order reordering, the grammatical twist. I'm sad for you, too, for the shame with which you store away—hide—a whole treasure box of other, mother, language. It's too rough-mannered, you say, too strange, too exotic, too untutored, too low class.

You're robbing us, robbing the young one saying her first sentence, reading her first book, writing her first poem. You're confirming her scorn of her cradle tongue. You're robbing her of a fine brew of language, a stew of words and ways that could inspire her to self-loving invention.

And you're robbing yourself . . . no, we're robbing ourselves, of selfness, of wholeness, of the joys of writing with *all* our words, of the sound of your Mama's voice, my Papa's voice, of the smell of the kitchen on the page.

I Am the Reasonable One

I am the reasonable one. I am the one you can say your spite to, the one you can ask the venomous questions. It's so hard to say your contempt of these loud, dirty, emotional people if you're white, rational, and liberal. Your self-expression is so limited by your self-repression, and what can you do with your bile?

I am the reasonable one and, best of all, I am your friend. We have sat together, talked together, given and received support, touched hands, touched cheeks. You know me to be kind, to be thoughful.

You know me to be reasonable, to be rational. You know me to be almost white, almost middle class, almost acceptable. You can count on me, hopefully, to answer quietly, reasonably, and if I don't, you can say, "Don't take it personally." You can ask, "You're not angry with me?" You can trust me, nearly, to answer "No."

I am the one Puerto Rican you can ask, "Why don't they learn

English?" And what I answer is full of love and understanding of all those people, your ancestors included, who were forced by the acculturated jingoist migrants of a previous generation to abandon their languages—yiddish, irish, chinese, japanese, tagalog, spanish, french, russian, polish, italian, german—to give birth to your acculturated jingoist selves.

I am the one who hears it all. You can speak freely about "them," about the lower classes, about puertoricans, about blacks, about chinese. When you lower your voice to ask about them, to talk about them, you don't lower it to exclude me. You know you can tell me.

I am the one you can say "people like us" to, meaning white middle class women who are fine, who are right, whose ways are the only ways, whose life is the only life.

And if I say, "not me"—oh, and I do say, "not me"—you do not need to listen. Surely! You can pooh-pooh my stubborn clinging to being different. You know me better than I know myself. You know I am white like you, english-speaking like you, right-thinking like you, middle-class-living like you, no matter what I say.

And through this all, I have ever been the reasonable one, never wanting to betray myself, to become before your eyes just exactly what you despise: a loud and angry spik, cockroaches creeping out of my ears, spitty spanish curses spilling out of my wet lips, angry crazy eyes shooting hate at you. All victims of all racist outrages look like that in your eyes, like your own evil personified, the evil you participate in, condone, or allow.

But now I tell you reasonably, for the last time, reasonably, that I am through. That I am not reasonable anymore, that I was always angry, that I am angry now.

That I am puertorican. That under all that crisp english and extensive american vocabulary, I always say *mielda*. I say *ai mami, ai mami* giving birth. That I am not like you in a million ways that I have kept from you but that I will no more.

That I am working class and always eat at the only table, the kitchen table. That taking things is not always stealing; it's sometimes getting your own back, and walking around in my underwear is being at home.

And I am angry. I will shout at you if you ask your venomous questions now, I will call you racist pig, I will refuse your friendship.

I will be loud and vulgar and angry and me. So change your ways or shut your racist mouths. Use your liberal rationality to unlearn your contempt for me and my people, or shut your racist mouths.

I am not going to eat myself up inside anymore. I am not going to eat myself up inside anymore. I am not going to eat myself up inside anymore.

I am going to eat you.

Spring Fever

You,
You're like a crocus, like a sugar maple
Your juices ooze in the tepid sun
Pushing against your flesh
Out to your eyes your hair your fingertips
Leaving you pulsing and vulnerable
To the ever returning frost.
And all on this faint promise of the warmth to come.

Not I.
I need steady warm breezes to unfreeze my blood
I need to sink my chilled bones in a soup warm sea
I need to soak my brittle flesh in the burning sun.

Oh! I will be a lizard and sit on a sun hot stone
I want to lie flat, lie lifeless
A cold and scaly sponge
Lie belly close to the dull rough stone
And twitch my tail in low, slow, lazy circles
Eyes closed
Limbs still
Soaking
Waiting
For the strong, slow baking heat
To stir me into life.

My Revolution

My revolution is not starched and ironed
    (Stand over the ironing board, wield the hot iron)
It is not ass-girdled and breast-bound
    (Wiggle and worm into it every morning, wiggle and worm out
    of it every night)
My revolution is not white-gloved and white-suited
    (Soak it and scrub it and bleach it . . . and wear it?
      Only with care!)

It's not thick-soled and heavy high-booted
    (Lift the left foot. Down. Now lift the other)

My revolution is comfortable
    hard-wearing
        long-lasting
            versatile!
I can wear it in the fields
I can wear it to go dancing
        do the dishes
        do the laundry
        see the movie
        do the marching

My revolution is not cut from a pattern, *I* designed it.

It's homemade and handcrafted
It's got seams to let out
    and hems to let down
        tucks to take in
            darts to take out.

My revolution is comfortable
    hard-wearing
        long-lasting
           versatile!

My revolution fits,
So well
Sometimes
I don't know I'm wearing it.

So, when your revolution doesn't fit
               ain't your size
               chokes
               binds
               climbs up your crotch
               bites into your breasts
               or rubs your heels raw

Give it back!
Turn it in!
Ask for a refund!

and make yourself another
    make one of your very own.

Africa

Africa waters the roots of my tree,
    pulses in my sap,
    seeps thru my heartwood.
Though my roots reach into the soils of two Americas,
Africa waters my tree.

Aurora Levins Morales

Born: 1954

Aurora Levins Morales was born in Indiera Baja, Puerto Rico, as she states, "one week before Lolita Lebron led the nationalist attack on congress, of a U.S. Jewish father and a New York Puerto Rican mother." She was raised on "books and social justice, on a coffee farm in the mountains, with interludes in Rochester, New York, Ann Arbor, Michigan, and New York City." When she was five years old, her mother taught her to read and at seven she began writing poetry.

At thirteen, living with her family in Chicago, she began writing a journal, filling four hardbound books a year. As the light-skinned mestiza daughter of a university professor she had been among the privileged of the island. In the United States she received what she calls "a valuable political education" by learning about racism from "the other side of the coin" and about the instabilities of class position.

In 1976, after moving to California, she began giving readings and publishing her poetry and other non-fictional work. She has appeared in *This Bridge Called My Back: Writings by Radical Women of Color* (Kitchen Table Press, 1981), *Cuentos: Stories by Latinas*, (Kitchen Table Press, 1983), *The Courage to Heal* (1989), and *Reconstructed American Literature* (1990). She also has worked in radio and theater.

She co-authored *Getting Home Alive* (1986) with her mother, Rosario Morales. This interwoven collection of poetry and prose is an exploration of the lives of two Puerto Rican women, one from each side of the water, "immigrants, writers, social activists, mother and daughter." It is a book that has been widely taught and excerpted.

Most recently Aurora Levins Morales has been writing fiction and raising a daughter. Her story "Vivir Para Ti" won an Oakland Arts Council Fellowship. She has a forthcoming collection of short stories, *Threads*, a "family mythology." She resides in Oakland, California.

Kitchens

I went into the kitchen just now to stir the black beans and rice, the shiny black beans floating over the smooth brown grains of rice and the zucchini turning black, too, in the ink of the beans. Mine is a California kitchen, full of fresh vegetables and whole grains, bottled spring water and yogurt in plastic pints, but when I lift the lid from that big black pot, my kitchen fills with the hands of women who came before me, washing rice, washing beans, picking through them so deftly, so swiftly, that I could never see what the defects were in the beans they threw quickly over one shoulder out the window. Some instinct of the fingertips after years of sorting to feel the rottenness of the bean with a worm in it or a chewed-out side. Standing here, I see the smooth red and brown and white and speckled beans sliding through their fingers into bowls of water, the gentle clicking rush of them being poured into the pot, hear the hiss of escaping steam, smell the bean scum floating on the surface under the lid. I see grains of rice settling in a basin on the counter, turning the water milky with rice polish and the talc they use to make the grains so smooth; fingers dipping, swimming through the murky white water, feeling for the grain with the blackened tip, the brown stain.

From the corner of my eye, I see the knife blade flashing, reducing mounds of onions, garlic, cilantro, and green peppers into sofrito to be fried up and stored, and best of all is the pound and circular grind of the pilón: *pound, pound, thump, grind, pound, pound, thump, grind. Pound, pound* (the garlic and oregano mashed together), THUMP! (the mortar lifted and slammed down to loosen the crushed herbs and spices from the wooden bowl), *grind* (the slow rotation of the pestle smashing the oozing mash around and around, blending the juices, the green stain of cilantro and oregano, the sticky yellowing garlic, the grit of black pepper).

It's the dance of the cocinera: to step outside
fetch the bucket of water, turn,
all muscular grace and striving,
pour the water, light dancing in the pot,
and set the pail down on the blackened wood.
The blue flame glitters in its dark corner,
and coffee steams in the small white pan.
Gnarled fingers, mondando ajo,
picando cebolla, cortando pan,
colando café,
stirring the rice with a big long spoon
filling ten bellies
out of one soot-black pot.

It's a magic, a power, a ritual of love and work that rises up in my kitchen, thousands of miles from those women in cotton dresses who twenty years ago taught the rules of its observance to me, the apprentice, the novice, the girl-child: "Don't go out without wrapping your head, child, you've been roasting coffee, y te va' a pa'mar!" "This much coffee in the colador, girl, or you'll be serving brown water." "Dip the basin in the river, so, to leave the mud behind." "Always peel the green bananas under cold water, mijita, or you'll cut your fingers and get mancha on yourself and the stain never comes out: that black sap stain of guineo verde and plátano, the stain that marks you forever."

So I peel my bananas under running water from the faucet, but the stain won't come out, and the subtle earthy green smell of that sap follows me, down from the mountains, into the cities, to places where banana groves are like a green dream, unimaginable by daylight: Chicago, New Hampshire, Oakland. So I travel miles on the bus to the immigrant markets of other people, coming home laden with bundles, and even, now and then, on the plastic frilled tables of the supermarket, I find a small curved green bunch to rush home, quick, before it ripens, to peel and boil, bathing in the scent of its cooking, bringing the river to flow through my own kitchen now, the river of my place on earth, the green and musty river of my grandmothers, dripping, trickling, tumbling down from the mountain kitchens of my people.

1930

My grandmother Lola, with her beautiful sagging face and her fine, black and silver hair, sits on the bed weeping as she tells me the story, tears and words spilling slowly. She loves the weeping and telling and the gestures she incorporates, rolling her eyes to heaven, casting them down. But the story is nonetheless true, and I don't move, so as not to break the thread.

The images, once heard, are unforgettable. My abuelo walking ninety blocks to look for work, saving the nickel so he could take the trolley home. The janitor's job opening up just in time, mijita. There was a group of Puerto Ricans, tú sabes, people who all knew each other and looked out for each other, not familia, but parecido, because, you know, there weren't so many of us in New York then. They said, "Who should get this job?" and someone said, "Manolin, because he has a new baby." So they sent for him and took him down there at night and taught him how to use the vacuum cleaner, one of those big industrial ones, and the next day he got the job. As soon as they paid him, he went straight to the store and bought food. We hadn't eaten in three days. Imagínate!, with Sari nursing. She was taking all that milk out and nothing was going in. I was así (she holds up her pinkie to show me how thin and laughs), así. He brought home a couple of eggs and a little butter. He had to cook them for me because I was too weak to get up, and then he fed them to me because I couldn't even hold the spoon. Sari and I just lay on the bed together. She'd be drinking the milk and I'd be just lying there, too weak to move. And she heaves a deep quavering sigh, absent-mindedly scratching the skin of my bare leg.

There is a memory of hunger in me, a hunger from before birth that aches in the hollows of my fingers, my hands, my arms, bones caving in on themselves from hunger, stomach swelling, teeth falling out. My mother is there, too, tiny and dark-haired and black-eyed, her mouth sucking and sucking.

This is a story I make up from the scraps my mother and grandmother have let fall, a story I tell myself over and over, embroidering it, filling in the missing details of wind and weather and smells, of how my grandfather's hands clutch at the coat against the cold, how he leans forward into the wind like a steamboat; the way my grandmother's face is drawn and thin, the dim light of the bedroom where she lay, and the sharp urgency of my mother's cries; the smell of those eggs cooking and how they felt in Lola's stomach, those first few bites. My mother is the infant in the picture, but this is not my mother's story. It is my story for her, told to myself as I invent the details of her history, the foundations of my own. I lean on my grandmother's bed in the heat and humidity of Bayamon in summer, gathering material.

"I had a brown dress," she says after a moment. "That's all I had to wear. Sí, mija! One dress. When I had to wash it, I took it off and wore my slip until it was dry. We called it 'wash and wear.'" She laughs again, that snorting laugh of my grandmother's that I love so much, the one that erupts into the middle of her best dramas. "I'll never forget that brown dress."

And I think of my mother loving brown, the rich, comforting earthy warmth of that color which was the only one her mother wore during the first year of Sari's life: and I think of Lola's closet now, packed to the point of explosion with clothing of brilliant colors mixed wildly, a tropical rainbow of rayon and cotton and polyester blends: knit pants and cotton housedresses and silky negligees and satiny synthetic blouses, never again just one brown dress.

There is this picture: my thin grandmother with her suckling child lying half starved together on a bed in a dark old tenement building. There is also another picture: long-limbed and graceful as a young stork, radiant with life, she stands on the roof with neighbors and cousins, her place near the sky. We look at it in silence, then, "I always wanted to sing," she says. "I used to pray that I would wake up able to sing. I always had this crooked little squeaky voice. Las nenas se burlaban de mí. But if I could wake up one morning singing, I would die happy."

South

Flying south, south, into the deepest south, there was the feeling of being pulled farther home than I've ever been. I began to wonder if the body does have its secret reservoirs of memory after all, cubbyholes in the cells, that pass on from generation to generation the smell of a place once loved, the feel of its air on the skin. Flying in the dark over Mexican desert and then later over the sea, my heart sang back to the heart of my continent, singing in the night, calling me, pulling me near.

First we crossed the high thundery places. Too dark, too cloudy to say for certain, "that was a peak," but now and again, flashing between gulfs of black air and mountainous piles of moonlit cloud, between sideways-stabbing strokes of lightning I saw what was too white, too sharp to be cloud. Something cold and crisp and clear as a quena song. My head grew light and the man next to me said the oxygen was thin up here, climbing over the spine of the world. Then the thunder fell behind us, the perpetual growling of those wild uppermost Andes, and we coasted slowly down into the richest air of the beginning.

In the beginning my blood traveled from this air, and returns to it in my deepest dreams: where the trees all but shut out the sun, and in a green dimness where the jaguar runs like a vivid flame along the branches and ground, my people still walk, still hunt, still stand mouth open, laughing up into the rain.

Taíno. Aruaca. Gauraní. I follow the thread of my blood back from the cave I once found in the hills near my home: the pottery shard, the painted wall, I follow it, bright and tremulous out of the coded messages of my bones, the archeology of my flesh. The Díaz clan coming down out of the hills to intermarry, carrying the precious drop that is mine, as they carried precious water in gourds and skin sacks on the long voyage (I remember it) out of the forests of the Orinoco, over the mountains and nearly to the edge of breathable air, then down to the swampy coast, a millennium ago perhaps, and up the chain of islands, a journey of many generations of hundreds of years, never spilling it, never leaving it behind.

To the villages in the coastal valleys of my island, netting fish from the sea, growing manioc, yuca, achiote, making palm wine, weaving hamacas, painting their faces red and black: seed juice and sap, dipping arrows against their marauding cousins the Caribs. How they journeyed from beach to beach until they came here, to Boriquén. Island of Crabs, and caught the crabs and roasted them, and roasted a jutía with achiote and wild onions, and feasted right there on the beach.

I feast with them and remember the time of copper and blood when the Spaniards came and you thought they must eat gold, they were so desperate for it, and you blew on the conch and rose up and fought them, and then the war was over and you said "jíbaro" meaning one who runs away to be free, and a small band of you fled up into the mountains I was born in, to Indiera, "place of the Indians."

Still you said guaraguao for hawk, guamá for the sticky sweet pod, guayaba for the small round yellow fruit, words sweet and round in the mouth that traveled with you from the place of many rivers, where you were a people of the Guaraní people, and life was wet and growing and you hunted for weeks at a time under the endless green shadows.

The shadows are not endless anymore. Each day the bulldozers bite out another piece of the jungle and the sun invades the green world and little rivers dry up in their beds and the fish die in the mud. But all night long one night, I flew above it, with not a single light below me. Nothing but the murmuring of a million rivers and a hundred million new leaves opening and breathing into the night . . . and myself, a late leaf of that ancient tree, opening and breathing a rich and heady oxygen out of my deepest root.

California

1.

In the middle of writing about the grimness of Chicago, about my disorientation as a newly arrived immigrant of thirteen, I look out the window and notice I am in California. That I've been here ten years, longer that I've lived in any one place before. I remember how strange the Spanish architecture on Chabot Street looked the day I arrived, and all the gardens full of succulents. How thrown I was by the odd mixture of vegetation from places I've loved––pine and hibiscus, bougainvillea and maple, and all sorts of strange Martian-looking, green deformities with delicate fringed and puffed blossoms poking out at odd angles. And the whiteness of the light. Eastern sunlight had been yellow, deciduous, moist. Here it was leafless and white and dry. Intense enough to imprint itself not only on my retina, but on the insides of my lungs. This is the place no one took me or sent me to. The place I chose for myself.

Place. How I always begin with place: the most potent imagery for a wandering Jew, an immigrant Puerto Rican. "What will this place give me, do to me? What landscapes, what houses will it leave in my dreams? What layers will it add to the collage of my identity, my skin, my permanent passport?"

Ten years later I am in California and it's summer. Soft air and warm breezes and fragrance on the streets. A whiff of honey this morning as I pass a tree with minute bunches of white hairs arranged in bouquets between dark green leaves. The showering down of Japanese incense from a plum tree in full pink blossom hiding the black branches from sight.

2.

I have filled a beautiful blue and turquoise cup with orange and golden nasturtiums with their peculiar musty scent of dank earth. The scent that surrounds old tin bathtubs set outside in the sun of twenty years ago on the cement in front of our house on the mountaintop in Puerto Rico. The water would sparkle in the sun while I splashed in the tub, and the air was hot and thick with the smells of flowering nasturtiums and cherry tomatoes heavy with small orange fruit, and all around me the hibiscus bushes rustled with lizards and reinitas, and the lichen-stained cement of the cistern was criss-crossed with the scurrying of ants.

As I wrote those words, a truck pulled up to this house and delivered two five-gallon bottles of spring water, sweet to quench thirst on hot California days. Water that doesn't need to be boiled or have the ten drops of bleach measured in it: poison just sufficient to kill the bacteria from the dead lizards and frogs that decayed in our water tank.

Today I notice I'm in California and I have survived the bacteria in the tank and the invasions of McCarthy and the FBI, survived the anger of my mother and the passivity of my father, survived the loneliness I thought I would die of, and the violence and fear and violations of my growing up. I have become taller than the nasturtiums, able to breath above them. Now I walk through them, picking and choosing, parting the flat floppy leaves to find the blooms I want, arranging them in this ceramic cup made by a Mendocino potter and glazed the color of the tropical sea at noon. The flowers I cull from the gardens of my mothers and fathers, but the cup is completely mine, and I have set the whole and glowing combination here on my desk to dazzle the eye.

3.

This is the life I chose before I was born, when the twin creature who floated beside me died and was reabsorbed into the pink walls of our world, and I decided to go on. The life I chose during the long, choking hours of labor before my first breath.

The life I chose the first time I picked up a pencil and saw that the page was absolutely mine, and as big as the world.

The life I chose when I promised my six-year-old self never to forget being a child, never to grow frightened and dishonest like the grownups I saw, nodding politely to each other without affection, and decided to put my true self in a time capsule for later use.

The life I chose when I filled notebook after notebook and promised to remember everything of importance.

The life I chose when I did not die of loneliness but fed myself crumbs I carefully gathered: six eggrolls worth of self-love, all at a sitting, and the deep golden cups of cheap tea, endlessly replenished for free.

4.

There is a picture before me of my great-grandparents standing in dark coats, black and gray, on the boardwalk in Brooklyn, in an older, colder immigrant community. I am an immigrant too, I tell them. Twice, thrice the immigrant. I was torn from the moist soil of Indiera, roots ripping, and transplanted to stony ground. I have dug myself carefully up and planted myself here. You would be proud of me, Leah. I have finally learned to make gardens.

There was a table with an umbrella over it on my great-grandmother's porch, always set with a bowl full of fruit, and we would sit there on long, warm afternoons. I remember Leah coming out from the shadows of the doorway into the blazing light of the porch in summer with a plate of knishes fresh from the oven: potato, cabbage, spinach, lemon, onion, kasha. For years I mourned the fact that she died without teaching me to make them, the secrets of dough and filling gone. But looking around me, I see that I know what I need to know: I have come into rooms with the same movements, carrying plates of tostones, crisp golden and garlicky, I have remembered her standing in sunshine, and I have begun to tell her story and mine.

5.

On my birthday I dream of a tablecloth, white and yellow in a large plaid, the corner lifting in a light breeze, flapping gently. On the table is your bowl, Leah, filled with the cool fruit of the temperate zone, plums and green grapes and nectarines and fuzzy peaches with red hearts. My table now. The table of the choosers of life.

Old Countries

New York is the Old Country to me. Childhood memories of the four years that I lived there, between the squirrels and stone walls of Riverside Park, and the thrilling roar, the musty winds, and glittering sidewalks of the subway, are laid, thin as silverplate on an old spoon, over an iron core of older memories. The garment district and my grandmother's hands at the sewing machine, stitching up bras and girdles with the other Puerto Rican women; my mother's fable about the essence of the city—a man she once saw leading a goat into the subway; my step-grandpa Abe's sister who died in the Triangle Shirtwaist fire; my great-grandma Leah and her husband Abe and her sister Betty, all working in the garment trade during the years of unionization; my aunt Eva the hatmaker and her radical Finnish husband Einar. They were the people who lived in my Old Country, who had lived there in the days of the big strikes. In the days of the big hunger called The Depression.

The names of streets and neighborhoods, spoken casually by native New Yorkers, are full of meaning to me, with bits of history clinging to them like earth to a shoe: Amsterdam Avenue and Harlem, a ferment of Black culture, politics, movement; Brownsville where my father was born among the other immigrants, and Coney Island home of Nathan's hotdogs and the big parachute ride; Bridgeport, where Pop worked in a factory and slept in a rooming house five nights a week, eating his meals at Chopick's; the Lower East Side, home of both my peoples, mysterious with smells and faces and eateries and the trailng threads of friends and cousins and neighbors last heard of in 1934 or '47 or '59.

I grew up in a rainforest, hearing, like earlier immigrant children, of the horrors and delights of the Old Country. Schools there were called PS and then a number. There were neighborhoods with lines as clearly marked as any international border: Italian, Irish, Polish, Black, Jewish, Chinese, and the new populations seeping in: Puerto Ricans, Dominicans, Haitians, Jamaicans, Cubans. In the old country they sold hot chestnuts on the street ("What's a chestnut, mami?" I think, sucking on a fresh-picked orange), and there were vendors who sold hot yams. My mother bought one every day she could and held it to keep her hands warm.

I heard that my father lived in his street the way I did on my hillside, knowing the neighbors and what they did when they grew up, each neighborhood a little homeland. That my mother loved kosher pickles and learned to knit from immigrant Eastern European Jews. How she watched her friend Moira smear forbidden lipstick on her mouth by the light of a street lamp, in the mirror of a glass door. How the Puerto Ricans called the police "la jara" after O'Hara, because so many of them were Irish. How the Irish kids beat up and insulted and threw stones at the Jews, my mother among them. How my father was beaten up by anti-Semites and learned how to fight.

I am earth and bone from the green mountains of Indiera. As my grandparents were from the hills of Naranjito. As my great grandparents were from the forests and farmlands of Yaza, where my great grand-father Abraham Sakhnin heard from his father stories of an older Lithu-anian home, left five generations before in the days of Tsar Nicholas I (ancestor, as Pop would say, of Tsar Nicholas the last).

I am a mountain-born, country-bred, homegrown jíbara child. But I have inherited all the cities through which my people passed, and their dust has sifted and settled onto the black soil of my heart. Kirovo-grad, the forbidden gentile streets where Pop bribed his way into a job. Granada of the Moors, where the great Mosque rises. Barcelona on the sea. Jerusalem the Holy, and Cairo, and Damascus. Bustling Ife, and Luanda, and Dakar. *Mine are great ports of the immigrants*: Odessa, Liver-pool, Bristol, Lisboa, Marseille, Cadiz, Amsterdam, Abidjan, Accra, Lagos. *The places of arrival are mine*: New Orleans, Montreal, Buenos Aires, Halifax, San Juan, Angel Island, San Francisco, Ellis Island, New York. They were no goldeneh medinas, no gold mountains, no lands of milk and honey, but in those crowded worlds of smoke and soot and hardship, of hunger and illness and ten-hour days, love sent its sturdy roots into the brick. A dozen languages rang out in song and argument between the tenement walls, bringing those dingy streets alive.

Even Chicago, grim old gritty dust heap of a city, had its blues its trains, had its Northern Black Irish Polish Russian Hillbilly Puerto Rican Ojibwe meatpacking railroad citylake city spirit, worthy of love.

I didn't yearn for the cities the way my mother did for greenness and quiet and trees. But I dreamt of them. The smell and confusion of them. The streets full of people. The alleys and avenues. The markets and neighborhoods. The stories hidden in their names, and the ingenuity of the people who made it home. The bustling variety of life, of lan-guages, of foods, of customs—the meeting of so many roads.

A Child's Christmas in Puerto Rico

Christmas day was the least of it then, when I grew wild on the mountainsides of Indiera, ranging the coffee farms and filling my skirt with stolen tangerines. Gifts must wait for the Three Kings on their plodding camels to pass wearily through our corner of the world on their way to Bethlehem and stable their beasts at our little offerings of green grass and pine needles. Meanwhile it was the dry season and we sat outdoors, in the yellow light that spilled from the kitchen while Tito Cruz from across the road slipped down to the store where the old men drank their shots of Don Q from paper cups and fetched back Cheo's cousin from Sábana Grande. And he appeared, melting suddenly into the circle of light. "Get him a chair," yells my mother and pours him a little red glass of the best while he tunes his guitar. I remember verse after verse, like dark birds rising from his quiet face with an echo of the moorish troubadours in the high sing-song of the Andalucian peasant and the black cane cutter from Angola all mixing, somewhere far away in his jíbaro blood while nearby, just across the valley, dogs barked at the shadows of the coffee branches skittering in the moon.

But Noche Buena the noise rose from every corner and hollow of the mountains, with the green and red jeeps roaring up and down the roads and Lencho Perez arguing with his wife about the basting of the pig that his son had butchered that morning, the pig that Tita and I had fed orange peels to all fall in the pen on the hill, careful always to walk on the uphill side to keep our shoes clean. All afternoon the pig turned in the pit, and the little boys fought for a chance at the crank, poking to see if it was done, until Chinita la de Ada pulled on its ear and it came off in her hand. Now it was night and the pig was carved into heaps of garlic-pepper-and-oregano-smelling slices, everyone diving for the bits with skin on them, with the smell of arroz con dulce in the oven and huge pots of rice and gandules steaming on top of the stove.

Best of all Spanish turrón and dulce de everything, quivering slabs of candied orange, mango, guava, coconut being sliced with cheese, until outside the bright house there was only soft light brushing the dark hills and the chickens' feathery shuffling under the orange tree, while the pigeons on the porch hummed softly to themselves in their wire cage.

Late, late in the night, sleepy children were bundled into blankets and the jeeps roared off into the scented dark. The road swayed in the headlights, and an owl swung like a brown pendulum across our path. Dogs' eyes lit up red at the roadside, and we thought they were unheard of beasts from the middle-of-the-night.

Down in the cities the fat jovial gringo in the red suit was pushing out the old men on their wise steeds. He spoke better English and had contacts in New York. Some people said he had a brother-in-law in the government. Blonde dolls and GI Joes poured into the small towns and came by mail even to backwaters like ours. Nowadays, my younger cousins wait for Santa with tinsel trees in their living rooms and unwrap Barbie dolls and machine guns and Three Chipmunks Christmas records and never hear the song rise into the dark air filled with the velvet flight of bats, or see the first light pour down the red hill while all the world sleeps it off and the church bells ring in the muffled dawn.

Sugar Poem

Poetry
is something refined
in your vocabulary,
taking its place at the table
in a silver bowl: essence
of culture.

I come from the earth
where the cane was grown.
I know
the knobbed rooting,
green spears, heights of
caña
against the sky,
purple plumed.
I know the backache
of the machetero,
the arc of steel
cutting, cutting,
the rhythm of harvest
leaving acres of sharp spikes
that wound the feet—
and the sweet smoke
of the llamarada:
rings of red fire burning
dark sugar into the wind.

My poems grow from the ground.
I know what they are made of:
heavy, raw and green.

Sugar,
you say, is sweet.
One teaspoon in a cup of coffee . . .
life's not so bad.

Caña, I reply,
yields many things:
molasses
for the horses,

rum for the tiredness
of the machetero,
industrial
alcohol to cleanse,
distil, to burn
as fuel.

I don't write my poems
for anybody's sweet tooth.

My poems are acetylene torches
welding steel.
My poems are flamethrowers
cutting paths through the world.
My poems are bamboo spears
opening the air.
They come from the earth,
common and brown.

Tita's Poem

Oh, brown skinny girl with eyes like chips of mica
what did we know, straddling the flamboyan branch
hanging dreamy eyed, shivering, in the sun?
What did we know, squatting
over the swollen roots of hillside ginger
tipping our wild little animal hips
to catch the stream of water from a roof
right between the legs?
Nothing had a name then.

I remember a photograph in Ladies Home Journal
two women, skinny, string haired, gaunt eyed:
"Lesbian Junkie Prostitutes in Jail" said the caption
I never connected that word with us   still
I remembered the picture.
Kiss my mouth you said, and wondered if you'd get pregnant
and said you didn't care.

What did we know that we don't know now?
When I come back, I grieved, you'll be married, with babies
and you said *no, no, espera pa' que tu veas, verás que no.*
All that last spring we gathered orchids deep in the rainforest
bringing them to our garden,
binding them to the wood with black thread:
green, fresh flowers never meant for the sun,
bouquets of dawn never touched
by the careless brutal burning of noon.

In the years since then you've spilled children from you
like wasted blood
half of them dying before you could learn their names.
Still, I imagine you, thin and dear,
gnawing at the rinds of green guavas,
tasting each orange to see if it was bitter
or sweet, your dark head bent to my breast.

If I were to find you now, with your thieving husband and three
surviving children   if I were to come to you now in some dark
and stuffy, overcrowded living room in New York
where photographs of your wedding and nieces and nephews
crowd the end tables
you sitting on the plastic-covered couch,
with the inner stillness of a girl still moving
in the shadows of trees
If I were to come to you now and take you   thin
into my arms   would you remember me
and be wild and daring again, reaching up into the sky
to pluck the sun?

Julio Marzán

Born: 1946

Julio Marzán grew up in New York and graduated from Columbia University's Graduate Writing Program. In 1986 he published his first book of poems, **Translations without Originals: poems by Julio Marzán** (I. Reed Books). He also has published his poetry in journals and magazines—**The Little Magazine**, **The New York Quarterly**, and **Images**—and in anthologies, **An Ear to the Ground: An Anthology of Contemporary American Poetry**, **New Letters**, and **Inventing a Word: Twentieth-Century Puerto Rican Poetry** (Columbia University Press, 1980) for which he is the author and translator. He recently completed a collection of stories, **Unforgettable Tangos, Indelible Pagodas**, the title story of which will appear in **Americas Review**. His critical reviews of Latin American writers regularly appear in *The Village Voice*.

He was chief consultant of National Public Radio's award-winning docudrama, **Faces, Mirrors, Masks: Twentieth-Century Latin American Fiction**, for which he wrote the scripts, "Juan Carlos Onetti: The Atmosphere of a Brief Life," "Luis Rafael Sanchez: Life as a Phenomenal Thing," and "Jorge Luis Borges: The Laughter of the Universe."

He has received a New York Foundation for the Arts Fellowship, a New York State CAPS Fellowship, the "Y" Poetry Center's Discovery Award, The New School's Dylan Thomas Memorial Award for Poetry, and a New York State Writer-in-Residence at the Rockland Center for the Arts, and a residency at the Edna St. Vincent Millay Writers' Colony.

Marzán was visiting poet at Cooper Union in New York in the fall of 1990. He resides in New York City.

Sunday Morning in Old San Juan

Now as the golden
Egg of morning

Cracks over the city
Spreading its transparent warmth

Coating everything with color
Atop the Spanish fortress wall

I walk over blue ocean
Under the tranquilizing blue over the world

So clean the horizon of blue on blue
I almost utter something to you

But cross to a bleached inland street
Shaded by wrought-iron balconies

Of house after house till suddenly
High over the bay

Flame-orange flamboyants
Vault a crescent of cobbled way

Descending to a sunlit
Circle of hyacinths

Street too unexpected for me to resist
Walking with you

In the red-orange rain
Of petals in the ocean breeze

To this scent of hyacinths
Blue enough to make you stop

And look at me
For how much do I know

You would have loved
This morning of colors

Blowing these flaming
Flamboyants in its breeze

In the Backyard

All to be said goes on every morning in this yard.
Near the yucca plant a lizard's eggs have hatched
Little lizards, each one inch long and black and terrified.
Close to the wall, the same faint trail of ants

That fossilized a perfect imprint of a beetle
(Under the pumpkin plant that's crawled
Beyond the garden and over the cemented floor)
Now devour a piece of steak, fallen unseen the night before.

Mosquitos bite, a chicken clucks, a small green bird
Drinks dew over a plantain frond, while I attempt
To concentrate on anything not you, and not forget
All to be said goes on every morning in this yard

Proceeding while my eyes are fixed on a tree frog,
His head caught in an iguana's throat,
Just four limbs dancing desperately as the neighbor's dog
Barks through the fence at the garbage truck

Till the tiny frog
Is in the iguana, in the guts of this yard
Holding his body beating a recurrent thought
As all to be said flows . . . to imageless eons of now.

Eve

Adam will never change. I
Don't believe he's strong enough for me.
Now take this snake: firm, independent,
Why with a pair of feet
He could've ruled this place at least as well as God.
Listen to the serpent, I tell Adam,
Do it for yourself, for me, I've
Had it up to here with God's bad jokes.
This fruit yes, this one no,

Down on your knees as I approach,
While He exudes his beatific fireworks,
Leading an endless entourage of feathered flunkies,
Frightening the animals half to death,
Without so much the courtesy to say
Good morning, Eve. O Adam,
Look how rich and red,
Think of what it means and take a bite.

Emergency

After my determined calendar of checkups,
My stoic brushings after every meal,
Another patched-up tooth rotten to the root.

Doctor, how do I stop this urge to diminish?

My hairline opened its campaign at seventeen,
Before my bones reached full maturity
My appendix chose to terrorize and disturb the peace.
Even as you drill to cure my tooth,
I contemplate my arches sapped of all morale,
My stomach ineluctably surrendered to an ulcer.
Sweet tooth, milk teeth, dandruff, pounds of it,
And look: I've worn glasses nearly all my life.

Yes, play with the root canal.
Save the tooth!
I need it for smiling.

Ed Vega

Born: 1936

Ed Vega was born Edgardo Vega Yunque, in Ponce, Puerto Rico. He moved to the South Bronx, N.Y., in 1949 when he was thirteen. After high school there he joined the United States Air Force and later attended Santa Monica College and New York University on the G.I. Bill. He has worked in many community service jobs—as Training Director at Black Communities, Inc., as Director of the Addiction Service Agency, Aspira—in addition to teaching creative writing and English to school children and adults. He has participated in many literary workshops and panel discussions dealing with a wide range of subjects, for example, "Are We Speaking the Same Language?" about the duality of written English and Spanish languages or about the meaning of migration or the feeling of being in permanent exile that many Puerto Ricans know; he has given lectures at colleges and universities such as Hunter College, Hostos Community College, the State University of New York at Old Westbury and Staten Island Community College. He was one of the organizers of the "Primera Conferencia de Poetas y Escritores Puertorriquenos en Nueva York/First Conference of Puerto Rican Poets and Writers in New York," a first formal meeting between Puerto Rican writers from Puerto Rico and from the United States at which they shared their work and their experiences.

Vega began publishing stories in 1979 with "Horns" in *Nuestro* and "Back by Popular Demand" in *Maize*. In 1980 he published both "The Kite" and "Spanish Roulette" in the *Revista Chicano-Riqueña* and "An Apology to the Moon Furies" in *Hispanics in the United States: An Anthology of Creative Literature*. He has a hilarious, satirical novel about a Puerto Rican/Eskimo hockey player's life in the United States, *The Comeback* (Arte Publico Press, 1985), and a book of short surrealistic fantasies about Puerto Rican Horatio Alger heros, *Mendoza's Dreams* (Arte Publico Press, 1987), his North American version of Latin American magical-realism. "The True Story Behind the Writing of the Conquest of Fructifera Soto" from *Mendoza's Dreams* is being translated into Dutch, and he is one of the writers included in the Dutch

319

anthology *Puertoricaanse Literatuur in Nueva York*, published in Holland in 1990. He has a great deal of work yet to be published: two generational novels, *Owlsong* and *Cartagena*; a science-fiction novel, *A Brief History of the Przewalski* about the first Puerto Rican President of the United States; two sports novels, *Hole* and *Sacrifice*, to mention but a fraction of it. An excerpt from a work in progress, "No Matter How Much You Promise to Cook or Pay the Rent You Blew It Because Bill Bailey Ain't Never Coming Home Again," appeared in *The Portable Lower East Side* (1988).

Mercury Gomez

People may say a great many complimentary things about me as a person or even as a writer, but these accolades are without justification because I lack common sense. I don't know how many times Esperanza told me to always check the weather before going out. I seldom remember and end up over dressed or without enough clothing to protect me from the elements. At my age I can ill afford nagging colds or a bout with pneumonia. So there I went one Monday morning to see my lawyer, Harold Gunderson, of the firm of Silverstein, Gunderson & Estes, about the business of translation rights for my non-ghetto novels which Layton Publishing refuses to grant on the grounds that I have maligned my own writing and therefore damaged their reputation.

I was fuming and, of course, did not listen to the weather report. Although it was June and the weather warm, the forecast had evidently included rain and out I went without either a raincoat or an umbrella. As I waited for the Second Avenue bus the air grew heavy, there was a thunder clap to the south, lightning streaked the darkened sky and quite suddenly it was pouring and the wind was howling, sending sheets of driving rain into the bus shelter. Even if the bus had arrived at that moment, I would have been soaked before I was able to board it. As I stood there cursing my stupidity for letting Layton push me around, a gray, stretch limousine, the word MERC on the licence plate, pulled up. Out of the driver's side there emerged a young white man dressed in livery, carrying an umbrella and urging me to get in.

Of course I refused, but then the window in the back seat of the limousine was lowered and one of the smallest, blackest faces I had ever seen on a man grinned out at me and motioned for me to get in.

"Come on, Mendoza," the man in the limousine said. "The meter's running. Get in!"

The man looked familiar but it couldn't be the person I was thinking about. My curiosity got the best of me. He evidently knew me. I had no enemies, other than Layton with his vendetta regarding my books, so I got under the umbrella, into the limousine and off we went through the downpour

"How's it going, Mendoza?" the little black man said. "Wet out there, ain't it? Want some coffee?"

I said I would, and a young, red headed woman seated across from us poured coffee, asked me what I wanted in it, and after I said cream and two sugars, executed the order, handed me the cup and returned to her work on a portable lap computer.

"I know you, don't I?" I said to my host, after taking a sip from my coffee. "How do you know my name?"

He chuckled and said of course I knew him and I had better remember quickly or else he'd put me out of the limousine and he wouldn't care how wet I got. I don't know whether he meant what he said or whether he was joking, but his manner was quite firm and intimidating. I

immediately knew who he was. The incongruity of the situation, however, made me feel as if I were dreaming the entire episode.

"You're Solomon Gomez," I said.

"In the flesh," he said, grinning and extending his small black hand.
"But nobody calls me that anymore."

"Evidently from the looks of things," I said, "they call you Mr.
Gomez."

"That too," he said. "But most people call me Merc. How you
been? You see the plates?"

"I did, Merc," I said, uncomfortably.

"So how you been?" he again said, grinning.

"I've been all right," I said. "How about yourself?"

"Can't say I have any complaints, except maybe some stock I
bought last month that just sits there like a lump. My broker wants me to
hold on to it. Other than that, everything's copacetic."

I said I was glad to hear that.

"You look like you're taking care of yourself. How's Mrs. Mendoza?" he said.

"You mean, Esperanza?"

"Yeah."

"She's back on the island," I said. "Couldn't take the cold anymore.
Went back about five years ago."

"So where are you headed?"

"Madison and Forty-fifth. My lawyer's," I said, and gave him the
address.

"No problem," Solomon said and spoke to his driver. "Hear that,
Vincent?"

"Yes, Mr. Gomez," the driver said.

Solomon Gomez grinned, turned to his secretary and began dictating, using words like satellite, micro chip, and rattling off Japanese
company names. I listened but felt very uncomfortable. I didn't want to
ask what Solomon Gomez was doing dressed in a six hundred dollar suit,
riding around in a stretch limousine with a secretary, talking about
stocks and yields and Japanese companies. But I was curious how the
oldest but the runt of the litter of my old friend Baltazar Gomez had
managed to attract such fortune into his life. I shuddered thinking of the
possibility that he had come by his wealth illegally. Although I'm not
generally concerned with the morality of people's life styles nor do I pass
judgement on them I, in all cases, keep my distance from people whose
criminal activity brings about the destruction of others. If Solomon
Gomez was a big time drug dealer and the words he was using were code
words I had to find out. His father, Baltazar, was a hard working man, a
man who did not tolerate sloth and corruption of any kind. He swept and
mopped and janitored buildings for the rich in exchange for a small
salary and a huge basement apartment where he and his wife, Altagracia,
could raise their ever increasing brood, twelve of them at the time when I
lost touch with him some twenty years ago. Solomon had to be close to

322

forty and his father in his sixties. Baltazar Gomez was a few years younger than me. Solomon finished dictating and appeared to be thinking, his tiny black face, filled with nooks and crannies from his concentration.

"How's the old man?" I said, breaking into his thoughts.

"Great," Solomon said, once more grinning. "I set him up in business down on the island. Bought him and Mom a big house. Swimming pool and all. Remember how he always talked about wanting to be a radio announcer?"

"Of course," I said. "He had a great voice and spoke Spanish with great care."

"*Un negro inteligente,* right?" said Solomon, chuckling. "Read a lot. Cervantes, Unamuno, everybody. And all the Latin Americans. Rulfo, Quiroga, Fuentes and all our people. Laguerre, Soto. And all the black writers. Met Langston Hughes and Zora Neale Hurston through Arthur Schomberg, who was from the island. There isn't one he hasn't read. He could be a literature professor." He stopped talking and looked directly into my eyes so that I felt as if he were reading my mind. He nodded several times and then said: "By the way, I read your last book. *Ghetto Mirror.* It was pretty good. I recognized everybody in it. Badillo and the rest of the politicians and ball players and even the people from the old neighborhood. You gonna put me in your next book, right?"

"Absolutely," I said, convinced that if I didn't my life would become very difficult.

"Anyway, I bought the old man a radio station down on the island."

"The whole thing?"

"You got it. Got some of the best people managing it. Pop's got a one hour interview show every weekday. He's had the governor on and Jose Ferrer, Raul Julia, Rita Moreno and all kinds of celebrities. You know, ball players and people in the news. Wednesday nights is devoted to writers, his other love. He always asks about you, but you're very hard to find these days. We're thinking of buying a television station or just starting our own and putting him on a talk show format. Maybe two hours late night. But something classy. 'Cause once in a while the producers screw up and go along with some of the sponsors who want to put on people in the news. You know, whackos. Like the lady down there that was pregnant and had a bunch of puppies and they all looked like the governor. You remember the old man. He didn't pull any punches with any of us kids and he hasn't changed. If it's bull, he'll get it out of you. That's the way he runs his show. If you try to snow him, he's got you. He goes right for the jugular."

"Amazing," I said, referring to my friend, Baltazar. "What does he think of your success?"

"He's proud as hell," Solomon said. "You know, his oldest kid and everything." He chuckled once more. "Tried to get me on his interview show."

"And?"

"Had to turn him down."

"How come?" I said.

"I don't give interviews," he replied.

I was about to inquire further when his secretary looked up from her work and gave me a warning look. Ever alert to the subtleties of a changing human environment, if not the weather, I understood immediately and withdrew from the conversation. We were turning up Forty-fifth Street and a few moments later we were in front of my lawyer's office building.

"Here we are, Mr. Gomez," said the driver, getting out of the car with his umbrella even though the rain had stopped and only a slight drizzle now fell.

"Well, it's been nice seeing you, Merc," I said, extending my hand to Solomon.

"My pleasure, Mendoza," said Solomon, shaking my hand and then handing me his card. "Give me a call tomorrow and we can have lunch. I'm calling the old man as soon as I get into the office. I'm gonna ask him to schedule you for an interview. The station'll pick up the tab for air fare and hotel. Everything first class. I think there's an honorarium. We'll do a whole hour on your work. How's that?"

"Sounds all right to me," I said, somewhat embarrassed by my lack of enthusiasm. At least I'd get a chance to look in on Esperanza and talk to her about coming back. It would probably end up being another long drawn out discussion of climate and politics and why I would insist on being in New York rather than on the island.

"Tomorrow, then?" said Solomon.

"Tomorrow," I said, and stepped out of the car.

The driver held the umbrella and walked with me until I was inside the lobby of the building. He then nodded politely and went back out.

In the elevator going up to see Harold Gunderson, I looked at Solomon Gomez' card. The first thing which struck me was the logo, a silhouetted figure of Mercury with his arm raised as if in a passing stance holding a package. Next to the logo, in slanted letters which instantly conveyed speed: MERCURY COMMUNICATIONS. Below that, Mercury Gomez, President. Down near the bottom edge, a Third Avenue address and a telephone number. My heart skipped a beat and I found myself smiling and shaking my head in disbelief. How had he done it?

Inside Gunderson's office I was greeted, as always, warmly and with great respect by Mrs. Fazio, Harold's secretary. She said Harold would be with me in a moment. I sat down and began looking through a magazine, flipping the pages absently, when I saw a big flashy ad for MERCURY COMPUTERS. "When accuracy is not enough," the ad said, and went on to compare the IBM PC and the Apple with its own and in the end touted the MERCURY PC as the state of the art computer. "Combine accuracy with the speed of 21st Century technology."

Next to a computer, on whose screen there was a six color graph, a statuesque blonde, with a bust big enough to feed the city of Boston, was smiling warmly, encouraging everyone to buy a MERCURY PC and she would forsake that fair city for whoever was reading the ad. On the corner of the computer, the little black Mercury passer. Damn, I thought, he's really done it. My friend's son had taken the American dream seriously and turned it into a full scale Hollywood extravaganza.

At that moment Harold Gunderson came out of his office and I stood up. We embraced and then went into his office, with the plush carpeting, the view of Manhattan facing west, the beautiful mahogany desk, matching conference table and chairs; the shelves filled with law books, the walls displaying diplomas and awards and pictures of Harold in all types of athletic gear from when he was a collegiate star at Princeton University. Mrs. Fazio came in and served coffee and a couple of assistants came in to discuss my situation with Layton.

As much as I tried I could not concentrate on the business at hand and kept thinking about Mercury Gomez. I could no longer call him Solomon. He had transformed his life to the extent of completely obliterating my consciousness of him as the diminutive teenager I had known. At noon, Harold suggested we send out for lunch and continue our discussion. By two o'clock we were finished and it had been decided that we would sue Layton Publishing and that when Silverstein, Gunderson & Estes were done with Layton he'd wish he's gone into ladies apparel rather than publishing.

"There's no way they can force you to honor that contract," Harold Gunderson said. "Enough is enough."

I felt quite good about taking on Layton and once and for all I would begin chipping away at the damage I had done in writing those ghetto books, but I still felt an enormous curiosity about Mercury Gomez. I asked Harold if he'd heard of him. He thought a moment and then shook his head. I told him the story and he found it remarkable. He buzzed Mrs. Fazio and asked her if Irving Silverstein was in his office. Mrs. Fazio said he was, Harold thanked her and then dialed Silverstein's number.

"Irving, Ernesto Mendoza's here in my office," Harold said, when Silverstein had picked up. "He wants some information on someone by the name of Mercury Gomez. Burgess handles his outfit, right?"

Harold listened intently, nodding several times and then breaking into a big smile. He thanked Silverstein and then, laughing uncontrollably, which for him was uncharacteristic, said I should go and see Silverstein.

I thanked Harold, we shook hands and I walked down the hall to see Irving Silverstein. He office was similar to Harold's, perhaps less formal. Silverstein greeted me and asked me to sit down. When I was seated he asked me about my health, said he was thinking of retiring and moving to Florida for good and letting his son take his place in the firm and then he mentioned Mercury Gomez.

"Little guy, right?"

"Four foot ten at the most," I said.

"Yep, some piece of work that kid was. You know him?"

I told him his father and I had known each other but that I hadn't seen him in more than twenty years. And then I told him how he'd picked me up in his limousine and how he'd set up his father in business on the island.

"Oh, sure. That's Fortune 500 stuff he's got there," Silverstein said. "Multinational corporation. Offices in London, Paris, Tokyo. You name it. Five years ago they were just electronics but now they've diversified and have their hands in everything you can name that's developing. There's even a rumor that they're ready to launch their own satellite."

"So buying that radio station for his father was no big thing," I said.

"Like going to Nathan's for a couple of hot dogs," Silverstein said. "A tax write off. My God, he owns more media stock than Ted Turner."

"How do you know him and how did he do it?" I said.

Silverstein shook his head.

"I don't know the answer to the second question, other than to tell you he's sharp. You've heard Harold talk about Bill Burgess and his firm, right? They handle big corporations and sometimes assign a hundred or more lawyers to work with one company. Well, they handle Mercury Communications and Bill says there isn't one thing that goes by the little son of a gun. He's on top of everything. Like a black Napoleon as a strategist and like Patton determination-wise. Any damn thing he puts his mind to turns to gold and they say he negotiates with the intensity of a starving cobra. I don't know anybody that's got the best of him. If they have, they're probably working for him right now."

"And the first part of the question?" I said.

"Yes, right. I don't know if I ever told you but my uncle Seymour used to have a messenger service," Silverstein said. "This is going back twenty, maybe twenty five years. The little guy worked for Seymour for two or three years. We'd use Seymour's firm to get stuff down to Wall Street in a hurry. You know, contracts and that. Light stuff but stuff you couldn't trust to the post office or needed to get a client in a hurry."

"He was just a messenger?"

"Right," Silverstein said. "But what a messenger. That's how he got his name. Seymour's the one that started calling him that and I guess it stuck."

"What do you mean?"

"Well, Seymour says that for about a year and a half he was just an average messenger. You'd give him something and he'd deliver it and come back two hours later and make another delivery. Never any problems. Always on time. No complaints from his clients. No disrespect. Always got the right signature. Never lost anything or damaged it. No accidents."

"And?" I said, growing anxious.

"Relax," Silverstein said. "I'm getting to it. All of a sudden, Seymour says, the kid's a whiz. Seymour would say, 'here, kid, this is gotta be picked up down on 34th Street near Macy's and it's gotta go across town to 666 Third Avenue, the Kent Building, 9th Floor.' 'No problem, Mr Silverstein,' the kid would say. 'Be back in no time.' And off he'd go. Ten blocks from Seymour's business down to 34th, another twelve to the Kent Building and five blocks back to Seymour's. How much time before the kid's back?"

"I don't know. Maybe . . ."

"Wait, don't answer right away. Think about it. Consider midtown traffic on both the streets and sidewalks in the middle of a weekday. Sometimes there's rain, sometimes snow and then slush. How much time?"

"An hour, maybe an hour and a half," I said.

"Fifteen minutes," Silverstein said. "Fifteen minutes before he was back in front of Seymour, grinning and telling him that he was ready for another delivery."

"You're kidding!"

"Nope. The first couple of times Seymour checked the clients and they said they'd gotten their deliveries. No problems at all. 'Who picked up?' Seymour would ask. 'Little black guy,' they'd say. And then he'd call the people the package was going to and ask who had delivered it. 'Little black guy,' they'd say. After a while he just gave up trying to figure it out and anything that needed prompt attention went to the little guy."

"Incredible," I said.

"That's not the end of it," Silverstein went on. "Inside of a month Seymour's business had doubled. If you wanted something delivered in a hurry, who did you call? Silver Streak Services. Three black S's with a white arrow through them."

"Symbolic," I said.

"I don't know from symbolic, but the following month business quadrupled. And then one day the kid walked in and asked Seymour for a raise. Seymour offered him fifty dollars more a week. He thought he was being fair and magnanimous. From what Seymour says the kid looked at him and shook his head. 'Seventy-five?' Seymour says. More shaking of the head. 'So, what do you want?' says Seymour. 'My heart? My liver? What?' The kid grins and says he wants to work on commission. Seymour says it's totally out of the question. The kid grins some more and tells Seymour thank you very much, Mr. Silverstein, and walks out never again to be in the employ of Silver Streak Services. So now Seymour's down again to two and three hour deliveries and clients are calling up asking for the little black guy and Seymour's going nuts looking for him and can't find him anywhere and then his clients start dropping off and pretty soon his business is down the drain because, guess what?'

"The kid went into business for himself," I said.

"With a vengeance, my friend," Silverstein said. "It served Seymour right. He died about ten years ago still trying to figure out the whole thing. We used Mercury for a while and then we heard he was getting out of the messenger business and that was it."

"Amazing," I said. "I'm having lunch with him tomorrow, maybe I can find out."

"Let me know."

We said goodbye and I went home totally obsessed with the riddle of Mr. Mercury Gomez. I woke up in the middle of the night after a terrible nightmare in which I was placed in a manila envelope and was being delivered from one office to another not knowing where I would go next.

The next day I called Mercury's number and his secretary said he was expecting me at noon. I wore my only dark suit and at eleven thirty I was on my way downtown. At noon I was met downstairs by one of Mercury's executives. The Mercury Building, a new glass and steel structure on Third Avenue, reeked of efficiency and wealth, two phenomena which have eluded my grasp for as long as I can recall. In the lobby, part of which was an arboretum, there was a thirty foot smooth black stone statue of the Mercury logo.

On the 60th Floor we went into a suite of offices and there was Mercury Gomez, seated behind a desk, signing papers. As if he had a secret, he came forward and greeted me with that ever present grin. He asked if I preferred going out or if I wanted to eat in his office, which had a dining table already set up for lunch. I took the hint and said the office would be fine. He pushed a button and moments later a waiter came in and went over several menus with us. I finally chose a light meal of chicken and wine.

Once we were seated Mercury thanked me for coming and told me he'd spoken with his father, Baltazar, and everything was set up. He gave me three or four possible dates in the fall and said I should decide which one suited me, but to let the producers know with at least three weeks notice so they could take care of the advertising. He added that Baltazar's television show was a certainty, although Mercury would most likely have to start his own television station down on the island. Four hot dogs, two knishes and a couple of orange sodas, I thought.

I then asked him how he'd achieved his success. I told him I was very impressed but rather intimidated by all the affluence. Mercury suddenly grew sad. He smiled and said he sometimes wished he were back at the beginning.

"With Silverstein?" I said.

He looked at me sternly and then seemed to think it over and relaxed. He chuckled and nodded several times.

"I don't do interviews," he said, mocking himself. "But the old man said I should trust you. I know you're dying to find out how I did it. By the way, who told you about me and Silverstein?"

"His nephew."
"The lawyer?"
"Yes."

Mercury Gomez nodded and then the food came. When we were seated and had been eating a while, he said I could ask him anything I wanted. I told him that although I would be interested in learning how he had managed to multiply his wealth, I was certain that he'd achieved it all through hard work, developed talents, risk taking, some luck and an indomitable will to triumph, and that he would have to forgive me, but that my primary concern was how he had managed to make those deliveries as quickly as he had when he first began.

He thought for a moment, mulling over, it seemed, how to answer my question. He chuckled and then began telling me what it was like working for Silver Streak Services, how grateful he was to have a job because his father had instilled in all of them the value of hard work, but how demeaning it had been to be treated with contempt and to hear all the racial jokes and the word "nigger," even though growing up he never thought of being black, notwithstanding the fact that both his father and mother were both blacks from Loíza on the island. And that this problem was what all of the people here in the United States had to confront.

"On the island," he said, "and even up in El Barrio you're black but it's no big thing. But once you get out into the world they make you decide. Even if you're a little bit black, they make you choose."

He said no matter how many years go by the people are gonna keep speaking Spanish and eating the same food and listening to the music and they're always gonna say they're from the island. "That's why being P.R.'s such a big thing. This society wants you to choose. Black or white and we refuse. It's a messed up system."

"I agree a hundred percent," I said.

And then he said that after working for about a year for Silver Streak Services he realized he was pretty much anonymous. "Just another black guy. And worse than that I was small. 'The little black guy,' I useta hear people say and I useta feel like saying *'puñeta, váyanse pa'l carajo, coño! Yo soy boricua! Negro pero boricua y si no le cae bien, cáguense en su madre!'* Know what I mean?"

"Of course," I said. "I've suffered similar discrimination."

"Everybody does. If you're real white, then you kinda slide in and become anonymous too, but there's little rewards here and there. But if you're black, forget it. That's it."

He became pensive again and then went on to tell me that back then he had spoken with his father and his father told him to just keep going and he'd figure it out because he had the brains and the courage to win and that he shouldn't feel sorry for himself because that's all they were waiting for. And then one day he was in Brooklyn visiting his girl friend and he went by a playground and saw a small black young man playing basketball, dribbling and scooting around and driving the other players crazy and then passing or shooting but always coming out on top and all of a sudden he had an idea. He waited until they were finished playing and spoke with him.

"Luther Robinson was his name," he said. "A little bit taller than me, but pure black and smart as a whip. High school dropout and part-time numbers runner. Street smart, that is, 'cause there's a difference. No matter how street smart you are, if you ain't got certain fundamentals for dealing in the bigger society, you're gonna get jammed somewhere along the way. Luther's been with me ever since. He lives in Nigeria right now and runs the entire African Mercury division from our offices in Lagos. I knocked all the NBA fantasies out of his head, made him go back to night school, graduate and then we both went to City College at night. I'll be damned if in his junior year he doesn't suddenly get a bug up his ass that he wants to study law and after we graduated we got him into Columbia Law and it was like a breeze. A genuine born legal mind. Photographic memory from the numbers racket."

He continued and said that for the next month he combed the city of New York, going into every neighborhood looking for small black young men. Five foot five and under, because as long as they were black and small they were totally anonymous in the greater society and nobody paid much attention to them; that he explained the scheme, informing them that at first they wouldn't make much money but that after a while nobody would be able to compete with them. Some of the young men thought he was crazy but that about a dozen or so figured it might work and stuck it out for the first few months while he was still at Silver Streak Services; and that they didn't make much money but had a lot of laughs at Silverstein's expense when he'd send him out and he'd be back in ten or fifteen minutes, when in the past the job would have taken at least an hour, if not more.

"So how were you able to accomplish this?" I said.

"I'd post them at different corners in midtown," he said. "Near telephones and I'd call in the address and off they'd go. Like the pony express."

"They must've been tired at the end of the day," I said.

"That's right and that's when Luther had a brainstorm and he said why didn't we start using real tall guys."

"Because they have longer strides," I said.

"No, nothing like that," Mercury said.

He explained how they started recruiting tall fellows in the playgrounds, only people with good hands and when they had a fair number of them they bought cheap footballs and cut them open and put zippers on them and used them as courier pouches and issued everyone whistles, so that now all he needed to do was get an order and phone it to one of the little guys near the pick up location. The little guy'd run up and get the letter or package, stick it in one of the footballs, blow the whistle and up the street one of the tall guys would blow his whistle and stick up his hands. "The little guy," Mercury said, "would let fly with a forty or fifty yard spiral that the big guy would catch and pass to the next guy until the package was delivered by another little guy."

"You're kidding, of course," I said, truly finding it hard to believe. "It didn't really happen that way."

"I swear on my mother," Mercury said.

That was enough for me. When the people swear on their mother there's no need to question a person's integrity. But that wasn't the end of it. Ideas continued to emerge from all the members of Mercury Gomez' messenger crew.

"One day Andre Covington, he's my West Coast man, shows up with his cousin on roller skates and tells me that Louis, that was his name, wanted to become a roller derby skater and he needed all the practice he could get and could we put him to work since he could really sharpen his skill skating in and out of Manhattan traffic. No problem, I said. So now we had passers, catchers, runners *and* skaters, and then it escalated and word got around and everybody though it was a big joke and they all wanted in. At one point I had a hundred and fifty of these guys. About twenty-five of them roller skaters. It was unreal. All of us that delivered always dressed the same. Day in and day out. Same pants, same sneakers, same jacket and cap. Three or four basic outfits. I bought them wholesale in the garment center. And then I decided to talk to Silverstein."

"You wanted a raise and he turned you down," I said.

"No, he didn't. He offered me raises but I turned him down. I wanted a partnership, but he wouldn't go for it and went into this song and dance about my wanting to deprive his children of an education and was I after his heart and so I figured I'd go into business on my own. I put on a suit and went back to our clients and promised to deliver in record time. MERCURY MESSENGERS 'On Time, Every Time.' That was our motto. For a while we worked out of phone booths around Grand Central Station and then I got my first office. I bet Silverstein, the lawyer, told you his uncle gave me the name, Mercury."

"As a matter of fact, he did say that," I said.

"Wrong. The fact is he started calling me Speedy Gonzalez. It pissed me off no end but I didn't show it. No, by that time I was at City, studying business at night. I had to take a humanities course and ran across Greek mythology and then I saw the Western Union logo. I had Bootsie Powell draw up our logo. He couldn't roller skate, run, pass or catch, but was a hell of an artist and we all dug him because he really wanted to be in on everything we did. I had business cards printed up and the rest is history. Bootsie's in charge of all our advertising and owns half of San Francisco's real estate. And that's the whole story. Bootsie began calling me Merc and it stuck."

"Amazing," I said. "What happened to the original messenger service?"

"A couple of years later I sold it to some smart ass types from Wall Street for a couple of hundred thousand and I took the whole amount and bought Polaroid and Xerox stock. The fellas that wanted to keep improving went off to go to school, came back and are still working for Mercury Communications. Luther and I went into the copying business all over the city. The Wall Street guys ruined the messenger service and six months later I bought the company back for peanuts. Just to have use of the name."

"You bought Polaroid and Xerox, before they went big?" I asked.

"You got it."

"How did you know?"

Mercury thought for a moment, shook his head and then chuckled.

"I guess I musta figured out two things about this country. They want everything in a hurry and they want everybody to kinda be the same. You know, carbon copies. Polaroid and Xerox. Fulfilling industrial fantasies for the American people. We always got a kick outta delivering. Nobody could tell the difference between us. It was always the little black guy that picked up the package or delivered it. It didn't matter whether it was me or Luther, Raul, Dolores or Cynthia."

"What?"

"Oh, sure," Mercury said. "We began getting more and more business and couldn't find enough little black guys, so we started using little black girls. No makeup, no earrings, no giggling and no falling for guys while on the job. And they had to wear the same clothes as the other messengers, hair tucked in. No exceptions."

"And the people in the offices still couldn't tell," I said.

"Nope," Mercury said. " 'The little black guy already picked it up,' they'd say."

"You've accomplished more than ten men do in a lifetime," I said. "What's next?"

Mercury Gomez was once again the super shrewd businessman. A stern look came over his face, his eyes took on their frightening look and his body radiated power.

"The electronics industry has unlimited potential," he said. "The sky's the limit."

My heart skipped several beats.

"Silverstein, the lawyer, said there was a rumor that Mercury Communications was planning to launch its own . . . "

I stopped speaking and watched Solomon Gomez bring the index finger of his right hand to his lips and silently issue a request that I keep my counsel. A knowing grin broke out behind the index finger and then he winked at me.

He offered to have me driven back to my apartment but I thanked him and told him I needed time to think and that I thought I'd walk for a while, but to be sure and tell his father that I would definitely be coming down to the island.

Out on the street I couldn't stop smiling. Those Rough Riders had definitely made a mistake back in 1898 when they landed in Guanica and annexed the island.

Boy, had they made a mistake.

The Barbosa Express

Several years ago, at the tail end of a big snowstorm, I was in Florindo's Bar on 110th Street and Lexington Avenue when Chu Chu Barbosa walked in cursing and threatening to join the FALN and bomb the hell out of somebody or other. Barbosa's name is *Jesús* but nobody likes being called Gee Zoos or Hay Siouxs, so it's convenient that the nickname for *Jesús* is Chu or Chuíto because Barbosa was a motorman for the last seventeen years with the New York City Transit Authority.

Barbosa is your typical working class stiff, bitter on the outside but full of stubborn optimism on the inside. He has gone through the same kind of immigrant nonsense everyone else has to go through and has come out of it in great shape. In spite of ups and downs he has remained married to the same woman twenty-two years, has never found reason to be unfaithful to her, put one kid through college and has four more heading in the same direction. He owns a two-family home in Brooklyn and on weekends during the summer, he takes Bobby and Mike, his two sons, fishing on his outboard, "Mercedes," named after the children's mother.

Usually even tempered and singularly civic minded, he lists among his responsibilities his serving as treasurer of the "Roberto Clemente Little League of Brooklyn," vice-president of the "Sons of Cacimar Puerto Rican Day Parade Organizing Committee," Den Father for the Boy Scouts of America Troop 641, Secretary of the "Wilfredo Santiago American Legion Post 387," and member of the Courtelyou Street Block Association.

That night Barbosa was out of his mind with anger. At first I thought it was the weather. The snowstorm was wreaking havoc with the city and it seemed conceivable Barbosa was stranded in Manhattan and could not get back to his family in Brooklyn. Knocking the snow off his coat and stamping his feet, Barbosa walked up to the bar and ordered a boiler-maker. He downed the whiskey, chugalugged the beer and ordered another one. I was right next to him but he didn't recognize me until he had finished his second beer and ordered another. Halfway through his third beer he suddenly looked at me and shook his head as if there were no reason for trying anymore.

"This does it, Mendoza," he said, still shaking his head. "It makes no sense, man. The whole town is sinking."

"Yeah, the snow is pretty bad," I said, but it was as if I hadn't even spoken.

"The friggin capital of the world," he went on. "And it's going down the d-r-a-drain. I mean, who am I kidding? I put on a uniform in the morning, step into my little moving phone booth and off I go. From Coney Island to 205th in the B-r-o-Bronx. Fifteen years I've been on the run. I mean, you gotta be born to the job, Mendoza. And listen, I take pride in what I do. It isn't just a job with me. I still get my kicks outta pushing my ten car rig. Brooklyn, Manhattan and the Bronx. I run through those boroughs four times a shift, picking up passengers, letting them off. School kids going up to Bronx Science, people going to work in midtown Manhattan, in the summertime the crowds going up to Yankee Stadium. And that run from 125th Street to 59th Street and Columbus Circle when I let her out and race through that tunnel at sixty miles an hour. Did you know that was the longest run of any express train between stops?"

"No, I didn't," I said.

"It is," he said. "Sixty-six b-l-o-blocks."

"No kidding," I said, suddenly hopeful that Barbosa was pulling out of his dark mood. "That's amazing."

"You're damn right it's amazing," he replied, his face angry once more. "And I love it, but it's getting to me. How can they friggin do this? I mean it's their trains. Don't they know that, Mendoza? They don't have to shove it down my throat. But who the hell am I, right? I'm the little guy. Just put him in that moving closet and forget about him. Jerónimo Anónimo, that's me. I don't care what anybody thinks. For me it's like I'm pulling the Super Chief on a transcontinental run, or maybe the old Texas Hummingbird from Chicago to San Antonio along all that flat land, eighty, ninety miles an hour. I give 'em an honest day's work. It's 'cause I'm Puerto Rican, man. It's nothing but discrimination."

I could certainly sympathize with Barbosa on that account. I had met severe discrimination in the publishing world and had been forced to write nothing but lies about the people. I was curious to find out what had taken place to make Barbosa so angry.

"I know how you feel, Chu Chu," I said.

"I mean you're a writer and it might sound strange, Mendoza. But I'm not a stupid man. I've read, so I know about words. When I'm in my rig going along the tracks and making my stops, it feels like I'm inside the veins of the city down in those tunnels. It's like my train is the blood and the people the food for this city. Sometimes there is a mugging or worse down there, but I say to myself, hell, so the system ate a stale *alcapurria* or some bad chittlins or maybe an old knish. Do you understand what I'm saying?"

"Of course I do," I said. "Subway travel as a metaphor of the lifeblood of the city."

"Right. It's the people, the little people that keep the city going. Not the big shots."

"Exactly."

"Then how can they do it? The trains belong to them."

"The graffiti's getting to you," I said, sympathetically.

"No, that's a pain in the ass but you get used to it. Those kids are harmless. I got a nephew that's into that whole thing. I wish the hell they'd find someplace else to do their thing, but they're nothing compared to the creeps that are running the system these days. Nothing but prejudice against our people, Mendoza."

I asked Barbosa exactly what had happened and he told me that nearly a thousand new cars had arrived. "They're beautiful," he said. "Not a spot on them. Stainless steel, colorful plastic seats and a big orange D in front of them for my line. Oh, and they also have this bell that signals that the doors are gonna close. Have you seen 'em yet?" I told him I had not since I avoid subway travel as much as possible, which he doesn't know nor would I tell him for fear of hurting his feelings. He then went on to tell me that even though he had seniority on other motormen, they didn't assign a new train to him.

"Why not?" I said.

"Discrimination," he said. "'Cause I'm Puerto Rican. That's the only reason, Mendoza. Just plain discrimination. Even *morenos* with less time than me got new rigs and I got stuck with my old messed up train. I'm not saying black people are not entitled to a break. You know me. I ain't got a prejudiced bone in my body. Man, I even told them I'd be willing to take an evening trick just to handle one of the new trains, but they said no. I'm burnt up, Mendoza. I feel like blowing up the whole damn system is how I feel."

I immediately counseled Barbosa to calm down and not be hasty in his response. I said that there were legal avenues that he could explore. Perhaps he could file a grievance with his union, but he just kept shaking his head and pounding his fist into his hand, muttering and ordering one beer after the other. At the end of an hour he began laughing real loud and saying that he had the perfect solution to the problem. He patted me on the back and said goodbye.

Of course I worried about Chu Chu for three or four days because you couldn't find a nicer guy and I was worried that he would do something crazy. Every time I stopped by Florindo's Bar I'd ask for him, but no one had seen him around. Once, one of the bartenders said he had seen him in Brooklyn and that he was still working for the Transit Authority. I asked if he had gotten a new train, but the bartender didn't know. I didn't hear from Barbosa or see him again for the next six months and then I wished I hadn't.

About a week before the Fourth of July I received a call from Barbosa. He was no longer angry. In fact he sounded euphoric. This made me immediately suspicious. Perhaps he had taken up drugs as a relief from his anger.

"How you doing, Mendoza?" he said. "How's the writing going?"

"It's going, but just barely," I said. "My caboose is dragging," I added, throwing in a little railroad humor.

He let loose a big roaring belly laugh and, speaking away from the telephone, told his wife, Mercedes, what I'd said. In the background I heard his wife say, "that's nice," and I could tell she wasn't too pleased with Barbosa's condition.

"Your caboose, huh?" he said. "Well, I got just the right maintenance for that. Something to get your engine going again and stoke up that boiler with fresh fuel."

"What did you have in mind?" I said, fighting my suspicion.

"A party, Mendoza. A Fourth of July party. We're gonna celebrate our independence."

This didn't sound too strange since Barbosa believed in the American Way of Life. He was a Puerto Rican, but he loved the United States and he wasn't ashamed to admit it. He didn't go around spouting island independence and reaping the fruits of the system. His philosophy was simple. His kids spoke English, were studying here and there were more opportunities for a career in the U.S. Whatever they wanted to do on the island was their business. "I don't pay no taxes there," he'd say. "I don't live there, I don't own property there, so why should I have anything to say about what goes on. Don't get me wrong. I love the island and nobody's ever gonna let me forget I'm from P.R., but it don't make no sense for me to be a phony about where I earn my rice and beans." I personally thought it was an irresponsible political stand, but I don't meddle in how people think or feel, I simply report on what I see.

"What kind of party?" I said.

"That's a surprise, but it's gonna be a party to end all parties. Music. Food. Drink. Entertainment. Fire works. You name it, we're gonna have it."

"At your house in Brooklyn?"

"Naw, too small. Up in the Bronx. Ralph, my nephew, can come pick you up."

"I don't know," I said. "I got a backlog of stuff and I'm not too good at celebrating the independence of this country," I found myself saying, even though I like to keep politics out of my conversations. He knew that and sensed that I was simply trying to get out of it.

"Aw, com'on, Mendoza," he said. "It's gonna be great. I wouldn't be inviting you if I didn't think you'd enjoy it. I know how hard you work and what your feelings are about this whole American and Puerto Rican thing, okay? Trust me. You'll never forget this. You're gonna be proud of me. Everybody's coming. The whole clan. You never seen my family together. I don't mean just my wife and the kids, but my eight brothers and five sisters and their husbands and wives and their kids and my aunts and uncles and my parents and grandparents. And Mercedes' side of the family which is not as big but they're great. You gotta come."

I couldn't help myself asking the next question.

"Where are you holding this party, Yankee Stadium?"

"That's funny," he said, and again laughed so loud my ear hurt. "No, nothing like that. You gotta come. My niece, Zoraida, can't wait to meet you. She's a big fan of yours. She's doing her, what do you call it, to become a doctor, but not a doctor."

"Her PhD? Her doctorate."

"That's it. She's doing it on your books. She's just starting out, so she wants to talk to you and get to know you."

All of a sudden I felt flattered, even though most of what I've written doesn't amount to much. I felt myself swayed by the upcoming adulation, but I truly wish I hadn't participated in what took place between early evening on the Fourth of July and some time around four o'clock in the morning when all hell broke loose on the elevated tracks near Coney Island.

"Where is she studying?" I said.

"Some college in Michigan," Barbosa answered. "I don't know. You can ask her yourself. Ralph'll pick you up about 6:30 on July 4th, okay?"

"All right," I said, suddenly experiencing a strange feeling of foreboding about the entire matter. "But I can't stay long."

"Don't worry," Barbosa said. "Once you get up there and the party starts you can decide that."

"What does that mean?"

Barbosa laughed and said he'd see me on the Fourth.

So on the Fourth of July I got ready. I put on white pants, polished my white shoes, got out one of my *guayaberas* and my panama hat and at 6:30 that afternoon Ralph Barbosa knocked on the door and down I went to one of my infrequent social activities.

I got into the car and off we went across the Willis Avenue Bridge into the Bronx. I asked him where we were going and he replied that his uncle had told him to keep it a surprise, but that it was up near Lehman College. I relaxed for a while, but still felt that feeling that something not quite right was about to take place. Some twenty minutes later we drove under the Woodlawn Avenue elevated line tracks and into the campus of Herbert H. Lehman College. Ralph parked the car, we got out and walked to a grassy area where a number of people were seated on blankets. Around them were boxes of food and drink, ice coolers, paper plates and cups, coffee urns and several other items that indicated we were to have a picnic.

I felt relaxed at once and as I was introduced to different members of the family I noticed that there were very few men. Out of the over 100 people gathered around several trees, most of them were women and children. I asked Ralph where I could find his uncle and I was informed that Barbosa was making final preparations. I was offered a beer, which I accepted gladly, was offered a beach chair which I also accepted, and then was introduced to Zoraida Barbosa, the PhD student, a lovely, articulate young woman with a keen intellect and, unfortunately, a genuine interest in my work. So enraptured and flattered was I by her attention that more than an hour and a half passed. I then realized that the sun was going down and Barbosa still had not shown up. I once again began to worry.

Another half hour passed and now we were sitting in the dark and some of the younger children began to get restless. And then the word came that we were ready to move. "Move where?" I inquired. "It's all right, Mr. Mendoza," Zoraida said, taking my hand. "Just follow me." Such was her persuasiveness and her interest in me that I allowed her to take my hand and followed her as we crossed the grassy field. We walked for nearly a half mile until we were at the train yards. At that point I knew I was heading for a major catastrophe, but there did not seem to be any way of turning back.

I soon found out why the men had not been in attendance. I saw the plan clearly now. We were to descend into the train yards, a rather hazardous undertaking from the place where our crowd had stopped. The men, however, had constructed a staircase, complete with sturdy banisters. This staircase went up over the wall and down some fifty feet into the floor of the train yard. I followed Zoraida and as we went I looked down on the nearly forty rails below, most of them with trains on them. This was the terminal of the Independent Subway System or IND as it is popularly known, a place where trains came to be cleaned and repaired or to lay up when they were not in use. Down we went and then guided by young men with flash-lights we walked along, seemingly dangerously close to the ever present third rails until we arrived at an enclosure where a train had been parked. I suspected this was where trains were washed.

Again, utilizing a makeshift staircase I followed Zoraida as we climbed up into a train. Although the light of the flashlights being employed by the young men was sufficient for us to find our way, it was impossible to see what I had walked into. I was directed to a place on the train and asked to sit down. Expecting to find a hard surface when I sat down, I was surprised to find myself sinking into a plush armchair. Moments later I recognized Barbosa's voice asking if everyone were on board. Word came back that everyone indeed had boarded the train. Then quite suddenly the motors in the car were activated. I heard doors close and lights came on. I found myself in a typical New York Puerto Rican living room, complete with sofas, armchairs with covers, little tables with figurines, lamps, linoleum on the floor and curtains in the windows. I thought I would have a heart attack and began to get up from my chair, but at that moment the train began moving slowly out and a loud cheer went up.

I turned to Zoraida sitting on the arm of my chair and she patted my should and said I shouldn't worry. A few moments later we were moving at fairly rapid rate and then the music came on, at first faintly but then as the volume was adjusted it was quite clear: Salsa, I don't know who, Machito, Tito Puente, Charlie Palmieri. I didn't care. This was outrageous. Moments later Barbosa came into our car and smiling from ear to ear greeted me.

"How do you like it?" he said, after I explained to him that my heart was nearly at the point of quitting. "It's pretty good, right? My nephew, Ernest, he's the interior decorator, did the whole thing. Wait till you see the rest of it. It's not a new train, but it'll do."

I wanted to tell him that I had seen enough, but was too much in shock to protest. With an escort of his two brothers who, to my great surprise, were members of the police department undercover detective squad, we went forward as the train began picking up speed. I asked who was driving and Barbosa informed me that he had another nephew who was a motorman on the IRT Seventh Avenue line and he was doing the driving. From the living room car we moved forward into the next car, which was a control center laid out with tables, maps and computers. I was introduced to another nephew, a computer whiz working on his PhD in electrical engineering. Several young people were busily working away plotting and programming, all of it very efficient. The next car, the lead one, was laid out as an executive office with a switchboard connecting the other cars by phone. There also were several television sets and radios, all tuned to the major channels and radio station. "We're gonna monitor everything that happens," Barbosa said, and introduced me to yet another nephew, an executive from AT&T, dressed in a business suit, seated at a big desk with wood paneling on the walls around him. Off to the side a young woman was transcribing from dictaphone onto an IBM Selectric. My shock was indescribable.

We retraced our steps through the train until we came out of the living room car into the bar car. How they had managed to get a thirty foot oak bar with matching wall length mirror on the train is beyond me, but there it was, stools riveted into the floor. I was introduced all around to the men and women at the bar, all of them relatives of Barbosa and all of them grinning from ear to ear about this adventure.

"I hope you're doing the right thing," I said.

"Don't worry, Mendoza," he said. "Everything's under control."

The next car was a kitchen with six different stoves, four refrigerators, two meat lockers, cutting boards, kitchen cabinets. Here I was introduced to Monsieur Pierre Barbosa, the chef for the Lancaster Hotel, on leave especially for this occasion. Dressed in white and wearing a tall chef's hat, he greeted me warmly and invited me to taste one of his sauces. I did so and found it quite agreeable, if somewhat tart. "Too tart?" he said. I nodded and he spoke rapidly in French to one of his assistants, another Barbosa nephew who moved directly to the sauce with several condiments.

In the next car there was a nursery with cribs and beds for the children and a medical staff headed by Dr. Elizabeth Barbosa, a niece who was a pediatrician in Philadelphia. There were also bathrooms for ladies and gentlemen in the next car. Two cars were devoted to dining tables with linen and candlesticks, each with its own piano. The last car was the most magnificent and modern dance establishment I've ever seen. The floor gleamed and there were lights beneath it and on the ceiling colored lights were going on and off and young people were dancing. "Our disco," Barbosa said, proudly. "With D.J. Mike, my son." His oldest son waved and Barbosa laughed. "I hope you know what you're doing," I said. "But I have to hand it to you. How did you do it?"

"This is a family, Mendoza," Barbosa said. "We'd do anything for each other."

Ten subway cars decked out for partying were moving through the Bronx, making stops but not letting anyone on, the Latin music blaring from loud speakers above four of the central cars. Every stop we made, people laughed and slapped their thighs and began dancing and very few people seemed angry that they couldn't board the train. All of them pointed at the train. I asked Barbosa why they were pointing and he explained that the train was painted. He described it but it wasn't until the following morning when the escapade came to an abrupt end that I truly was able to see what he was talking about. Each of the cars had been sprayed a different color: orange, red, yellow, pink, green, several blues, white (I think that was the nursery) and the disco which was black and even had a neon sign with the letters *El Son de Barbosa*. All along the cars in huge graffiti letters each car said *The Barbosa Express* and each one, rather than having the Transit Authority seal had BTA or Barbosa Transit Authority on it. All of them were decorated with beautiful graffiti "pieces," as I learned these expressions were called when I was introduced to Tac 121, the master "writer," as these young men and women are called. Tac 121 was in reality Victor Barbosa, another nephew, studying graphic design at Boston University.

The party began in full and we kept moving through Manhattan and then into Brooklyn and the elevated tracks. Everyone had eaten by now and it was then that all hell began to break loose. It was now close to midnight. At this point one of the dining rooms was cleared and converted into a launching pad for a tremendous fire works display. I was introduced to yet another nephew, Larry Barbosa, who was a mechanical engineer. He had managed to restructure the roof of the car so that it folded and opened, allowing his brother Bill, a member of Special Forces during the Vietnam War and a demolitions expert, to set up shop and begin firing colored rockets from the car so that as we made a wide turn before coming into the Coney Island terminal I could see the sky being lit up as the train made its way. The music was blaring and the rockets were going off in different directions so that one could see the beaches and the water in the light from the explosions.

I was exhausted and fell asleep while Zoraida was explaining her project and asking me very intricate questions about my work, details which I had forgotten with the passage of time. Two hours or so must have passed when I woke up to a great deal of shouting. I got up and went to the control car where Barbosa, dressed in his motorman's uniform, and some of his relatives were listening to news of the hijacking of a train, the announcers insinuating that the thieves had gotten the idea from the film "The Taking of Pelham 123." One of the television stations was maintaining continuous coverage with interviews of high officials of the Transit Authority, the Mayor, pedestrians, the police and sundry experts, who put forth a number of theories on why the people had commandeered the train. They even interviewed an art professor, a specialist on the graffiti culture, who explained that the creation of art on trains was an expression of youths' dissatisfaction with the rapid rate at which information was disseminated and how difficult it was to keep up with changing developments. "Using a mode of transportation to display their art," he said, "obviously keeps that art moving forward at all times and ahead of change."

In another corner a couple of young men and women were monitoring the communications from the Transit Authority.

"We gotta clear channel, Uncle Chu Chu," said one of the girls. "They wanna talk to somebody."

Barbosa sat down and spoke to some high official. I was surprised when the official asked Barbosa to identify himself and Barbosa did so, giving his name and his badge number. When they asked him what was happening, he explained how the hijackers had come to his house and kidnapped him, took him down to the train yards and forced him to drive the train or they would kill him.

"What do they want?" said the official.

"They wanna a clear track from here to the Bronx," Barbosa said. "And they want no cops around, otherwise they're gonna shoot everybody. They grabbed some women and children on the way and they look like they mean business."

"Can you identify them?"

"The women and children?"

"No, the perpetrators."

"Are you crazy or what!" shouted Barbosa, winking at me and the rest of the members of the family around him, most of whom were holding their sides to keep from laughing. "Whatta you wanna do, get me killed, or what? There's a guy holding a gun to my head and you want me to identify him?"

"Okay, okay," said the official. "I understand. Just keep your cool and do as they say. The Mayor wants to avoid any bloodshed. Do as they say. Where are you now?"

"Kings Highway," Barbosa said.

I was amazed. The train had gone to Coney Island, backed up, turned around and had made another trip to the end of the Bronx and back to Brooklyn. I looked above and saw news and police helicopters, following the train as it moved.

"Okay, we'll clear the tracks and no police," said the official. "Over and out."

"Roger, over and out," said Barbosa, clicking off the radio. He raised his hand and his nephew, leaning out of the motorman's compartment, waved and ducked back in, let go with three powerful blasts from the train whistle and then we were moving down the tracks at top speed with the music playing and the rockets going off and people dancing in every car.

"We did it, Mendoza," Barbosa said. "Son of a gun! We d-i-d-did it."

I was so tired I didn't care. All I wanted to do was go home and go to sleep. I went back in to the living room car and sat down again. When I woke up we were in the Bronx and Barbosa's relatives were streaming out of the cars carrying all their boxes and coolers with them. There were no policemen around. Zoraida Barbosa helped me out of the train and minutes later we were in Ralph's car. A half hour later I was in my apartment.

The next day there were pictures of Barbosa dressed in his uniform on the front pages of all the newspapers. The official story as it turned out was that graffiti artists had worked on the old train over a period of three or four weeks and then had kidnapped Barbosa to drive the train. Why they chose him was never revealed, but he emerged as a hero.

Unofficially, several people at the Transit Authority were convinced that Barbosa had had something to do with the "train hijacking."

A month later I was in Florindo's Bar and in walked Barbosa, happy as a lark. He bought me a beer and informed me that shortly after the train incident they had assigned him a new train and that in a year or so he was retiring. I congratulated him and told him that his niece had written again and that her dissertation on my work was going quite well. One thing still bothered me and I needed to find out.

"It doesn't matter," I said. "But who thought up the whole thing?"

"I thought up the idea, but it was my nephew Kevin, my oldest brother Joaquin's kid, who worked out the strategy and brought in all the electronic gear to tap into the MTA circuits and communication lines. He works for the Pentagon."

"He does what?" I said, looking around me to make sure no one was listening.

"The Pentagon in Washington," Barbosa repeated.

"You're kidding?" I said.

"Nope," Barbosa said. "You wanna another beer."

"I don't think so," I said. "I gotta be going."

"See you in the subway," said Barbosa and laughed.

I walked out into the late summer evening trying to understand what it all meant. By the time I reached my apartment I knew one thing for certain. I knew that the United States of America would have to pay for passing the Jones Act in 1917, giving the people automatic U.S. citizenship and allowing so many of them to enter their country.

As they say on the street: "What goes around, comes around."

Acknowledgments

Grateful acknowledgment is made for permission to reprint the following copyrighted material:

"Ending Poem" from *Getting Home Alive* by Rosario Morales and Aurora Levins Morales. Copyright © 1986 by Rosario Morales and Aurora Levins Morales. Published by Firebrand Books.

"Felipa, La Filosofa de Rincon que Nació a los 98 Años" from *Noo Jork* by Jose Angel Figueroa. Copyright © 1981 by Jose Angel Figueroa. Published by Instituto de Cultura Puertorriqueña, San Juan de Puerto Rico.

"Murdered Luggage" by Jose Angel Figueroa. Copyright © 1981 by Jose Angel Figueroa.

"Puertoricanness" from *Getting Home Alive* by Rosario Morales and Aurora Levins Morales. Copyright © 1986 by Rosario Morales and Aurora Levins Morales. Published by Firebrand Books.

"Immigrants" from *Getting Home Alive* by Rosario Morales and Aurora Levins Morales. Copyright © 1986 by Rosario Morales and Aurora Levins Morales. Published by Firebrand Books.

"Today Is a Day of Great Joy" from *Snaps* by Victor Hernández Cruz. Copyright © 1969 by Victor Hernández Cruz. Published by Random House.

"Traffic Misdirector" from *Traffic Violations* by Pedro Pietri. Copyright © 1983 by Waterfront Press.

"Christmas Eve: Nuyorican Cafe" from *Mongo Affair* by Miguel Algarín. Copyright © 1978 by Miguel Algarín. Published by Nuyorican Press.

"This Is Not the Place Where I was Born" from *La Bodega Sold Dreams* by Miguel Piñero. Copyright © 1980 by Arte Publico Press.

"The Idea of Islands" from *Terms of Survival* by Judith Ortiz Cofer. Copyright © 1987 by Judith Ortiz Cofer. Published by Arte Publico Press.

"Poem" from *Tropicalization* by Victor Hernández Cruz. Copyright © 1976 by Victor Hernández Cruz. Published by Reed, Cannon & Johnson.

"The Man Who Came to the Last Floor" from *Tropicalization* by Victor Hernández Cruz. Copyright © 1976 by Victor Hernández Cruz. Published by Reed, Cannon & Johnson.

Cruz. Copyright © 1976 by Victor Hernández Cruz. Published by Reed, Cannon & Johnson.

"Mountain Building," "For the Far-Out Experimental Writer," "Two Guitars," "If Chickens Could Talk," "The Swan's Book," "Ironing Goatskin," "The Physics of Ochun," "Anonymous," "Don Arturo: A Story of Migration" from *By Lingual Wholes* by Victor Hernández Cruz. Copyright ©1982 by Victor Hernández Cruz. Published by Momo Press.

"It's Miller Time" from *Rhythm, Content and Form* by Victor Hernández Cruz. Copyright © 1989 by Victor Hernández Cruz. Published by Arte Publico Press.

"A Lower East Side Poem," "Running Scared," "La Bodega Sold Dreams," "On the Day They Buried My Mother" from *La Bodega Sold Dreams* by Miguel Piñero. Copyright ©1985 by Arte Publico Press.

"Mr. Mendelsohn," "The Wrong Lunch Line" from *El Bronx Remembered* by Nicholasa Mohr. Copyright ©1975 by Nicholasa Mohr. Published by Harper & Row.

"The First Day of Spring," "Intermission from Monday," "Intermission from Wednesday," "Intermission from Thursday," "Intermission from Friday," "Intermission from Saturday," "Intermission from Sunday," "1st Untitled Poem," "10th Untitled Poem," "The Night Is out of Sight," "The Title of This Poem Was Lost," "How Do Your Eggs Want You(?)," "3rd Untitled Poem," "7th Untitled Poem," "9th Untitled Poem" from *Traffic Violations* by Pedro Pietri. Copyright ©1983 by Waterfront Press.

"For Lolita Lebron," "From Fanon," "For Fidel Castro," "1st Poem for Cuba," "Some People Are about Jam," "Ahora," "Here," "Take the Hearts of Children" from *Yerba Buena* by Sandra Maria Esteves. Copyright ©1974 by Sandra Maria Esteves. Published by Greenfield Review Press.

"It Is Raining Today," "In The Beginning," "A Celebration of Home Birth: November 15th, 1981," "Lil' Pito" from *Tropical Rains* by Sandra Maria Esteves. Copyright ©1984 by Sandra Maria Esteves. Published by African Caribbean Poetry Theatre.

"One Woman" by Sandra Maria Esteves. Copyright ©1973 by Sandra Maria Esteves. Published by La Sangre Liama.

"Happy New Year," "Meeting Gaylen's 5th Grade Class," "A Salsa Ballet" from *Mongo Affair* by Miguel Algarín. Copyright © 1978 by Miguel Algarín. Published by Nuyorican Press.

"Trampling," "Rosa," "Infections," "Tiger Lady," "'Always throw the first punch'," "El Jibarito Moderno," "Wire Tap," "Talking," "Broadway Opening," "Dante Park," "Taos Pueblo Indians: 700 strong according to Bobby's last census" from *On Call* by Miguel Algarín. Copyright © 1980 by Arte Publico Press.

346

"They Never Grew Old" by Judith Ortiz Cofer. Copyright ©1990 by Judith Ortiz Cofer. Published by Kenyon Review, Vol. 12, No. 3, (Summer, 1990), 69–70.

"Counting" by Judith Ortiz Cofer. Copyright ©1989 by Judith Ortiz Cofer. Published by Passages North Review, Vol. 10, No. 2, (Summer, 1989), 16.

"The Dream of Birth" by Judith Ortiz Cofer. Copyright © 1989 by Judith Ortiz Cofer. Published by Southern Poetry Review, Vol. 29, No. 11, (Spring, 1989), 20.

"The Hour of the Siesta" by Judith Ortiz Cofer. Copyright ©1990 by Judith Ortiz Cofer. Published by The Americus Review, Vol. 18, No. 2, (1990).

"Saint Rose of Lima" by Judith Ortiz Cofer. Copyright © 1990 by Judith Ortiz Cofer. Published by The Americus Review, Vol. 18, No. 2, (1990).

"Seizing the Day" by Judith Ortiz Cofer. Copyright ©1987 by Judith Ortiz Cofer. Published by Zone 3, Vol. 2, No. 1, (Winter, 1987), 24.

"Correspondence" by Judith Ortiz Cofer. Copyright ©1986 by Judith Ortiz Cofer. Published by Poetry Miscellany, No. 16, (1986), 49.

"How to Get a Baby" by Judith Ortiz Cofer. Copyright © 1989 by Judith Ortiz Cofer. Published by Southern Poetry Review, Vol. 2, No. 2, (Fall, 1988), 22.

"Why There Are No Unicorns" by Judith Ortiz Cofer. Copyright ©1985 by Judith Ortiz Cofer. Published by Negative Capability, Vol. V, No. 2, (Spring, 1985), 122.

"Learning to Walk Alone," "The Drowned Sailor" from *Penelope's Journal* by Judith Ortiz Cofer. Copyright © 1988 by Judith Ortiz Cofer. Published by Kenyon Review, Vol. 10, No. 4, (Fall, 1988).

"The Dinner," "I Recognize You," "I Am the Reasonable One," "Spring Fever," "My Revolution," "Africa" from *Getting Home Alive* by Rosario Morales and Aurora Levins Morales. Copyright ©1986 by Rosario Morales and Aurora Levins Morales. Published by Firebrand Books.

"Kitchens," "1930," "South," "California," "Old Countries," "A Child's Christmas in Puerto Rico," "Sugar Poem," "Tita's Poem," from *Getting Home Alive* by Rosario Morales and Aurora Levins Morales. Copyright © 1986 by Rosario Morales and Aurora Levins Morales. Published by Firebrand Books.

"Sunday Morning in Old San Juan," "In the Backyard," "Eve," "Emergency" from *Translations Without Originals* by Julio Marzán. Copyright © 1986 by Julio Marzán. Published by I. Reed Books.

"Mercury Gomez," "The Barbosa Express" from *Mendosa's Dreams* by Ed Vega. Copyright ©1987 by Ed Vega. Published by Arte Publico Press.

About The Editor

Faythe Turner was born in Port Clinton, Ohio in 1938. She holds a B.A. in History from Denison University (1960), an M.A. in English from the University of Rhode Island (1966), and a Ph.D. in English (1978) from the University of Massachusetts. She has contributed to the subject of Puerto Rican Literature with numerous articles in scholarly journals and a doctoral dissertation on Nuyorican Writers. Currently she teaches American Literature at Greenfield Community College and lives in Amherst, Massachusetts.